Waging War on Corruption

Praise for *Waging War on Corruption*

"Frank Vogl presents a fascinating account of the emergence of the worldwide anticorruption story over the last two decades. It is a long-missing contribution, adding the personal touch to the usual fare." —**Mark Pieth**, chairman of the OECD Working Group on Bribery in International Business Transactions

"If corruption is a 'crime against humanity,' as Frank Vogl asserts, nothing less than the future of human civilization is at stake here. Frank's authentic account of this struggle— the challenges and the accomplishments—should inform and inspire everyone fighting 'the war' against corruption today and tomorrow." —**Devendra Raj Panday**, a leader of the Nepal Citizens' Movement for Democracy and Peace; former minister of finance

"*Waging War on Corruption* provides a much-needed retrospective and overall assessment concerning the contemporary anticorruption movement. Transparency International and related groups seemingly came out of nowhere a generation ago, but Frank Vogl shows how long-term influences have shaped anticorruption agendas and strategies. Today, political events, new technology, and the movement's own successes in shifting the global agenda are creating fresh challenges. Vogl's book offers an essential discussion of those dynamics, and of what those concerned with justice and accountability must do in the years to come." —**Michael Johnston**, Charles A. Dana Professor of Political Science, Colgate University

"Frank Vogl describes the global rise of awareness of the devastating effects of corruption on millions of people around the world. Through the lens of fascinating human stories, he vividly illustrates the importance of individuals standing up against corruption and making the demand for transparency and accountability in politics and public life one of the key social challenges of our time." —**Cobus de Swardt**, managing director, Transparency International

"I always wished for a book like this: a book about where Transparency International came from, how we all became a part of it, what we stand for, and what we all are doing to make our dreams come true. There is a big need for this story in Russia these days, because Frank Vogl's book shows that everything is possible; that civic activism has a chance to push through even the hardest of agendas; that there are heroes among us such as TI's founders, who decided to make a difference and here we are—TI chapters now actively work all over the globe; that more and more people are joining our cause; and that governments in more and more countries are putting anticorruption at the top of their agenda. I plan to buy many copies of this book and give it to my students, to my colleagues, to people in government and in business—I will give it to all those who lost hope, who think that the David of civic activism is too weak to confront the Goliath of injustice, poverty, and corruption. This book proves that this is simply not true." —**Elena A. Panfilova**, general director, Center for Anti-corruption Research and Initiative Transparency International–Russia

"Frank Vogl's book is an important contribution to the fight against corruption—it will especially help young people to see the film and not just the photo, and so recognize that although slow and difficult, change is possible. As the author beautifully describes it, 'There is an Everest of corruption still to climb. Two decades ago we could look at the mountain from afar and dream. Today, we have reached base camp. We are living the dream.'" —**Delia Ferreira Rubio**, political scientist, Argentina; winner of the 2011 Joe C. Baxter Award from the International Foundation for Electoral Systems

"An invaluable account of the origins of Transparency International and its evolving role as a global movement, sharing his rich insights gained from continued and active involvement in the movement." —**Kamal Hossain**, former UN special rapporteur on Afghanistan and current member of the UN Compensation Commission

Waging War on Corruption

Inside the Movement Fighting the Abuse of Power

Frank Vogl

ROWMAN & LITTLEFIELD PUBLISHERS, INC.
Lanham • Boulder • New York • Toronto • Plymouth, UK

Published by Rowman & Littlefield Publishers, Inc.
A wholly owned subsidiary of The Rowman & Littlefield Publishing Group, Inc.
4501 Forbes Boulevard, Suite 200, Lanham, Maryland 20706
www.rowman.com

10 Thornbury Road, Plymouth PL6 7PP, United Kingdom

British Library Cataloguing in Publication Information Available

Library of Congress Cataloging-in-Publication Data

Vogl, Frank, 1945–
Waging war on corruption : inside the movement fighting the abuse of power / Frank Vogl.
  p. cm.
Includes bibliographical references and index.
ISBN 978-1-4422-1852-9 (cloth : alk. paper) — ISBN 978-1-4422-1854-3 (electronic)
1. Corruption—Prevention—International cooperation. 2. Bribery—Prevention—International cooperation. 3. Political corruption—Prevention—International cooperation. 4. Corruption. 5. Bribery. 6.
Political corruption. I. Title.
JF1525.C66V64 2012
363.25'9323—dc23
2012017547

Printed in the United States of America

To the remarkable people who created, built, and lead Transparency International (TI), founded in 1993. Through their vision, bravery, and tenacity, TI has become the world's leading not-for-profit anticorruption organization.

This book is also dedicated to the individuals who have established and expanded the Partnership for Transparency Fund (PTF), which has become a superb catalyst for channeling finance and knowledge to civil society organizations across the developing world that are on the front lines in the war on corruption.

Contents

Acknowledgments

This book started on the day in late 1990 when Peter Eigen and I sat down in his home in Nairobi, Kenya, to chat about corruption. Peter's passion for launching a global fight against graft was contagious. The motivation and the thinking behind much of this book owes much to Peter's vision and energy and to other good friends who worked so hard twenty years ago to launch Transparency International (TI). I owe a great deal as well to friends and acquaintances in other not-for-profit organizations and in the media in many countries whose bravery and insights have convinced me to take an optimistic view on the prospects of securing substantial victories in the long war against corruption.

Many of the ideas and findings in this book owe much to the people who labor quietly behind the scenes at TI and the Partnership for Transparency Fund (PTF) at their respective head offices in Berlin and Washington, DC. I owe a particular debt to Stan Cutzach in TI's Berlin secretariat, whose services to TI's board of directors and its global membership have been invaluable; to TI managing director Cobus de Swardt and his Berlin team; and to TI chair Huguette Labelle. I am most grateful to Kathleen White and Colby Pacheco at PTF, and also to PTF's president, Daniel Ritchie, whose tireless efforts are enabling the organization to reach new heights.

I am indebted to Jeremy Pope, Pierre Landell-Mills, Miklos Marshall, Delia Ferriera Rubio, and Raymond Baker, who provided valuable comments and advice on drafts of various sections of this book and improved them substantially. I am also most appreciative of the time Laurence Cockcroft took to comment on the text, especially as he was finalizing his own excellent 2012 book, *Global Corruption—Money, Power, and Ethics in the Modern World.*

I am likewise grateful to my literary agent, Ronald Goldfarb, for his advice and for bringing me together with Rowman & Littlefield, where Jon Sisk, Darcy Evans, Patricia Stevenson, and their colleagues have been hugely helpful.

This book would not have been possible without astute editorial advice from Michael Schaffer and shrewd comment and constant encouragement from Julia Vogl and Marc Vogl. And *Waging War on Corruption* benefited beyond measure from the constant encouragement of my wife and partner, Emily Vogl. She read and commented on drafts and egged me on when I thought the project was going off track. Without Emily's patience and support, there would not have been this book.

Introduction

The "Arab Spring" was a seminal event. It inspired public protests from New Delhi to New York and from Minsk to Moscow, and in time the protests will multiply and embrace dozens of countries. Tens of thousands of Tunisians and Egyptians started it, risking their lives and overcoming their fears to denounce their illegitimate governments.

Now, people in many countries are taking action on an unprecedented scale in what is emerging as a war on the abuse of power. They are standing up for their dignity and for integrity. They are demonstrating for justice and for honest government. They are confronting corrupt leaders and elites.

The hundreds of thousands of protesters in many countries know that the journey will be long and hard. Few of their aspirations are likely to be achieved in the short term. Building new, accountable, and strong institutions of justice, civil society, and democracy will be difficult everywhere. Politicians keen to take advantage and to enrich themselves at the public's expense will abound. Yet corrupt leaders in all countries have now been warned as never before—citizens are more able and more willing now to demand reform and to make their actions count.

The voices of anger have risen, and will rise still higher, to confront the vile conspiracies between crooked businessmen and crooked public officials. Across the Internet, global TV, and the print media, we see the despots and their cronies enjoying lavish luxuries, oblivious to the misery and the hardship they create, and we all recognize the ugly face of greed and arrogance.

The protests are not just directed at the masters of grand corruption at the zenith of power. They also express the frustration and anger of hundreds of millions of people who are routinely the victims of extortion at the hands of mid- and low-level police and other officials who should be serving the public, rather than serving themselves.

The clarion call emerged from Tahrir Square and it was heard every-where. In the White House, the voices of the poor in North Africa and the Middle East turned strategic policies on their heads. President Obama de-cided to side with the citizens and against the dictators who for years were viewed as the "friends" of the West.

Trust among people to take heart, to overcome fears and go to the streets, was built via Twitter and Facebook and other social media. This was not the first time that new technology was deployed for this cause. Exactly one decade before the events in Tahrir Square, in January 2001, massive texting by thousands of Philippinos sparked huge demonstrations in support of the full force of justice against President Joseph "Erap" Estrada, who was forced from office on charges of corruption. But the scale and the global impact of the "Arab Spring" marked the coming of age in the arena of public protest against corruption in the new age of transparency.

Now, thanks to myriad media channels and new technologies, what was long opaque in government and business is becoming transparent. In this new age, the public is being increasingly well informed on the practices of the powerful. The eyes of the world are now more focused on the deals that governments and businesses do together, on the ways public procurement contracts are determined and who benefits, and on those actions by people in power that have hitherto not been sufficiently subject to public scrutiny and oversight. This new age of transparency that is dawning is seeing levels of government and public-sector accountability rise. Increasingly, the corrupt villains, whose best friend is secrecy, find that they have ever fewer places to hide.

The message that the protesters are sending is clear: the anticorruption train has left the station and it is gathering speed toward a destination called good governance. The journey will be long, there will be interruptions and setbacks, and some carriages may not make it all the way, but many will.

Every individual has a fundamental right to be treated by those who hold governmental power with respect and with honesty. Accordingly, all people engaged in public service need to serve the people and all of their interests. Public officials who serve their own interests and abuse their offices and the public trust are corrupt. They should face justice for their crimes, as should all those who pay bribes.

As discussed in this book, corruption is the abuse of public office for private gain. Corruption involves the following elements:

- theft of public funds by government leaders, senior public officials, and their cronies;
- bribes being paid to those who hold public-sector power—at even the lowest levels of the civil service—by those seeking special favors; and

• extortion by politicians and civil servants to obtain illicit payments from ordinary people and from businesses by threatening them with bitter consequences if they do not pay or by withholding basic services from them.

At the inaugural conference of Transparency International (TI) in Berlin during May 1993, Professor Robert Klitgaard (then of the University of Natal, South Africa) inspired participants by arguing that our cause would succeed if we could adopt a thoroughly practical approach. Klitgaard, now at Claremont Graduate University, California, said much the same thing in an article on Southern Sudan in 2011: "Put the fight against corruption at the center of creating a new government. Create a core of qualified, well-paid government leaders. Demonstrate that impunity is over by frying some big fish."[1]

This is a long war. There will always be corrupt politicians and government officials. Moreover, the scale of the problem is enormous. At the end of 2011, TI published its annual Global Corruption Barometer survey covering 105,500 people in one hundred countries, which noted that almost one in four (24 percent) people surveyed reported paying a bribe in the previous twelve months to one of nine institutions and services, from health to education to tax authorities. The police were the worst offenders—almost 30 percent of those who had contact with the police paid a bribe. In many countries corruption is seemingly all-pervasive across politics, the civil service, and the military. TI's Corruption Perceptions Index ranked the ten countries perceived as the most corrupt in a survey of 183 countries in 2011 as Venezuela, Haiti, Iraq, Sudan, Turkmenistan, Uzbekistan, Afghanistan, Myanmar, North Korea, and, worst of all, Somalia![2]

The "Arab Spring" awakened the world to a mounting understanding that a revolution is unfolding against corruption and in support of cleaner government. There is a momentum now toward greater transparency and accountability in public life and in big business. More battles are being waged than ever before.

There is a vastly diverse range of courageous heroes and Machiavellian characters bestriding the global corruption stage. Like a great Shakespearean play, there are major plots and significant diversions, stars and bit-players, the valiant who are cut down in their prime, and scoundrels who create awesome misery.

This is a story of anticorruption activists, victims of corruption, and the villains. As the tale evolves, the building blocks of which have been put in place over a generation that runs from the demolition of the Berlin Wall through the Arab Spring, so a bold conclusion comes into focus: we are living now at a moment when, perhaps for the first time, we can cautiously conclude that a tipping point has been reached. Many of the gains being made in the anticorruption war are solid and greater victories are in prospect, even though, as I note below, some crucial outstanding issues need to be addressed far more comprehensively.

The positive story of so much of this book is shaped by people who are making a remarkable difference to the course of our civilization. These heroes are the women and men who are fearlessly demonstrating in the streets; the investigative reporters and their courageous editors who tell the story as it is; the bold civil society activists; the academics who are strengthening our understanding of the complexities of curbing corruption; the public prosecutors who are challenging powerful tycoons and politicians; the philanthropists who are funding so many good works in this area; and those business people and public servants who are determined to hold true to values of integrity, irrespective of peer pressures.

I do not minimize the obstacles in the path of formidably reducing corruption. In the latter chapters of this book I focus on some of these and introduce policy recommendations to contribute to a reduction in money laundering, to strengthen transparency in the defense and natural resources sectors, to build fairer and more honest systems of justice, to enhance the effectiveness of the anticorruption work of the World Bank, and to make far more meaningful the implementation of many of the new anticorruption laws and conventions that have been agreed upon by national and multilateral authorities in recent years.

No area on the corruption stage is more complicated and more important than the relationship between corruption and international security. In addressing this issue I offer no clear solutions but strive to make the case that a major debate should now be launched on this vital topic that involves senior intelligence and foreign policy officials of many nations. For too long, great powers have bribed foreign "friends" in the name of pursuing strategic goals. Such policies are increasingly backfiring. Afghanistan is only the latest vivid example. As this book was being written, more than ninety thousand foreign troops were engaged in Afghanistan, a country whose government/business/mafia elites shipped, according to official government records, more than $4.6 billion in cash from Kabul airport to Dubai and other foreign places in 2011 (almost as much as the total national budget). The undermining of security efforts by the corruption perpetrated by Afghan officials has become a leading concern for Western military leaders, yet a full and open debate about the issue and the lessons we need to learn for the conduct of future international relations and the building of security remains elusive. Speaking to the US Senate Armed Services Committee in March 2011, Marine Corps General John Allen, who commands the International Security Assistance Force (ISAF) with overall responsibility for all foreign forces in Afghanistan, stressed the threat of corruption to ISAF's mission: "We know that corruption still robs Afghan citizens of their faith in the government and that poor governance itself often advances insurgent messages."

In Afghanistan, Pakistan, and Iraq, and in other strategically important places, the massive scale of corruption is often fueled by the inflow of great sums of US taxpayer cash. It spawns anti-Americanism, which becomes a proxy for anti-modernism, anti-democracy, and anti–women's rights. The costs to our civilization's prospects may be enormous.

As more people become aware of the full risks that corruption poses, the prospects of finding effective solutions is likely to rise. Today, more people in more countries have a keener sense of being able to confront abuses of power while fully recognizing the dangers that speaking truth to power often involves. Thousands of citizens died in 2011 as they were gunned down by the armies of their corrupt leaders in Egypt, Libya, Syria, and Iran. Many individuals working as investigative journalists, as advocates of human rights and anticorruption, have been beaten by the authorities and sometimes assassinated.

It is easy to be cynical about the prospects of curbing corruption. But the reality is that the many people who are risking their lives now are not doing so in vain. I believe they are on a winning trajectory. There is also a good deal of good news around that underscores the intensity of public interest in corruption, the rising levels of information about particular corruption episodes, and insightful media reporting. As this book was being written, a plethora of new developments on the corruption front was hitting the headlines: more money was going into the US elections than ever before, and no doubt those providing the largest single amounts of cash will be seeking benefits for themselves from the politicians they have so lavishly sponsored; UK investigations moved into high gear over the bribery of senior Scotland Yard policemen by UK journalists; the Independent Commission Against Corruption in Hong Kong was building a major case against billionaire real estate developers and former top officials; an enormous corruption scandal was shaking the top echelons of China's Communist Party; and international media reports were detailing multimillion-dollar stock-market profits through alleged insider trading by top Kremlin officials. Meanwhile, on Wall Street, bribery was being seen in major insider-trading prosecutions; Walmart, the world's largest retailer, came under investigation by the US Department of Justice for alleged widespread illicit pay-offs to public officials in Mexico; and massive bribery of government leaders in Ireland was resolutely confirmed by the final report of the "Corruption Tribunal: The 'Tribunal of Inquiry into Certain Planning Matters and Payments.'"

There have always been corruption conspiracies in many countries, but now we are witnessing extraordinary zeal by public prosecutors, armed with excellent forensic e-mail/computer technologies, cooperating with each other across national borders, and keenly aware that they enjoy strong public support for their efforts.

And, most importantly, despite the many dangers and despite the seemingly awesome obstacles in the path of corruption fighters, every day sees a strengthening of national anticorruption movements in dozens of countries. More people are joining the ranks of the demonstrators and campaigning organizations are growing as the spirit of the "Arab Spring" takes hold.

NOTES

1. Robert Klitgaard, "Making a Country," *Foreign Policy*, January 2011.
2. Transparency International's Corruption Perceptions Index 2011. See appendix 1.

Part 1

Drama

Chapter One

Waking Up

Imran Khan stood before a crowd of perhaps as many as one hundred thousand people in Lahore, Pakistan, in November 2011 and castigated his country's politicians for corruption. The former captain of his country's cricket team, with rugged, movie-star good looks, has been building political support across the nation with blunt accusations: "Because of corruption there is unemployment, because of corruption there is inflation, because of corruption, we are in a state of slavery with the United States."[1]

As never before, the anticorruption message is being blasted across public squares in dozens of countries and via the Internet. The war on corruption did not start in Tunisia and Egypt in January 2011, but the demonstrations provided the fight with an enormous forward momentum that has ricocheted across the world. The timing could not have been better. Many initiatives, in many countries, have been launched over the past twenty years and now they are coming together with force and focus. The stage is being set for a new era of mass anticorruption public engagement.

What makes the 2011 ouster of Tunisia's and Egypt's leaders so important is the fact that they reflected the power of the new age of transparency. This enables people to exchange information beyond the reach of official censors. The tools of this era of transparency are freeing citizens everywhere to voice their frustrations, to share their ideas, to call on each other to act, to overcome their fears of ruthless authorities, and to spread news of government theft, extortion, and coercion. These tools are the fuel of the assault on corruption.

On January 25, 2011, over fifty thousand Egyptians gathered in Tahrir Square in central Cairo. On one side of the vast square is the National Museum, where spectacular collections of past Egyptian greatness mostly collect dust in largely neglected rooms. Now, the crowds had massed to topple another pharaoh, President Hosni Mubarak. They were inspired by the successful mass protests in Tunisia just a few days earlier that saw long-term President Zine el-Abidine Ben Ali, seventy-four, and his family and cronies flee into exile in Saudi Arabia on January 16. They came to Tahrir Square to tell the world that their national leaders were betraying them and had done so for decades, and that they had had enough.

Writing in the *New York Review of Books* in September 2011, Hussein Agha and Robert Malley stressed that for years the citizens of numerous Arab states saw their governmental systems as counterfeit:

> Citizens were put off by how their rulers took over public goods as private possessions and made national decisions under foreign influence. When that happens, the regime's very existence—the merciless domination they impose on their people and the debasing subservience they concede to outsiders—becomes a constant, unbearable provocation.

Ordinary Egyptians rallied as word spread across Facebook and Twitter and through e-mails and text messages sent from one person to another. They overcame their fears of reprisals by the ever-present government security forces and the police. They had had enough—the "unbearable provocation" of their rulers had come to its logical end.

Hundreds of the Egyptian protesters would die in the following days and many more would be beaten. These brave Egyptians stood their ground and voiced their protests because they needed jobs, they needed some hope for the future, and—most compellingly—they needed to secure for themselves a measure of personal dignity after years of continuous disrespect from those who held political power. They came to Tahrir Square to demand an end to the massive corruption perpetrated by President Mubarak, his sons, his immediate subordinates, his friends, and the business personnel with whom they conspired to cheat the people.

I went to Cairo exactly to the day two years earlier at the invitation of a courageous young Egyptian woman, Omnia Hussien, who had covertly been striving to create a network of influential Egyptians who shared her view that corruption had to be confronted. Omnia's goal was to establish an Egyptian national chapter of the global anticorruption organization Transparency International (TI).

Omnia worked to put together a conference that would be all about corruption, but would appear to be about the international financial disarray that had exploded in the fall of 2008. A meeting on "transparency and disclosure in the global financial and economic crisis and its impact on Egypt" took place at a prestigious think-tank, the Al Ahram Centre for Political and

Strategic Studies. Omnia had convinced the US Agency for International Development (USAID) to fund the event, but she had prudently ensured that this did not become public knowledge.

About one hundred people came together and none of them was interested in discussing the global financial crisis. They all wanted to talk about corruption: the abuse of public office for private gain. The participants complained openly about the scale of corruption in every corner of the government. Omnia explained later that such talk was so commonplace that the authorities made no effort to quash it as long as it was within the confines of respectable institutions, such as this think-tank. But, as I was to learn at a meeting that she also convened of just a dozen people, the authorities would not tolerate for an instant any effort to organize an anticorruption campaign or allow the registration of any nongovernmental organization engaged in governance issues.

I was also to learn that the economic conditions in Egypt were turning from bad to worse and that the greater the underemployment and joblessness of hundreds of thousands of well-educated young people, the more frustrations rose. One illustration of the worsening conditions, I was told, was a sharp increase in street crime. I was left in little doubt that the situation was widely seen as explosive. I was mugged on my way to the airport—a portent, perhaps, of the desperation that unleashed the historic events precisely two years later.

The enormous unemployment in the Arab world, the seeming disregard of the poor by their governments, and the intense daily humiliations of ordinary citizens by the police and the security services all combined to build the eventual explosion of public frustration. The use of social media to foster and promote the protests was hugely important. Its full impact was due to the fact that the time was right after years of outrageous abuses of power.

The "Arab Spring" did not end corruption in the Arab world. The risks of serious reverses are ever present in a region that has scant history of democracy or governmental accountability. Yet the protesters in Tunisia and Egypt at the start of 2011 sent a wake-up call throughout the Middle East and North Africa and far beyond.

US President Obama understood the protests and the evils of corruption. On May 19, 2011, in a speech on the Middle East, the president said, "We will help governments meet international obligations, and invest efforts at anti-corruption—by working with parliamentarians who are developing reforms, and activists who use technology to increase transparency and hold government accountable."

CORRUPTION IS UNIVERSAL

All governments are vulnerable to corruption and no government can claim that it does not harbor officials who abuse their office for their personal gain. While it is almost certainly true that corruption in government will never be ended, it is equally true that much can be done to reduce its prevalence.

Michael Elliot, a veteran British journalist, was one of the first reporters to look in-depth at the progress being made by then one-year-old TI when he wrote a cover story for *Newsweek International* that started with these words:

> You're driving in Accra, capital of Ghana, minding your own business, when a traffic cop decides you've made an "illegal" left turn. The spot fine? Fifty bucks, and no receipt. Your company needs telephone repairs in Beijing. The price? A fishing trip for everyone in the local telephone and telegraph office. You spend a day at the Venezuelan port of La Guaira, filling in forms so you can export mangoes. At the last minute, an official spots a typo. So sorry, all the paperwork has to be redone: that, or pay a "special fee." Or watch your mangoes rot. *Baksheesh* in Egypt, *dash* in Kenya, *mordida* in Mexico—corruption is everywhere, and ancient. Mercury probably ran a crooked messenger service on Mount Olympus. Anti-corruption laws are just as old: "Neither shalt thou take bribes," god told Moses, "which blind the wise and pervert the words of the just." [2]

Corruption is not a single event, but a continuum, perpetrated day in and day out against citizens by crooked politicians and civil servants who enjoy positions of power. They can be heads of state who demand a pay-off of millions of dollars on major government contracts. Or they can be lowly civil servants in small towns who have the power to grant building permits or allow access for children to schools or reserve hospital beds, and who use such powers to extort cash payments from poor people.

Corruption is a political, social, and economic issue of global proportions. Today, as never before, it is a major cause of the global crises of poverty, human rights, justice, and security. It impacts us all.

Corruption, of course, exists beyond the realms of public officials. Corrupt practices of diverse kinds are pursued solely among private enterprises, without involvement of public officials, and do have severe consequences. My concern in this book, however, centers on the abuse of governmental power, including the interaction between business and government, and on the immense damage this does to the human condition and to our global security.

When American financier Bernie Madoff builds a phony investment fund and provides kickbacks to associates who supply his fund with major infusions of new cash, then that is corruption and we have laws and investigative agencies to deal with this. When rival firms collude and secretly agree to secure payoffs among themselves so that one firm can be a successful bidder on a contract at an inflated price, then that is a form of corruption. Many others have written about these and other kinds of private-sector corruption. It is important to acknowledge its existence. The extent to which business-to-business corruption is investigated, prosecuted, and ultimately reduced will largely depend, I submit, on the degree to which the war on governmental corruption succeeds.

I have no doubt that corruption in many countries can be curbed and will be curbed. This will contribute enormously to an improvement in the quality of our civilization and to relationships between peoples both within and across national borders. It is easy to view the anticorruption struggle as a Sisyphean endeavor, where no sooner have victories been attained than losses follow, so that over time one has made no progress. There are many examples to support such a view, from Kenya to Ukraine.

When, in 2002, Mwai Kibaki took the helm of government in Kenya and replaced Daniel arap Moi, who had been president for twenty-four years, there was a widespread expectation in the country and beyond that a new era of honest government was dawning. That impression was strengthened by the government's actions in its first year. But old habits resurfaced and before long the top echelon of the Kibaki administration was feeding as fully and illegally from the governmental trough as Moi's ministers had done.

Corruption is often the product of envy. Opposition leaders see the luxuries enjoyed by the rulers and when they themselves become the rulers then they feel that now they should taste the riches of power. Ethnic and tribal pressures can promote the envy and the greed and theft that are born when, as Michela Wrong has declared in the title of her book on graft in Kibaki's Kenya, "It's Our Turn to Eat."[3]

Corruption can mount as despots become ever more accustomed to the trappings of power. A decade ago the "Orange Revolution," prompted by massive public protests in Ukraine, led to the coming to power of what looked like an honest and democratic set of leaders. But they gradually lost their reforming zeal as they came to enjoy their high offices. They lost favor with the public and were replaced at the polls by politicians who made no pretense of being reformers. Today, Ukraine is again under the tyranny of a corrupt government and ranks among the world's most corrupt nations.

The bad news on corruption always overshadows the good news on anticorruption. Nevertheless, there is a lot more progress being made toward curbing corruption than is widely realized. As more people understand this, popular cynicism that argues there has always been corruption, and that there always will be, may be reduced. Instead, we may see heightened levels of public engagement dedicated to the goals of increasing transparency and accountability in all aspects of government.

The pace of anticorruption action is accelerating. Over the last generation we have seen developments that are transforming the once hopeless cause of fighting corruption into a viable proposition. We are now seeing a powerful combination of forces:

- A robust set of civil society organizations operating nationally and internationally—headed by courageous professionals—that are dedicated to curbing corruption.
- A complex of national and international anticorruption laws and conventions, backed by world leaders, which set benchmarks and standards for enforcement that are being monitored with mounting impact. The conclusions of the Group of 20 summit meetings in 2010, 2011, and 2012 with specific anticorruption agendas illustrate the momentum behind official-level anticorruption actions today.
- The rapid development of new information and media technologies that are creating a level of interconnectivity between peoples of all ages and all countries that, by building a new age of transparency, leaves the corrupt bribe takers and bribe payers with ever fewer places to hide.
- Rising support from philanthropic foundations, plus formidable increases in academic research, which are adding greatly to the operational capacities and to the focus of those civil society organizations, large and small, that are at the core of the war on corruption.

GREED

The giant corporate scandals that unfolded from 2001 onward, starting with the collapse of Enron, once the seventh-largest company in the United States, and then the Wall Street financial crisis in 2008/2009, which spread across all mature industrial economies, heightened public awareness of grand-scale corporate malfeasance. So many of the business debacles that grabbed the headlines highlighted extraordinary greed on the part of a relatively small number of titans of industry and finance. The protests on Wall Street in late 2011 were triggered in part by a general sense that the leaders of big business were engaged in conspiracies with politicians for their mutual benefit at the expense of the public at large. The American capitalist system, or at least its most prominent parts, was perceived as corrupt.

The "Occupy Wall Street" movement was one more mass public protest inspired by the Arab Spring. It described itself as "a leaderless resistance movement with people of many colors, genders and political persuasions. The one thing we all have in common is that 'We Are The 99%' that will no longer tolerate the greed and corruption of the 1%. We are using the revolutionary Arab Spring tactic to achieve our ends and encourage the use of nonviolence to maximize the safety of all participants."[4]

A visitor to the protesters down on Wall Street in the fall of 2011 was Nobel-prize-winning economist and Columbia University professor Joseph E. Stiglitz, whose lectures and writings—notably, an article in the May 2011 issue of *Vanity Fair* magazine[5]—were an influence on the Occupy Wall Street movement's core thinking and protest. The article, titled "Of the 1%, by the 1%, for the 1%," started by noting the following:

> Americans have been watching protests against oppressive regimes that concentrate massive wealth in the hands of an elite few. Yet in our own democracy, 1 percent of the people take nearly a quarter of the nation's income—an inequality even the wealthy will come to regret. . . . In terms of wealth rather than income, the top 1 percent control 40 percent. Their lot in life has improved considerably. Twenty-five years ago, the corresponding figures were 12 percent and 33 percent.[6]

Professor Stiglitz is by no means the only member of the American economics and business establishment to be concerned about the rising greed and trends toward extraordinary income inequality in America. Such thoughts concerned quite a number of leaders a decade earlier after the convictions of a host of top US executives who had wrecked such once giant companies as Tyco, WorldCom, and Enron. On the first anniversary of the 9/11 tragedy, President William J. McDonough of the New York Federal Reserve Bank took to the pulpit of Trinity Church in Manhattan to speak about the virtues of American leadership in the world and the risks to such leadership when the values of those at the helm of American business go astray. He noted that a recent study showed that twenty years earlier the average chief executive officer of a publicly traded company made forty-two times more than the average production worker, but the multiple today (2002) was over four hundred times the average employee's income. McDonough then said:

> It is hard to find somebody more convinced than I of the superiority of the American economic system, but I can find nothing in economic theory that justifies this development. I am old enough to have known both the CEOs of twenty years ago and those of today. I can assure you that we CEOs of today are not ten times better than those of twenty years ago. What happened? Sadly, all too many members of the inner circle of the business elite participated in the overexpansion of executive compensation. It was justified by a claimed identity between the motivation of the executives and shareholder value. It is reasonably clear now that this theory has left a large number of poorer stockholders, especially including employee stockholders, not only unconvinced,

but also understandably disillusioned and angry. The policy of vastly increasing executive compensation was also, at least with the brilliant vision of hindsight, terribly bad social policy and perhaps even bad morals.

There is nothing new about the vilification of business tycoons. The American "robber-barons" did not win their title for nothing. Even Britain's Conservative Party leader and prime minister Edward Heath, in 1993, felt bound to hit out as he learned of the bribery and intrigues involved in the African mining deals spearheaded by businessman Tiny Rowland. Heath declared this is "the unacceptable face of capitalism."

Be it in the public parks or from the pulpit of a great church in Manhattan, the protests over corporate greed ring loud. They contribute compellingly to a public sense of outrage and injustice and so fortify those leading anticorruption efforts. The news of the excesses of greed now travel faster and wider than ever before, thanks to the Internet, and the better informed the broad public becomes, the more support anticorruption campaigns can secure.

GLOBALIZED NETWORKS FOR REFORM

The broader context of all of the diverse developments that are impacting the anticorruption war is the rapid evolution of globalization, which sees not just goods and services crossing national borders at a record pace, but also people and information flowing across the globe as if national barriers no longer meaningfully existed. Brent Scowcroft, US National Security Council chief in the administration of President George W. Bush, described the situation well when he said:

> I believe we've had a more abrupt change in the international environment than at any time in recent history, a fundamental change that goes under the broad heading of globalization. It's a change in the way people communicate and interact. That is what's revolutionizing the world . . . The important point is that it is really changing the status of the nation-state, how it cares for its people, and how it can manage its overall responsibilities for its citizens. The fact is that the role of nation-state, while still predominant, is steadily diminishing.[7]

The pace of the globalization process of which Scowcroft speaks intensified in the 1990s as the Internet came into widespread use. Suddenly, people in distant places could connect with others at minimal cost. As the era of the fax gave way to e-mail, civil society organizations could expand at a pace that had previously been unthinkable. Networks started to develop across nations—indeed, across the world—between ordinary people who shared common interests.

And this coincided with the collapse of the Soviet Union, the end of the Cold War, and the rise of major efforts in many countries to plant the seeds of democratic institutions in countries that hitherto had only known dictatorships—not just in Central and Eastern Europe, but also in Latin America and, following the end of apartheid and the example of newly democratic South Africa, through sub-Saharan Africa as well. The pro-democracy efforts involved initiatives to broaden press freedom, to curb state directed censorship, to encourage free speech and contested elections, and to teach civics to tens of millions of people who had never before had the opportunity to cast a free and secret vote for their governments.

As anticorruption actions across the world become better understood, they will build even larger public pressures for fundamental governance changes. The Arab Spring is just a foretaste.

Over time in many countries, if not all, the scale of public demonstrations and calls for meaningful governance changes will increase, and the risks of exposure for corrupt officials and politicians will rise. The crooks will find it ever more difficult to retain office, to keep their schemes secret, and to hide their ill-gotten gains.

The years ahead will see a rising tide of investigations into the illicit activities of the bribe payers and the corporations that aid and abet corrupt politicians and officials to launder their stolen cash. There will be an unprecedented assault on money-laundering, to put a halt to the illicit activities of the financial intermediary institutions that help crooks, including corrupt officials, to wash hundreds of billions of dollars each year through the global financial system.

Sensing that the anticorruption war is not a fly-by-night endeavor, but here to stay and gaining in strength, the world's most powerful leaders are indicating ever more strongly that they are willing to sign up. In 2010 in Seoul, South Korea, and in 2011 in Cannes, France, the leaders of the world's most powerful countries met at summits of the Group of 20 to agree and develop specific anticorruption action plans. Their commitments ranged across the landscape from tax evasion and money laundering to uses and abuses of foreign aid. Their agreements were unimaginable a generation earlier when not a single global anticorruption civil society organization existed and there were no international anticorruption conventions. The G20 agreements represent not just a vital landmark in the long war against graft, bribery, and kickbacks but also a roadmap for future action (see chapter 13).

This is an acknowledgment of the pressures, led by civil society, that are changing the corruption equation in favor of those who are fighting this crime. The G20 declarations are calls for further, more intense and effective anticorruption actions ahead. It will be challenging to hold the feet of the

G20 to the fire to ensure that actions follow rhetoric, yet it is a challenge that civil society organizations across the world are better prepared to pursue than ever before.

We are on the cusp of a new era where the rising pressures on bribe takers and bribe payers will become increasingly evident to growing numbers of people across the world. This will provide vital encouragement to support civil society action, law enforcement, and positive political change.

In the lead in the journey that is unfolding are people of enormous drive and courage. People matter when it comes to changing the course of national and international events. And when it comes to smashing the corruption that traps tens of millions of people in absolute destitution, then the bravery of individuals is making—and I believe will continue to make—an extraordinary contribution. This is why this book features a number of those individuals from across the world who have emerged as the heroes in the anticorruption battles.

In late 2010, I had a meeting with a young man from Zimbabwe who was working with TI; in response to a question he said, "My mother is really scared. On the one hand she likes what I do, but each time she sees me she is happy because she is not sure she will see me again. My fiancée is even more worried. I do this because my country is too rich to see so many people living so badly. We have enormous wealth in our country, but the government has diverted all the funds. When you work in this area [anticorruption] you know you are being watched by the police and the security agents all the time. Sometimes they take you in for a few hours, sometimes they make threats. But we know that if we can resolve the governance problem, then we can move to the promised land."

Elena Panfilova is at the forefront of the Russian anticorruption movement. Major efforts by TI's founder and first chairman, Peter Eigen, were made in the mid-1990s to set the foundations for a TI chapter in Russia, which were subsequently formalized and carried forward by Elena. "When I started to become concerned with the issue of corruption it was an intellectual challenge," she told me. "I wanted to understand it—how it is organized, what impact it has. Gradually, by 1997 and '98, I started to realize that Russia was not alone and that we had many problems in common with many other countries, like Colombia and Philippines. I learned a lot about the general problems of corruption when I was working at the OECD in Paris. My friends in Russia said that it must be nice and academic being in Paris, but shouldn't I do something for my country?"[8]

Elena continued:

> In 1999, we packed up in Paris and moved to Moscow and I met with others who had similar views to me and on December 19, 1999, we started TI-Russia. None of us knew anything about NGOs, but we had a combination of talents.

And, right from the beginning, I had the irrational belief that I could always be smart and not endanger my family. I hated the constant talk that we Russians are more corrupt than others, that it is our nature. I felt a compelling urge to show that we Russians can do something about corruption and that we could bring corrupt people to justice.

So we started and we met people who were victims of corruption, and we discussed with good businesses that were in trouble and we looked for opportunities to speak on big stages and to build support to change things. After ten years we can really say that we brought anticorruption onto the national agenda—people at many political levels now talk about it in contrast to the silence of the 1990s. And, we have brought younger people into the movement. More and more people have become attracted to our dual mission of helping ordinary people and at the same time pushing the big agenda.

Elena questions, "Are we in danger? There have really been three stages. In our first five years we were ants and we were not seen as significant by the authorities. From 2004–2008, we faced constant pressures, people followed me, my computer was hacked, our office was watched. More recently, there has been less pressure. We still have official checks on what we are doing and on our finances and we could be closed and arrested at any time. But, [former] President Medvedev recognized TI and acknowledged our issues publicly and that gives us some cover. Today, I feel deep pleasure in what I do."

This book starts by describing the corruption drama: the damage wrought by corruption, the victims, the game-changing activists, the villains in politics and in business, and the enormous influence that the leading Western governments wield on ties between corruption, peace, and security. In the second part of this book we travel back in time to trace the major milestones that have been put in place to bring us now to a point of real hope of curbing corruption. The third part of this volume looks at the current agenda of major anticorruption issues and seeks to recommend initiatives, programs, and policies that can take us closer to victory while also recognizing some of those individuals who are true heroes of the war against corruption.

TRANSPARENCY

I have felt driven to write this book by the courage of many of my friends in many countries who are leading TI. TI, launched in 1993, was the idea of a small group of dreamers who believed that civil society action could curb corruption. It has grown to become a world leader with a highly professional staff at its global secretariat in Berlin, Germany, and more than ninety nationally based organizations led by individuals whose zeal, intelligence, and pragmatic skills combine to translate the early dreams into modern realities. Their approaches and successes need to be better understood.

TI's founders, and I was fortunate to be among them, recognized that corruption thrives in secrecy. We knew that if we could make the business of government publicly transparent, then we could make real progress. Create sunshine on the hidden corridors of public power and it will act as a powerful disinfectant.

I share the view of Jeremy Pope, the first managing director of TI, who noted once that "knowledge is power, and those who possess it have the power to rule. Perhaps that is why an obsession with secrecy persists across the world."

But the defenders of secrecy are in retreat. The citizens of many countries no longer accept the arrogant "trust us" claims of those who govern. Increasingly, people want to be able to judge for themselves about the degree to which they can trust those in power. The demands for access to governmental information are rising across the world and civil society and the media are pushing hard, not just to obtain information that has been held secret in the past, but also to disseminate it as rapidly and as widely as possible. The rationale is simple, as Pope has written:

> If our objective is transparent, accountable and honest governance—govern-
> ment we can trust and a private sector that is trustworthy—then clearly the less
> information that is kept from us, and the greater the confidence we have in its
> accuracy, the more likely we are to achieve our aim. Transparency has become
> a substitute for trust. [9]

Today, within the context of fighting corruption, the degree of transparency in public life is far, far higher than anyone imagined it would be just a couple of decades ago. Yes, there are some key areas that remain opaque—notably, the operations of assorted governmental intelligence agencies and the international financial machinery that efficiently launders one trillion dollars of illicit funds every year and turns the loot into respectable investments. But even in these areas there are cracks.

Wikileaks, Twitter, Facebook, texting, old-fashioned e-mail, and assorted related new technologies have transformed and will continue to transform the information landscape. At the time of this writing, hundreds of millions of people now use Facebook, enabling them, through a single platform, to communicate without any sense of national barriers and talk about whatever enters their minds. The Internet and social-media tools in particular are real power in hands of civil society activists. There are now a rising number of websites dedicated to raising public awareness of corruption and asking people to participate, to lodge their complaints, and to find volunteer experts who can help them with their own cases as victims of corruption; www.bribespot.com and www.ipaidabribe.com are just two of many such sites that are generating rising interest.

With the support of a quilt of anticorruption laws covering more countries than ever before, the public at large in scores of countries is learning more every day about corrupt politicians and civil servants and those that bribe them. And this knowledge is a source of power and a driver of action. Increasing numbers of people, appalled about what they are learning, are now willing to go into the streets to protest, to sign petitions, to join campaigns, and to be counted.

In early 2009, TI's chair, Huguette Labelle, and the TI secretariat managing director, Cobus de Swardt, set about crafting a new multiyear TI strategy that placed people engagement at its center. Central to this strategy would be the Internet and social media.

These are extraordinary leaders from radically different backgrounds. Huguette is the chancellor of the University of Ottawa and served for nineteen years as deputy minister of different Canadian government departments, including secretary of state, Transport Canada, the Public Service Commission, and the Canadian International Development Agency. Huguette, who has been elected three times as the chair of the TI board of directors (elected by the global membership of TI) since 2005, has traveled tirelessly to dozens of countries to learn about corruption firsthand, to confer with national activists, and to understand their risks and their challenges. She has then spoken on their behalf at the highest councils of the World Bank and the United Nations (UN) and to government and business leaders. At the same time, she has been leading lengthy TI Board discussions aimed at strengthening the global movement and forging a far-reaching new TI strategy.

Her prime partner, running the operations of the Berlin-based TI secretariat with its staff of over 130 people, is Cobus. As a young man in his hometown of Cape Town, South Africa, he was highly active in the antiapartheid movement, often being arrested and beaten. An academic sociologist who has taught in several countries, he has also been engaged in several civil society organizations and joined TI in 2004 and became managing director in 2007. In the course of 2009 and 2010, he arranged dozens of meetings of TI staff and members of TI national chapters to evaluate the movement's strengths and weaknesses and to build an understanding of where they would like to see the movement go in coming years. These were vital inputs for the eventual new TI strategy.

What both Huguette and Cobus learned, above all, was that the many members of the movement believed that it was now time for a dramatic broadening of the movement's reach and focus. In its first dozen years, understandably, TI had been highly engaged in its relationships with elites, be they in governments, business, academia, other civil society organizations, philanthropic foundations, and major media. Now, it was time for TI to become a far more grassroots-based movement, harnessing mass publics to the anticorruption cause.

In November 2010 (by coincidence just two months before the dawn of the Arab Spring), 350 delegates from over one hundred countries came to TI's annual meeting in Bangkok, Thailand, and ratified the new strategy. As was to be seen in the streets of Tunisia and Egypt shortly thereafter, TI's new strategy was not ahead of its time, but in sync with the times. The leading aspiration of TI-Strategy 2011–2015 reads as follows:

> People standing up to corruption: We recognize that for change to be sustainable, it is essential that it be underpinned by widespread public support. It is people who must demand accountability from those who are in positions of entrusted power. To this end, we aspire to stimulate and support the emergence of a broad-based social movement of millions of people standing up to corruption, especially where it violates human rights and threatens the most vulnerable.

Under the direction of TI's highly creative communications chief, André Doren, a mass-marketing, advertising, and publicity campaign was launched to support the mass public strategy called "Time to Wake Up." People everywhere need to wake up to the fact that they can come together and protest the outrages cast upon them by corrupt leaders.

People everywhere are waking up. The brave actions of tens of thousands of Tunisians and Egyptians against their corrupt governments at the start of 2011 inspired public protests in many countries. First, Arabs in Libya, Syria, Bahrain, and in other Arab countries overcame their fears to go into the streets and demand a just society. Then, in Iran, where thousands of citizens had marched against the corrupt regime the year before, new protests started and once again many people were hauled off to prison by the authorities. The public protests across the Middle East and in North Africa gave courage to victims of corruption on an unprecedented scale.

Thousands of people took to the streets from Belarus, where the regime of President Alexander Lukashenko is decidedly more rotten and criminal than most, to the other end of the alphabet in Venezuela, where the nation's vast oil income disappears into the pockets of President Cesar Chavez and his associates, while the country suffers ever more power shortages. In India, where a free press has persistently reported alleged business-government corrupt dealings for years and where the authorities have ignored the issue, the public demanded change. Speaking to thousands of his supporters after his release from prison in New Delhi on August 19, 2011, Anna Hazare, age seventy-four, said, "You have lit a torch against corruption. Don't extinguish it until India is free from corruption."

He vowed to continue campaigning until the parliament passed an anti-corruption law (which it has yet to do) and, speaking to more than fifty thousand people at a rally, he declared, "There is corruption in land being forcibly taken away from farmers for builders and companies. Farmers are being forced to commit suicide. We have to fight for them. The education system has become so corrupt that we have to pay money to get our children admitted in schools and colleges. This chain of corruption has to be broken. We have to change the system."[10]

The message from one street to another, from Tahrir Square to even the horridly repressed peoples of Myanmar, is the new reality of our times. In late September 2011, Lex Rieffel, a Brookings Institution scholar with a passionate interest in one of the most corrupt countries in the world, Myanmar, suggested in an e-mail that even the Burmese are now waking up:

> Myanmar has been irrelevant in the international economy for the past 60 years, and it has been one of the most horribly governed (and least transparent) countries in the world during this period. And we're talking about a country of 50–60 million people. . . . But something worth watching is happening in that country now. Steps have been taken by the new government, installed in April 2011, that people did not believe were possible three months ago, and even less a year ago.

The mass demonstrations in so many places pose a mounting challenge to the leaders of corrupt Third World regimes. But they are not alone in having to face the new reality of people power in the new age of transparency. Much of the corruption on this planet stems from the willingness of the governments of rich nations to provide exceptional support to corrupt overseas leaders in exchange for arms deals; rights to oil, gas, and mining resources; and strategic relationships.

As these pages were being written, the corrupt leaders of many nations were being cordially received at the White House, at tea with the Queen of England, at military parades with the French president, and before the General Assembly of the United Nations. The hospitality is seen by foreign policy strategists as part of broad-based efforts to secure "friends" in foreign governments, irrespective of what crimes these leaders may be doing to their own citizens. For example, it was as recently as June 2009, when then Italian prime minister Silvio Berlusconi hosted the summit conference of the Group of 8 in Italy and invited Libya's Colonel Qadhafi to join the festivities, shake hands, and chat with leaders, including President Barack Obama and then UK prime minister Gordon Brown.

Many foreign-policy experts in Western capitals are complacent about corruption either because they believe nothing can and will be done about it, or because they see it as a useful short-cut to achieving short-term strategic goals. They are wrong. Their ostrich-like obstinacy meant that they failed to see the Arab Spring coming, just like they fail right now to understand that we will see extraordinary public protests leading to major government changes in Azerbaijan, Belarus, Afghanistan, Iraq, and in many other countries in coming years.

The eradication of corruption is a global challenge. The Arab Spring is a call to action.

NOTES

1.   Report by Julie McCarthy from Pakistan for US National Public Radio's "Morning Edition," November 24, 2011.

2.   Michael Elliot, "Money Talks," *Newsweek International*, November 14, 1994.

3.   Michela Wrong, *It's Our Turn to Eat—The Story of a Kenyan Whistle-Blower* (London: Fourth Estate, 2009).

4.   See occupywallst.org.

5.   Joseph. E. Stiglitz, "Of the 1%, By the 1%, For the 1%," *Vanity Fair*, May 2011.

6.   At the conclusion of his article, Professor Stiglitz noted, "The top 1 percent have the best houses, the best educations, the best doctors, and the best lifestyles, but there is one thing that money doesn't seem to have bought: an understanding that their fate is bound up with how the other 99 percent live. Throughout history, this is something that the top 1 percent eventually do learn. Too late."

7.   *America and the World—Conversations on the Future of American Foreign Policy* (New York: Basic Books, 2008)—conversations with Zbigniew Brzezinski and Brent Scowcroft, moderated by David Ignatius.

8.   The Organisation for Economic Co-operation and Development (OECD), headquartered in Paris, serves as a "think-tank" for the world's largest economies. It also administers a series of specialized official governmental agencies concerned with international economic issues, such as the Financial Action Task Force (FATF), which is the leading multilateral agency engaged on money-laundering issues.

9.   Jeremy Pope's essay in Transparency International's *Global Corruption Report: 2003* (London: Profile Books, 2003).

10.   *The Hindu* (India), August 21, 2011.

Chapter Two

Corruption Crimes

Ngozi Okonjo-Iweala is a strident and courageous anticorruption advocate who served some years ago as finance minister and foreign minister of Nigeria, then became a World Bank managing director, and later was appointed again as her country's finance minister in July 2011. Ngozi gave a lecture in June 2007 in Washington where she told the story of Rose, a twenty-one-year-old university student in Nigeria:

> Rose, from a poor rural family, could not purchase the series of class notes sold by her lecturer to students as part of the reading material for her class. The lecturer, who used these moneys to supplement his income, noticed that Rose was not purchasing the notes and penalized her through low grades for her work. When she explained she couldn't pay she was asked to make up with other favors, which she refused. The failing grade she was given was instrumental in her withdrawal from the university, which put an end to her higher education. An individual and an entire family lost their hope and pathway to escape poverty. When I followed up on this story, I found that it was by no means an isolated case. It was part of a systemic rot that had befallen what had once been a very good tertiary education system in Nigeria.

The crimes of corruption are not abstract issues. Every time an official steals from the public purse, then someone suffers. Every time an official acts as a villain, then there is a victim. There are tens of millions of young people like Rose. They are the victims of extortion. They have been cheated of their rights. They and their families, through no fault of their own, have had their lives wrecked by officials who care only about enriching themselves. When you travel to India and Pakistan, to Central America and to China, to Egypt and to East Africa, you see firsthand the many dimensions of the corruption crime.

Of course, payoffs to governments have a very long tradition. I recall participating in a TV discussion some years ago with a Russian journalist who, smilingly and loudly, declared, "We have a one-thousand-year glorious tradition of corruption."

He was telling the truth, but Russia is not alone. Powerful potentates down the ages have bribed and corrupted opponents to gain territory and treasure. Speaking at the launch conference of TI in May 1993, Professor Joseph LaPalombara of Yale University said that "corruption may not be the world's oldest profession," but it was thriving in the Roman Empire. He noted that there are records of actions going back to 67 BC that made the "treating" of votes a punishable offense and that Roman politicians used political go-betweens to make payoffs to secure their elections.

In almost all countries until the birth of the United States of America at the end of the eighteenth century, people wielding political power—despite rhetorical flourishes about serving the people—served themselves first and the people second. The abuse of power in government was the norm. Bribery of public officials was the means to gain power and to maintain power. Bribing public officials was the route to seeking influence with those in power and winning government business. Kingdoms were routinely won and lost through bribery.

In the early sixteenth century, for example, Charles V of Spain beat King Francis I of France to gain the support of Pope Leo X to become Holy Roman Emperor. He bribed everyone he could and he won. That was the game back then and well before. It was also a game that the Bush administration played as it sent troops into Afghanistan and into Iraq. In both cases, the United States looked for and found nationals whom it saw as useful leaders: it supported and promoted them, it showered them with cash, and it surrounded them with "advisors" (diplomats, generals, and officers from the Central Intelligence Agency [CIA]).

What is new is that we now know far more about the crimes of corruption than ever before and this knowledge is powerful for those who are standing up today and fighting for reform. What inspires their activism is the wreckage they see in their own countries that corruption has caused and continues to cause.

CORRUPTION IS A CRIME AGAINST HUMANITY

In October 2011, the leaders of TI from more than one hundred countries met for their annual meeting in Berlin and one of the topics under discussion was whether corruption was a crime against humanity.

The International Criminal Court (ICC) in The Hague has the mandate[1] to prosecute such crimes, and there are anticorruption activists who believe that the ICC's remit should embrace corruption. The TI leaders were divided. Some believed that campaigning for the ICC to acknowledge the horrors that corruption causes would be a major milestone in the anticorruption fight. Then Emir Djikic, leader of TI's national chapter in Bosnia-Herzegovina, spoke and, clearly thinking about the ethnic cleansing in his own country, stressed that as horrible as corruption is, it cannot be equated with genocide.

I agree and I do not seek to make the case here for a strict ICC-like understanding of the term "crimes against humanity." But in a more general sense there are crimes of corruption that unquestionably do count among the most vicious crimes that abound.

More people have died in bloody violence in recent years in the Democratic Republic of the Congo (DRC) than in any other country. They are the victims of ethnic strife and vicious power struggles. At the very core of the carnage is the determination of rival leaders with their own armies to obtain power and to massively enrich themselves as a result—there is hardly a country in the world so well endowed with mineral wealth.

An estimated 5.4 million people in the DRC have died over the last handful of years, with half of those murdered being children; tens of thousands of women have been raped; and in the first three months of 2010 alone more than 150,000 people were displaced. Those who hold power in the DRC engage in vastly lucrative sales of minerals to international companies, mostly in secret contracts and almost certainly with clauses calling for payments into bank accounts in Switzerland and other places where bank secrecy is guaranteed under the law. Politicians, senior civil servants, and customs officials are all part of a huge bribery chain so that criminals can deal with international firms and sell and ship the DRC's mineral wealth. Corruption is at the heart of the crimes against humanity that continue in the DRC.

Hundreds of millions of people lack clean water, decent sewage, and access to reasonable healthcare, housing, and education. These people also lack the opportunity to earn a decent wage. They live in Afghanistan and Pakistan and Bangladesh and Nicaragua and Zimbabwe in absolute squalor and on the edge of survival. Many of these people find themselves in such desperate conditions because public funds that should go to providing services and economic opportunities are siphoned off into the private bank accounts of politicians and public officials.

International media headlines frequently highlight large-scale corruption, for example, at the helm of Afghanistan's Government, but my friend Karen Hausman, a founding member as well as a board director of "Integrity Watch Afghanistan," once noted, "Often, the ordinary people in Afghanistan are far more concerned with petty corruption that impacts their daily lives, such as extortion by the police, than by grand corruption at the top of the government."

The fact is that in every country where grand corruption by top politicians and senior public officials is widespread, there is rampant petty corruption where low-level officials in every village and municipality extort bribes from the poor.

• Corruption is when HIV/AIDS medication is too expensive for many people who need it in Ukraine because of all manner of kickbacks between importers and public officials.
• Corruption is when policemen stop ordinary citizens driving along the roads of Ghana and threaten them with prison unless they immediately pay a "fine" in cash.
• Corruption is when dealers in counterfeit medications pay off health officials in Nigeria so that out-of-date or counterfeit pharmaceuticals are distributed to hospitals.
• Corruption is when the government of South Africa entered into major purchases of weapons systems (some of these involved alleged bribes to top officials) at a time when the government of the day said it did not have sufficient budget resources to fund medicines for HIV/AIDS.

Some of the worst poverty is in countries that have vast oil and gold resources and where honest governments could lift their peoples out of poverty and give them the chance to build decent lives for themselves. From Sudan and Angola to Nigeria and Myanmar, and a host of countries in the former Soviet Union, the mineral wealth is stolen by the elites who hold all the power while the people are neglected and trampled on.

There is a close correlation between abuse of human rights, levels of individual freedom, and the scale of corruption. This is underreported.

It is noteworthy that many of the most corrupt countries in the world are also the ones with the worst human rights records. The Freedom House organization, which has been tracking global human rights since 1972, found that in 2009 a total of forty-seven countries ranked "Not Free," with nine countries and one territory receiving the survey's lowest possible rating for both political rights and civil liberties: Myanmar, Equatorial Guinea, Eritrea, Libya, North Korea, Somalia, Sudan, Tibet, Turkmenistan, and Uzbekistan. Many of these countries also find themselves close to the foot of the rankings of the annual TI Corruption Perceptions Index (CPI), which was created in 1995 and analyzes a range of independent opinion polls to gauge perceptions of the degree of bribe taking by officials in over 180 countries.

Countries that rank badly in each of these areas are almost identical. In order to steal from the state, powerful rulers believe they must go to great lengths to curb all forms of criticism, and so the human rights of individuals are stripped away, just as the basic rights of individuals to assemble, to speak openly, to obtain information from their government, and to enjoy a free press are rudely denied.

CORRUPTION IS AN ECONOMIC CRIME

When corruption raises the costs of goods and services, as it almost always does, then it damages living standards and undermines economic growth and the functioning of market forces. When public procurement contracts are won as business people pay bribes to officials, then fair trade and competition are cast aside. When traders and government officials secretly fix prices of commodities so that the officials can become very rich, then everyone suffers.

In July 2011, Financial Action Task Force (FATF), the international official organization that works to counter money laundering, published a report that noted, "The most prominent economic effect of corruption seems to be diversion of money from the government budget to expenses with lower multiplier effects. If money that is meant as an investment in economic development or poverty relief is diverted as result of embezzlement or other forms of public corruption towards private spending, it will in most cases incur a transfer towards expenditures with a lower multiplier effect, such as imported Hummers instead of medicines in the hospitals, or foreign fittings in newly built middle-class city mansions instead of school materials."[2]

- Corruption is when the former Halliburton subsidiary, KBR of Texas, conspired with French and Italian business partners to pay $180 million in bribes to Nigerian government officials in return for $2 billion of energy-sector engineering contracts.
- Corruption is when customs officials in Russia routinely hold up machinery in the docks that is destined for major factories until the buyers pay handsome bribes.
- Corruption is when Siemens AG of Germany, Europe's largest engineering and electronics company, organized and implemented marketing plans to win deals and sell products in a host of countries by paying bribes to officials and by creating a secret multimillion-euro slush-fund in an offshore banking center for this purpose.

A facet of the economic criminality is that each year billions of dollars obtained by corrupt officials are illicitly sent via all kinds of offshore financial centers, banks, and other financial institutions across the globe in various money-laundering schemes designed to hide their real ownership. This weakens the global financial system, erodes confidence in banks, and makes a mockery of efforts by official banking regulators to effectively supervise finance in the public interest.

Raymond Baker, the director of the Global Financial Integrity (GFI) think-tank in Washington, DC, estimates that more than one trillion US dollars in illicit cash flows across national borders every year. This comes from the mispricing of trade in goods and services, from trade in counterfeit goods, from illegal sales of arms, from tax evasion, and from corruption.

GFI's research suggests that about seventy tax havens and secrecy jurisdictions are in operation across the globe, which shelter tens of thousands of shell companies whose real ownership is difficult to trace (and the Tax Justice Network has concluded that more than an estimated $11.5 trillion of illicit cash is deposited across the globe outside of its country of origin[3]). Raymond Baker's analysis leads to the following conclusion:

> For every $1 poor nations receive in foreign aid, an estimated $10 in dirty money flows illicitly abroad. With such great amounts of capital draining from weak economies, there is little hope of significant development or of curtailing poverty. Without mechanisms to curtail illicit cash flows, the benefits of foreign aid are undermined and the potential for drug cartels and terrorist groups using the banking system to their advantage is greatly increased.[4]

CORRUPTION IS A CRIME AGAINST TAXPAYERS EVERYWHERE

When citizens pay taxes they expect public services, be it in New Jersey, United States, or in New Delhi, India. When instead those taxes are pocketed by politicians and public officials, citizens are cheated. When the taxpayers in the mature industrial countries, from Australia to Sweden, support annual global foreign-aid programs worth more than $100 billion, they expect the funds to reduce poverty and promote economic and social development.

- Corruption is when foreign-aid funds flow into the pockets of the governments of developing countries and from there into real estate from the high-rent area of central London to the super-luxury of the South of France and the high-rise condominiums in Dubai.

- Corruption is when British members of Parliament cheat on their expense accounts, charging British taxpayers for second homes, for travel on government business that never happened, and for luxury additions to their country estates.
- Crucially, taxpayers across the developing world and in Central and Eastern Europe routinely find that public services are failing or that civil servants demand bribes to provide public services.
- Corruption is when the last two governors of the US state of Illinois take and demand kickbacks and secret campaign contributions—each of them was tried and sent to prison. It is when Antoin Rezko, a property developer, becomes a political campaign fundraiser (he even raised funds for President Obama's campaigns) in Chicago and arranges all manner of kickback schemes to win contracts from state and local governments in Illinois. He was found guilty on sixteen charges, including fraud, money laundering, bribery, and influence-peddling, and sentenced to ten and a half years in prison. As the sentence was announced in the federal district court in Chicago on November 22, 2011, Judge Amy J. St. Eve deplored his "selfish and corrupt actions" and stated, "You defrauded the people of Illinois, you engaged in extensive corruption throughout the state of Illinois." The judge added, "This sentence must send a message that enough is enough."[5]

CORRUPTION DAMAGES PEACE AND SECURITY

- When officials in Pakistan are bribed to provide their country's nuclear secrets to the governments of North Korea and Iran, then our lives are placed at highest risk.
- Corruption and security come together when key politicians and leaders of the military and intelligence services in Pakistan take tens of millions of dollars of US aid and also use such funds to provide support to the Taliban and terrorist organizations that the United States is fighting in Afghanistan.
- Our security is placed at risk when Chechnyan terrorists bribe lowly officials at a Moscow airport to get on board planes, blow them up, and kill hundreds of people.
- Corruption that undermines global security is when international arms dealers pursue secret deals to supply all manner of terrorist and rebel organizations with the weapons needed to create instability.

Steve Killelea is an Australian businessman and philanthropist who several years ago set out to create a Global Peace Index (GPI) to rank countries and build public understanding of the nature of violent and less peaceful countries. He has done a stunning job and the quality of the GPI today, with expert research by the Economist Intelligence Unit (EIU), is a mine of valuable data. Matching the rankings of the GPI to those of TI's CPI finds a close correlation. The countries seen as the most corrupt in the world are also those with the least peace and the most violence. Steve sees corruption as a key factor in the environments in which security is lowest. He believes that if corruption can be reduced, then the prospects for greater peace can be improved.

As we consider the range of humanitarian, economic, and security problems entwined with corruption, we can see a reform agenda that is both vast and compelling. Tracking the plight of the hundreds of millions of people who are victims of the crimes of corruption, and seeking to bring the villains to justice, is one of the great dramas of our age. An enormous amount is at stake for our civilization in securing the success of the fight against corruption. As former UN secretary-general Kofi Annan has noted:

> Corruption is an insidious plague that has a wide range of corrosive effects on societies. It undermines democracy and the rule of law, leads to violations of human rights, distorts markets, erodes the quality of life, and allows organized crime, terrorism, and other threats to human security to flourish.[6]

NOTES

1. The Rome Statute of the ICC, adopted on July 17, 1998, restricts the investigative work of the ICC to crimes of genocide, crimes against humanity, war crimes, and the crime of aggression, but it does not mention corruption.

2. FATF, "Laundering the Proceeds of Corruption" report, Paris, July 2011.

3. The Tax Justice Network is a US not-for-profit organization of economists and tax experts that has pioneered work on international tax evasion. In its reports and on its website (www.taxjustice.net) it has noted, "How big is the problem, and what is its nature? Assets held offshore, beyond the reach of effective taxation, are equal to about a third of total global assets. Over half of all world trade passes through tax havens. Developing countries lose revenues far greater than annual aid flows. We estimate that the amount of funds held offshore by individuals is about $11.5 trillion—with a resulting annual loss of tax revenue on the income from these assets of about 250 billion dollars. This is five times what the World Bank estimated in 2002 was needed to address the UN Millennium Development Goal of halving world poverty by 2015. This much money could also pay to transform the world's energy infrastructure to tackle climate change."

4. Raymond W. Baker, *Capitalism's Achilles Heel—Dirty Money and How to Renew the Free-Market System* (London: Wiley, 2005).

5. Annie Sweeney, "Rezko Gets 10 1/2-Year Sentence," *Chicago Tribune*, November 22, 2011.

6. UN Secretary-General Kofi Annan, first paragraph of his foreword to the report on the UN Convention Against Corruption, United Nations Office on Drugs and Crime, Vienna, Austria, 2004.

Chapter Three

Victims

We are all victims of corruption. Be it in the poorest countries where hospitals and schools and clean water and decent housing are denied the very poor because dictators have looted the national treasuries, or be it in the wealthiest industrial countries where money and politics undermine governance integrity.

Mary Jane Ncube is a petite, young woman from Zimbabwe with enormous courage and toughness. She is the executive director of TI-Zimbabwe. She told me once that each day, knowing full well that the authorities could take her away at any time, she seeks to work with some of the six million people of her country that the regime of Robert Mugabe has made destitute. These people, she said, once paid taxes and earned decent livings and today remain alive only because of the good work of international humanitarian organizations. They are the victims of corruption. Their tax payments were stolen. The public services they were promised never arrived. They now live on the edge of survival in a country that not long ago was among Africa's most prosperous agricultural producers. Their misery is due solely to the greed and criminality of public officials.

Mary Jane sees in the faces of starving Zimbabweans the cruelty and evil of corrupt regimes and this drives her to act with great compassion and great courage. There are others like her in many poor countries who work to assist those in greatest need and campaign to fight corruption at the same time.

Nuhu Ribadu places Africa's victims of corruption in a comprehensive context of misery and culpability. He told the Financial Services Committee of the US House of Representatives on May 19, 2009:

> The corruption endemic to our [African] region is not just about bribery, but about mismanagement, incompetence, abuse of office, and the inability to establish justice and the rule of law. As resources are stolen, confidence not

just in democratic governance but in the idea of just leadership ebbs away. As the lines of authority with the government erode, so too do traditional authority structures. In the worst cases, eventually all that is left to hold society together is that someday it may be your day to get yours. This does little to build credible, accountable institutions or put the right policies in place.

He continued: "The West must understand that corruption is part of the reason that African nations cannot fight diseases properly, cannot feed their populations, cannot educate their children and use their creativity and energy to open the doorway to the future they deserve. . . . The crime is not just theft. It is negligence. Wanton negligence, the full impact of which is difficult to know."

Ribadu also became a victim of corruption. As the executive chairman of Nigeria's Economic and Crimes Commission (EFCC), Ribadu relentlessly went after some of the most corrupt politicians in the country, seized vast funds, and secured special powers for policemen and judges to investigate top officials. His success was due in part to the support he enjoyed from then Nigerian president Olusegun Obasanjo. But his was largely a lonely battle and his days were numbered when Alhaji Umaru Yar'Adua became Nigeria's president in May 2007. First, Ribadu was assigned to special training at the police academy, then demoted, and then faced ever-more serious death threats. He left his family behind and fled to the United Kingdom but continued to campaign against corruption in Africa, writing statements and making speeches to strengthen international understanding of the massive scale of hardship that the victims of corruption endure in Africa. In late 2010, he felt it was safe enough to return to Nigeria, where he entered the political fray as a would-be presidential candidate.

When corruption becomes excessive, it can have consequences that spread rapidly and dangerously across many countries at the same time. The 2010–2011 Eurozone sovereign financial crisis, which saw financial losses for millions of investors in financial markets and had still graver consequences as it contributed to plunging Europe into recession, started in Greece.

In December 2009, the government of Greece announced that previous public budget statements were inaccurate and that the national budget deficit was far greater than had previously been disclosed. It soon became evident that Greece was unable to service its large foreign debts. For many Greeks the fudged budget figures were no surprise. The citizens of Greece have long given up believing their governments. They knew that most Greeks tried to find ways to reduce their tax payments and that most Greeks also believed that taxes they did pay went into the pockets of politicians and officials and not to support basic services.

According to survey data compiled by TI-Greece in 2010, on average more than one in ten people report having to pay a bribe for some kind of service, predominantly to public-sector institutions. For example, more than a third of people surveyed who used a public-health-sector facility reported paying a bribe to secure a service or jump a queue. Seventy-five percent of Greeks surveyed in June 2010 thought corruption was increasing. The majority of the respondents (92 percent) respectively thought that Greek society was corrupted.

The TI-Greece report noted that concerning the ranking of the most corrupted services in the public sector, the hospitals are the champions, followed by the tax offices, which are just ahead of the construction-licensing bodies. According to a "2010 Corruption Pricelist" that the national chapter developed as a result of the survey, the bribery cost for surgery ranges from €150 up to €7,500; the cost for tax arrangements is between €300 and €15,000.

The fight against corruption in many countries of the world is inseparable from actions to explicitly address the lack of basic needs and the resulting human suffering. This was made explicit to a larger global audience than ever before by the thousands of Arab victims of corruption who rose in protest in the Arab Spring. Their voices expressed anguish about many injustices, including the following:

- People are too accepting and complacent about government leaders serving themselves at the public's expense to do anything about this.
- If pushed too far, there comes a time when ordinary people overcome serious fears of vicious government security forces to take to the streets in protest.
- Even though the dictators have the ability to kill their own people, they will be defeated.

The Arab protesters did not go into the streets for some broad, general political cause. They were not organized by a political party or an established movement. Every single one of them had an intense personal sense of victimization. The impact of the Arab Spring will continue to reach right across the developing world and across Central and Eastern Europe, where hundreds of millions of people are the victims of corruption.

"When the public at large demonstrate for more accountable and decent government in so many countries or the world they are motivated, to no small extent, by anger over corruption." These words were not spoken after the Arab protests of 2009, but in November 1993 in Berlin, not long after the collapse of the Soviet Union. The speaker, who saw mass public demonstrations across Latin America in the 1980s in support of democracy and honesty in government, saw even more dramatic demonstrations for the same core causes as Communism collapsed. The speaker was Nobel Peace Prize winner and former Costa Rican president Oscar Arias Sanchez, and he continued:

> By anger over corruption: corruption that humiliates the poor who must bribe small officials for minimal services; corruption that bankrupts the honest trader; corruption that empowers unscrupulous captains of commerce and their partners, dishonest politicians; corruption which spreads like a cancer to kill all that is decent in society.[1]

Dr. Arias has often stressed that corruption is, above all, a humanitarian issue and it is a view that slowly, but surely, is becoming widely understood. Aid agencies and many academic researchers often discuss corruption in the jargon of economics and social science. But increasingly the media who report the protests, as well as the protesters themselves, speak more directly about the personal hardships that corruption inflicts. The stories range across the multitude of circumstances of diverse victims, from a beautiful, young, and desperately poor woman called Rina Das, who has suffered as a victim of public officials in Orissa, India, to a multimillionaire international financier, William Browder, who has been the victim of Kremlin extortion.

POVERTY

Rina Das lives in Raghupati Nagar in India. Like many others, Rina Das depended on municipal services, which so often were inadequately funded despite payments of taxes. A group of civil society organizations is now changing this. They are educating ordinary people like Rina Das to exercise their rights under India's 2005 Freedom of Information Act. Civil society organizations in many parts of India have been holding workshops for groups of people in small communities to teach them about their rights. Then these groups start to demand transparency from their local government officials. Thousands of women like Rina received government public-works cards that entitled them to menial jobs, if such jobs were available. But Rina was told there was no job for her. Then, together with many women just like her, she demanded to exercise her freedom of information rights and request that local officials open the public-works employment master rolls. Often, as Rina discovered, those rolls are full of dead people—the pay packets have disappeared.

Uncovering local corruption does not always lead to sustained reductions in corruption. Some officials get fired and people like Rina get jobs, but in time new corrupt officials gain positions that enable them to steal and cheat and extort and abuse their offices. Corruption is rampant in India. Everyone knows it. But far too little is done to protect the Rina Dases. Often it is poor women who suffer the most. But this is not just a problem for India; it is one that you find in dozens of countries.

What is the cost of corruption?

The African Union once estimated the cost of corruption at 25 percent of Africa's gross national product. At differing times, analysts have used numbers like $100 billion and even $1 trillion a year to quantify the toll that corruption takes.

Striving, however, to find the cost of corruption in terms of dollars and cents misses the real point: the costs of corruption need to be seen in terms of the full scale of the human misery that it creates. Corruption traps hundreds of millions of very poor people in utter squalor. Corruption kills.

Building contractors in Haiti paid off officials to circumvent building codes. Offices, houses, and apartment buildings were, as a result, quick to collapse in the earthquake of January 2010, killing tens of thousands of people. Similar forms of corruption allowing subcode construction were the cause of thousands of deaths in earthquakes in China and in Turkey in recent years.

We know more today about the scale and scope of bribery in individual countries and how it most affects the general public because of extensive national surveys. Foremost among these are regular studies by the World Bank Institute, and also by TI and its national chapters. These surveys track the trends and the staggering scale of human impoverishment that can directly and indirectly be attributed to bad governance.

TI publishes an annual Global Corruption Barometer, which found that poorer people are twice as likely to pay bribes for basic services, such as education, than wealthier people. A third of all people under the age of thirty reported paying a bribe in 2010, compared to less than one in five people aged fifty-one years and over. Eight out of ten people said political parties are corrupt or extremely corrupt, while half the people questioned said their government's action to stop corruption is ineffective.

HEALTH CATASTROPHE

In the 1980s, I traveled extensively in sub-Sahara Africa and visited many health projects funded in part by the World Bank. I asked experts why so many national health programs failed and they had a blunt answer: corruption. In many of the countries that I visited the elites had quite good healthcare with decent hospitals located in major capitals. But in one country after another, public funds earmarked for public health had been stolen by officials.

Rural health clinics and hospitals—and in the poorest countries the majority of the people live in rural areas—are few and far between, badly equipped, and grossly understaffed. On a tour in rural Zambia in 1985 to see a number of hospitals, my African expert companion told me that most people feared going to hospital because they saw it as the fastest route to the cemetery. As Dora Akunyili, former head of Nigeria's Food and Drug Authority, has remarked, corruption in healthcare "kills en masse and anybody can be a victim."

In the 1980s, the World Bank and the World Health Organization refused to speak publicly about corruption or take the governments in poor countries that they supported to task. They turned a blind eye to massive thefts of their funds and to the failures of projects that they had designed. They felt that they lacked the political power and support to ring the alarm bells. Today, they do speak out, but on the ground in dozens of poor countries the conditions remain terrible.

Upward of one billion people on our planet have exceptionally poor access to basic healthcare services, not only because insufficient money is available to support such services, but also because in many countries the cash that should be allocated is misappropriated.

In dozens of countries—and not just the very poorest—the "free" healthcare services are never free. Nurses seek bribes to allow patients to even stand in line for an appointment to see a doctor, and doctors, often paid atrocious official wages, seek cash payments to treat patients. Those who cannot pay just suffer. This is the story from Bangladesh to Bolivia, from Nigeria to many parts of Central and Eastern Europe. Surveys of health services from Peru to Greece and in many other countries repeatedly show how bribes to administrators and nurses and doctors are widely seen by the public as routine.

Deborah Solomon of the *New York Times*, in questioning Nigerian novelist Chinua Achebe, asked, "As a professor at Brown University, in Providence, Rhode Island, you yourself live in exile, as do many other Nigerian writers, including the playwright Wole Soyinka and the young novelist Chimamanda Ngozi Adichie?" The writer responded, "If you were in Nigeria and had cause to go to a hospital or to see a doctor, you would then immediately understand why so many people are abroad."[2]

In TI's *2006 Global Corruption Report: Special Focus Corruption and Health*, scholars Liz Taylor and Clare Dickinson wrote:

> While it is difficult to draw a casual link between corruption and the spread of HIV, there is ample evidence that corruption impedes efforts to prevent infection and treat people living with AIDS in many parts of the world. The mechanics of corruption affecting the prevention and treatment of HIV/AIDS are not substantively different from those affecting the health sector more general-

ly: opaque procurement processes, the misappropriation of funds earmarked for health expenditure and informal payments demanded for services that are supposed to be delivered free. What are different are the scale of the problem and the nature of the disease—a chronic, usually fatal and often-stigmatized disease that can be contained only with expensive drugs.

In the health sector, as in many other public-services areas in poor countries, the government pay to employees is often so low that they feel they have no alternative but to supplement their incomes by extorting fees from all who seek to use the services. This is what one former official, Te Kuy Seang, who was the director general of administration and finance in the Ministry of Health in Cambodia, described as "survival corruption." He noted that in the case of healthcare, the survivors he had in mind were not only the patients but also the nurses and other healthcare workers.[3]

BROADER PUBLIC SERVICES

When foreign-aid funds to the poorest countries are not effectively monitored by the donors, then the governments that obtain the funds often pocket some of the cash and the clinics and other public services for the poor are short-changed. When governments of oil-producing countries obtain royalty payments from multinational oil companies and deposit some of the funds in their foreign bank accounts, then it is the poor citizens of these oil rich nations that are deprived.

A score of countries today are what *Foreign Policy* magazine annually review as "failed states," where the rule of law is absent and where those wielding power take all the funds they can steal, equip private armies, and trap the mass populations in devastating conditions. These countries, such as North Korea and Somalia, are probably hopeless cases when it comes to curbing corruption. At the moment it is not safe for anticorruption organizations to try and establish themselves in these failed states. And in these wretched nations almost the entire populations are victims of daily extortion by officials, while those who hold power steal what little public funds are available.

Funds officially earmarked in national budgets, or in foreign aid agreements, to support rural hospitals and clinics, schools, basic housing, clean water, and jobs frequently are not delivered in many of the world's very poorest countries. Too many greedy hands have clasped the cash. But it is not just in the very poorest nations that the toll on the very poor is staggering. Both Brazil and India are among the fastest-growing emerging-market economies in the world. But that is not the impression that people get when they visit the vast acres of squalor that are shanty homes for millions of people in and around cities like Rio de Janeiro and Mumbai, which attests to incredible government failures (the horror is evident in unforgettable film footage in the 2008 Oscar-winning movie *Slumdog Millionaire*).

Government programs in scores of countries intended to build schools, supply books, and pay teachers are more fiction than fact. Often, parents have no choice other than to bribe teachers to get one of the few available places at a school. Those who cannot pay have no hope of seeing their children educated.

In its "Asia-Pacific Human Development Report" in 2008, the United Nations Development Program (UNDP) noted, for example, "In many countries corruption is widespread in the hiring of teachers, which in the most extreme form, results in the recruitment of 'ghost teachers' or even in the creation of entire 'ghost institutions'—with the allocated salaries and other expenses going into the pockets of corrupt officials." The UNDP report then added:

> Just as families may need to pay bribes to get into hospitals, they may also have to pay bribes to get their children admitted to schools. In China, in 2003 audits of nearly 3,000 primary and 1,500 secondary schools in Jianxi found 125 cases of illegally collected fees worth $2 million. Nationwide the government uncovered over $20 million in illegally collected school fees . . . this problem is also common in South Asia where students are often required to make unofficial payments for admission to schools, for books, sporting or religious events, examinations, or promotion to higher classes. Bribes for tuition or a better grade may also be extorted in the form of sexual exploitation.

Whenever a commodity is in short supply, then those who control its distribution and its use have the potential to abuse their positions by allocating resources on the basis of the kickbacks they receive, not on the basis of need, conspiring with gangsters to mutually enrich each other at the public's expense. No commodity is as vital as water, and here mismanagement is rampant. The depth of the problem starts to be grasped by noting that in its *Millennium Report 2000*, the United Nations stated, "No single measure would do more to reduce disease and save lives in the developing world than bringing safe water and adequate sanitation to all."

As Nobel Peace Prize laureate Wangari Maathai describes in TI's *2008 Global Corruption Report: Corruption in the Water Sector*:

> The global water crisis destroys sources of water and waterways, and leaves a large portion of the world without access to safe drinking water, that destroys lives and livelihoods all over the world and that continues to create ecological disasters at an epic and escalating scale is a crisis of our own doing. It is a crisis of governance: man-made, with ignorance, greed and corruption at its core. But the worst of them all is corruption. Corruption means power un-

bound. It gives the powerful the means to work against and around rules that communities set themselves. This makes corruption in water particularly pernicious.[4]

BUSINESS'S VICTIMS

Bribe-paying corporations create hosts of victims: from the citizens in the countries where the bribes are paid and whose governments now pay inflated prices for products, to rival firms that lost deals because they were honest, to the company's shareholders, who have to pay the fines when the criminal acts of their enterprise are investigated and prosecuted.

A number of years ago I sat down with a top executive of GE Canada, who told me that in a fair competition for a major foreign government contract, his company was the winner. Before the signing of the deal, however, he was called in for a meeting with a senior government official who asked him to raise the contract price and suggested that the difference between it and the original bid should be deposited in a separate account. The Canadian executive said he refused to do this and a rival firm signed the deal. GE Canada became a victim.

William Browder is a business victim of corruption and his Russian lawyer, Sergei Magnitzky, was murdered for the crime of being honest. Browder is an American resident in the United Kingdom who saw enormously profitable investment possibilities in Russia. He established Hermitage Capital, which attracted substantial funds that were invested in a range of Russian industries, and this attracted the curiosity of senior Kremlin officials. They asked Browder for payments and he refused. Hermitage Capital was then investigated for tax fraud and $230 million of its assets were impounded. Threats to his life forced Browder to stop paying visits to Russia, but he refused to be plundered by the Kremlin.

Browder hired Sergei Magnitzky, a thirty-six-year-old Moscow lawyer, to represent Hermitage Capital's interests. It was not long before Sergei began to publicly complain that not only were the tax charges without merit but that Kremlin officials had also stolen the $230 million. He accused the Russian government of corruption and in November 2008 he was arrested. He refused to recant his accusations.

You can be imprisoned for up to one year in Russia without facing a trial. Sergei died in prison in November 2009, just before the first anniversary of his arrest. The authorities said he died of natural causes.

I had not met Sergei, but I did meet his mother, Natalia Magnitskya, a year after Sergei's death. She said she would never give up fighting for justice and for an honest explanation from the authorities about how her son died. She knew the dangers to herself and to those in the Russian human rights and anticorruption community who were aggressively helping her. Her courage and that of her friends has been remarkable. They have also demonstrated great skill in first ensuring that the foreign press kept the story alive, and then using every diplomatic and political channel they could find to keep pressing President Dmitry Medvedev to secure the release of the truthful report on how this young lawyer died.

In July 2011, President Medvedev did order the release of a report that acknowledged that Sergei had been beaten to death in his prison cell. Two prison doctors were arrested. They have not been put on trial. No prison guards have been arrested. Hermitage Capital's cash has disappeared.

· As we consider the hundreds and hundreds of millions of victims of corruption, we should never forget that each one of them has a story to tell. Some are wealthy like Browder, some of them are murdered like Sergei, some are threatened like Sergei's mother, Natalia, and most are horribly exploited and cheated of their basic rights.

As Kathy Lally reported in the *Washington Post*, the treatment that Browder and Sergei received at the hands of Russian justice is replicated in different ways with outrageous outcomes in today's Russia. Honest business people are constantly fearful of becoming victims. Police, prosecutors, and judges are bribed and then conspire to jail business people on false charges to enable their competitors to secure major business advantages:

> When a compliant judge denies bail, detention gets a businessman out of the way while his company is stolen. It's a powerful tool for corrupt officials to extract a bribe: Pay up or go to jail. Detainees are held in intolerable conditions. The water is usually undrinkable—the fortunate use electric coils brought by relatives to boil it. Cells are damp and dark. Medical care is routinely denied. Many suffer, and for no reason. Last year, according to court records, 404,333 people were convicted of economic crimes, but only 146,490 received prison terms. The rest paid fines or got suspended sentences. At the same time, 59 people died in Moscow's pretrial prisons, half a dozen more than the year before. [5]

When one company pays a bribe to win a contract, then its competitors suffer and become the victims of corruption. A determination to ensure fair competition and to support honest corporations is the prime motive behind the substantial efforts of the US Department of Justice and the US Securities and Exchange Commission to investigate corporations that violate US law and pay bribes to foreign government officials.

When Europe's largest weapons systems' manufacturer, BAE Systems of the United Kingdom, or Europe's largest electronics company, Siemens AG of Germany,_allegedly pay bribes to foreign government officials to win contracts for themselves, they make a mockery of free enterprise. The victims include all those competitors of BAE and Siemens that strive to play by the rules, to win deals on merit, and refuse to pay bribes.

When companies conspire with government officials and factor bribes into contracts, then those contracts are inflated and the citizens of the countries of the bribe takers are cheated. Hospitals and schools and water systems and public housing are not built because there are no funds—the cash has gone to foreign crooked corporations and their co-conspirators, crooked public officials. And should the companies be caught and prosecuted and agree to pay fines—Siemens has paid fines of over $1.6 billion and BAE Systems has paid around $450 million in fines—then the shareholders of these companies are also victims.

Sometimes, executives of companies offering goods and services that a country does not need call on senior politicians to propose crooked deals. I was once told about a Latin American government that placed a very large order for railroad tracks that were a different gauge to the national rail system and thus useless. I once found myself in a bizarre situation listening to how a variety of governments were striving to convince the government of Kenya to make enormous purchases of products that Kenya did not need. In this case, it seemed foreign companies were conspiring with their own governments to convince the Kenyans to misuse public funds.

On a visit to Nairobi in 1985, when I worked for the World Bank, I was invited to breakfast by the US ambassador. He said he wanted the World Bank's help to ensure that the Kenyan government spent its money wisely. He said that there was a competition for some funds that Kenyan president Arap Moi controlled between the French government, which was promoting cement factories for Kenya (the ambassador said Kenya already had plenty of these); the British government, which was promoting naval frigates (he said that Kenya faced absolutely no threats in the Indian Ocean); and the German government, which was promoting Airbus wide-bodied aircraft (that the ambassador said did not have the range to fly nonstop from Frankfurt to Nairobi). At first, the envoy did not mention what US companies planned to sell the Kenyans. But before long, having dismissed the competitors, he suggested that the World Bank should convince President Moi that it would be greatly beneficial if Kenya purchased American Boeing 747 planes. Naturally, he added, the deal would be a good one with the US Export-Import Bank providing financing.

I never did discover what the Kenyans eventually purchased, but a few years later, after I had left the World Bank, I visited Nairobi to be told by friends there that no major government deal was ever transacted without top officials pocketing substantial sums of cash.

Government money is often fungible and when the competition for contracts is intense, then it is not just diplomats who get to work to influence decisions, but also business agents of major firms who have experience in arranging deals advantageous to government ministers. The country's citizens, especially the poor, always suffer as a result.

Often the bribes are extorted from businesses, as officials create all kinds of rules and regulations and red tape that make it difficult to obtain business licenses and permits and as these officials suggest that problems can be fixed with some under-the-table cash. Such payments may often be quite small, but when they become pervasive they wreck the efficiency of government, business, and the economy and the costs are inevitably large.

But, as is evident from so many of the Foreign Corrupt Practices Act (FCPA) cases, such as the huge bribe payments made in Nigeria by Halliburton's subsidiary KBR, businesses do not wait for extortion threats. They approach public officials with offers of bribes to smooth the path toward gaining advantages. Kickbacks for contracts between businesses and officials at national governmental levels, and also at municipal and local government levels, are far too commonplace across the world.

In many developing countries, for example, top politicians, including military leaders, use the term "national security" to block transparency of defense contracts. Then, these officials determine how to use the defense budgets not to protect their citizens but to enrich themselves. They award contracts to vendors offering the best bribes, not the best equipment. In this process, national budgets are distorted, funds that should go on public services of all kinds are siphoned into secret military budgets, and generals and top government officials get rich as the citizens suffer.

The impact on trade and competitiveness may well range significantly by both the nationality of the bribe-paying firms and the business sector that they are involved with. Honesty in major contracting with governments in the construction and defense sectors, for example, is far more rare than in many other sectors. The more we learn about bribe paying, the more we can understand about the scope of the problem overall and the difficulties that honest firms must have as they seek to compete.

VICTIMS IN LEADING INDUSTRIAL COUNTRIES

Of course, the victims of corruption do not only reside in the developing and emerging-market countries. Hundreds of millions of middle-class people in most countries of the world are to some extent victims of corruption. They pay high taxes and receive inadequate services from local governments, and often this is due to officials taking kickbacks from contractors who then fail to deliver what is promised. Moreover, they believe they have democratic rights, yet these are frequently undermined by the corruption strategies of cunning politicians.

For a decade, French investigative magistrates built a case against some of the nation's leaders. Their prime target was Jacques Chirac, who, so long as he enjoyed the position of president of France, was immune from prosecution (from Chile's Pinochet to Italy's Berlusconi, presidents cling to office as a means of securing their immunity against prosecutors determined to nail them on corruption charges). The charges against Chirac, alleging breach of trust and misuse of public funds, stemmed from his eighteen years as the mayor of Paris prior to being elected president in 1995. He was found guilty and given a two-year suspended sentence, which took into account his frail health. He ran a pay-to-play scheme, collecting contributions for his political party and his campaigns from business people in return for an assortment of favors. Chirac is the first president in the history of France's Fifth Republic to be found guilty by a court on corruption charges.

It is unlikely that another municipal politician with grand ambitions had been inspired by Chirac's Paris capers, after all he had more than enough examples of political corruption in his own neighborhood. Rod Blagojevich, former governor of the State of Illinois, was found guilty in 2011 on eighteen charges of fraud and corruption. His version of pay-to-play adds new twists and new levels of arrogance to the game. For example, he tried to use power to, in effect, sell a US Senate seat. The governor had the right to appoint someone to fill the vacancy created when Illinois Senator Barack Obama was elected president in 2008. Blagojevich sought to shop the seat to whoever would pay him the most for it. Now, he is starting a fourteen-year prison term—the longest given to any US politician found guilty of corruption.

From Illinois to New Jersey and New York State to Alabama, California, Florida, Louisiana, Ohio, and the US capital of Washington, DC, prominent politicians and public officials have been indicted for corruption. Most of the cases involve officials in municipal governments padding their bank accounts at taxpayers' expense.

Frequently, the corruption relates to construction, property development, and public-works contracts. In New York State, top politicians are being investigated and prosecuted for seeking kickbacks from Wall Street bankers in return for contracting with them to manage parts of the state's public pension fund; in New Jersey, a clutch of mayors are facing trial for taking bribes from local construction contractors; and in Illinois, Alabama, and Louisiana, for example, there are long histories of governmental corruption.

In many countries corruption in party political finance is widely seen as undermining democratic legitimacy. In the United States, the scale of money in politics dwarfs that of any other country and the public perceptions of corruption are rife. The 2008 US elections involved close to $1.8 billion of campaign cash—how much of it bought special access, special favors, and special influence for those who made particularly generous contributions and those who "bundled" the mega-contributions on behalf of candidates?

The mixture of money and politics is toxic everywhere. And in most countries there is a sense that deals are done between the privileged and the politicians that benefit these players at the public's expense. Politicians in the United States, mostly through organizations that support their election campaigns, are the beneficiaries not only of such assorted powerful groups as the US Chamber of Commerce, the National Rifle Association, the AFL-CIO national trade union organization, and many others like them, but also from vastly wealthy institutions and individuals who need not reveal themselves as campaign donors. As a result of a 2010 US Supreme Court ruling, the scale of interest group funding of US elections is rising substantially. The Court asserted that as part of the constitutional right to free speech, organizations and individuals could use their money as they wish, privately and anonymously, in support of whatever political views they might hold. This is a huge blow to transparency and an invitation to corrupt practices.

It is difficult to express just how massive an invitation to corruption in American politics has been provided by the highest US court. Over many years, Fred Wertheimer, the founder and president of Democracy 21, a nonprofit, nonpartisan organization dedicated to transparency in the US political system, has been widely seen as the dean of American experts on every facet of money and politics. In September 2010, he wrote an article that summed up just how serious the decision of the Court is:

> When the Supreme Court in the *Citizens United* decision struck down the ban on corporate expenditures to influence federal elections, five Justices radically changed our political system. The 5-4 Court decision elevated the status of corporations in our democracy and freed them to use their immense, aggregate wealth to flood elections and buy influence over government decisions. The Justices built the legal rationale for this radical change, however, on a purely fictional premise.
>
> The Court held that corporate campaign spending, if done independently of a candidate, could not corrupt the candidate. Therefore, the Court found, such independent expenditures by corporations cannot be constitutionally restricted. This legal rationale, however, belies reality. Does anyone reasonably doubt that if a corporation spends $10 million to defeat the congressional opponent of a federal officeholder, that spending creates the opportunity to buy influence with the officeholder, or, at a minimum, creates the appearance of the opportunity for such influence-buying? The overwhelming majority of Americans recognize this is simply a fact of life. According to a recent Survey USA poll, more than 75 percent of voters, including 70 percent of Republicans and 73 percent of independents, view corporate election spending as an attempt to bribe politicians rather than as free speech protected by the First Amendment.[6]

The Republican primaries in the first half of 2012 saw unprecedented amounts of cash being deployed on behalf of candidates to take out advertisements for the sole purpose of damaging the credibility and integrity of their rivals. The 2012 US elections will no doubt be seen as involving far more cash than previous elections, with a considerable portion of the cash being filtered through "Super PACs," often from anonymous donors and used to run sharply negative ads. The smell of so much cash in American politics gives rise to legitimate concerns about potential corruption and undue influence on politicians by very rich individuals and special interest groups. It heightens the sense that elections can be bought and creates cynicism among the electorate. It undermines efforts by the US government, through foreign aid programs and support for pro-democracy not-for-profit organizations, to promote fair elections and honest governance overseas.

Lobbying is a legitimate—indeed, an important—part of a democracy where advocates for all manner of causes have the opportunity to "educate" elected officials on their issues. But when the lobbyists pledge elected officials large sums for their election campaigns, provide them with private corporate jets for their weekend use, and entertain them extravagantly, then there are grounds for concern.

What Fred Wertheimer is to money and US politics, Professor James Thurber of American University is to US lobbying. His books, lectures, and seminars attract an influential following and shape the broader public's understanding of both how valuable lobbying is and how dangerous it can be for the health of the political system. He has stated, "By official estimates, the lobbying industry is the third largest enterprise in our nation's capital, after government and tourism . . . the number of persons employed in Washington who either are lobbyists or are associated with all dimensions of the advocacy industry (registered and unregistered advocated and supporting institutions) has been estimated to be well over 100,000. Spending by registered lobbyists has more than doubled in the last 10 years, from $1.56 billion to $3.49 billion in 2009, and that is just for the visible registered activities."

Professor Thurber has also noted, "The $3.49 billion is just the tip of the lobbying expenditures iceberg, because it includes only what is recorded by registered lobbyists in public records. These expenditures average to more than $20 million in lobbying expenditures each day the Congress is in session in 2009, or over $65 million per member of Congress. . . . There are estimates that the total spent on lobbying is closer to $9 billion per year in Washington—or about three times the officially reported amount. None of these figures include the additional $4 billion spent for the 2010 congressional campaigns."[7]

Professor Thurber served as an advisor to the Washington, DC–based think-tank the Committee for Economic Development (CED), as its trustees worked on a report on the US political system. In early 2008, CED published its report and concluded:

> Washington is broken. Civic debate has become uncivil invective; analysis has been displaced by ideology; and vital public issues are not solved, but rather stored for future partisan use. Our political system has not addressed the rising public debt, ballooning and crippling health-care costs, a looming Social Security shortfall, and serious energy and environmental problems. Efforts to deal with our educational system are woefully inadequate. If our political system cannot confront these visible challenges, where will it find the reserves of comity and trust to face the unknown crisis that can erupt at any time?

Well before individual billionaire Americans were bankrolling their favorite presidential candidates, the scale of abusive influence-peddling in American politics had become formidable. More than a decade ago, John Carey reviewed a book about the US tobacco industry by David Kessler, which Carey said painted a picture of a world where congressmen read whatever scripts the tobacco industry and its lawyers gave them, and where the companies would openly declare "we've got more money than God."[8]

According to the US Center for Responsive Politics, the presidential candidates in the US 2008 election campaign spent a total of $1,759,227,339. Candidates in the campaigns for the US House of Representatives that year spent $938,040,528. US Senate candidates, meanwhile, in 2008 spent $418,618,638. The precision of these numbers is due to laws (which now have been undermined by the Supreme Court) that demanded full transparency on all fundraising and campaign spending by politicians. But transparency is no anticorruption guarantee. The big contributors enjoy exceptional access to the candidates, and the time they spend with them, which is gained solely because of their money, buys them influence.

That influence expresses itself in two ways. First, coalitions of big spenders can have great influence on seeking to kill legislation that they do not like; vast sums, for example, were spent on campaign contributions and on lobbying by US health insurance companies in 2008/2009 and 2010 to try and ensure that new national legislation did not undermine their profitable preoccupations. Second, large contributors to campaigns often "suggest" to the politicians whom they helped that they would like a variety of government contracts. Via the appropriations process of the US Congress, so-called "earmarks" surface where members explicitly write into voluminous and complex legislation a special deal. Sometimes these are added to the legislation in the middle of the night before a final vote is taken.

In early 2010, Boeing, which has plants and suppliers in many parts of the United States and is a generous contributor to the campaigns of many politicians, found itself as the only bidder on a massive $50 billion multiyear contract for the US Air Force. One potential bidder that was forced out of the running and complained of foul play (because it lacked Boeing's political weight) was the European Airbus consortium, EADS. While UK prime minister Gordon Brown and French president Nicolas Sarkozy loudly protested, they lacked the lobbyists and the political cash available to Boeing and thus had no effect. Is this corruption?

Of course. Are the interests of American citizens well served when there is only one bidding company on a vast government contract?

Of course not.

Funding political campaigns in scores of countries is rife with opacity. Politicians seek funds legally and often illegally from those who all too often want some government favor in return. We know more about the scale of US political financing than that of any other country because US campaign laws in this area, prior to the Supreme Court's ruling in 2010, tended to be more explicit and demanding.

Because of the new age of transparency the public in many countries has greater information on finance and politics. One result is seen bluntly in opinion polls that show the same conclusion: politicians are held in low esteem and are not trusted.

Corruption in politics robs everyone. It not only cheats voters and taxpayers and all who depend on them in our society, but also undermines confidence in democracy itself. And the damage it does to public understanding of the potential benefits of democratic government runs still deeper. At the launch of TI in Berlin in May 1993, for example, Nigerian leader Olusegan Obasanjo said it was time that Africa faced up to the rampant corruption in its midst and that Africans joined with others across the globe in a major campaign to fight corruption. He said that in too many countries young people believe that the only reason for a person to go into politics is to get very rich. He called for an unprecedented international effort to change this and bring honesty and accountability to politics for the sake of the children of the world.

When we see the abuse by politicians in so many countries, when we see how our civilization, which has placed a man on the moon, cannot rise to the challenge of global poverty and establishing basic freedoms for all peoples, then we know that we are all the victims of corruption.

NOTES

1. Speech by former Costa Rican president and Nobel laureate Oscar Arias Sanchez on the opening of the Transparency International office in Berlin, Germany, November 1993.

2. Deborah Solomon, "Questions for Chinua Achebe—Out of Africa," *New York Times*, March 26, 2010.

3. From a paper by Te Kuy Seang presented at a seminar at the 2002 International Anti-Corruption Conference in Prague.

4. Transparency International, *Global Corruption Report 2008*, "Corruption in the Water Sector," foreword by Hon. Professor Wangari Maathi (Cambridge: Cambridge University Press; developed in conjunction with the Water Integrity Network).

5. Kathy Lally, "Laws to Rein in Russia's Pretrial Detention System Are Ignored," *Washington Post*, November 28, 2011.

6. Op-ed by Democracy 21 President Fred Wertheimer, "Voters Have a Right to Know Who Is Behind the Money Being Spent in Elections," *The Hill*, September 17, 2010. See http://thehill.com/blogs/congress-blog/civil-rights/119385-voters-have-a-basic-right-to-know-who-is-providing-the-money-being-spent-in-their-elections.

7. James A. Thurber is distinguished professor of government at American University, Washington, DC, and founder (1979) and director of the Center for Congressional and Presidential Studies. His most recent book is *Obama in Office: The First Two Years* (St. Paul, MN: Paradigm, 2011). See especially pages 132 and 133 of chapter 8, "Obama's Battle with Lobbyists."

8. Book review by John Carey of *A Question of Intent: A Great American Battle with a Deadly Industry*, by David Kessler (New York: Public Affairs, 2002), *Business Week*, February 5, 2001.

Chapter Four

The Activists

In the early 1990s, fighting corruption was the province of dreamers with grand aspirations. There were no civil society organizations operating on a regional or global basis that were dedicated to fighting corruption, there were no international laws against corruption, and the United Nations and the World Bank refused to even acknowledge that corruption was an economic development problem.

At that time, the United States was alone in prosecuting multinational companies for bribing foreign government officials (Germany allowed its corporations to deduct their foreign bribes from their taxes, as did, in effect, both France and the United Kingdom). There was minimal international cooperation between public prosecutors to investigate bribe-paying multinational corporations. There was no Internet or efficient technologies beyond the fax, the phone, and the teletype machine to assist investigative reporters to get their stories, disseminate them widely, and exchange information across the globe with their peers and their sources.

The changes seen in less than twenty years are staggering. Today, there are dozens of anticorruption civil society organizations; there is a plethora of new anticorruption laws, and even the United Nations General Assembly has approved an international anticorruption convention; more bribe-paying corporations than ever before are being successfully prosecuted; progress is being made in anti–money-laundering efforts, and Siemens of Germany has paid the largest fines in history, exceeding $1.2 billion; and more politicians in more countries than ever before are being prosecuted and/or hounded from public office because of their corruption crimes. In addition, journalists are finding more ways to get their stories out and secure support for investigating corruption. There were no not-for-profit investigative organizations a genera-tion ago, such as Global Witness and Pro Publica, which now are revealing volumes of information that relate to corruption.

TI, officially launched in May 1993, was the first global nongovernmen-tal organization exclusively concerned with the fight against corruption. Its influence has been formidable on public awareness and public attitudes, on countless campaigns in dozens of countries, and on the shaping of landmark legislation and important public statements by governments and official international institutions.

To understand the core dynamics behind so much of today's worldwide anticorruption, civil society activism requires insights into the origins and development of TI, as well as an understanding of the extraordinary individu-als engaged in the TI movement. It is no exaggeration to state that their work of more than twenty years equates in the corruption field with that achieved on behalf of other vital causes by such Nobel Peace Prize–winning non-governmental organizations as Amnesty International, the International Cam-paign to Ban Landmines, and Médecins Sans Frontières.

What drives such organizations and what gives the TI movement—and other key organizations such as the Partnership for Transparency Fund (PTF) and Global Witness—such power is the courage and tenacity of dedicated individuals across the globe to improve the human condition and to reduce the poverty and insecurity that abound in our world.

INDIVIDUALS MAKE THE DIFFERENCE

In 2000, I had the privilege to present Lasantha Wickramatunga from Sri Lanka with TI's annual Integrity Award. He was a prominent and tenacious newspaperman with the courage to ask tough questions, call for government accountability, and expose corruption. He had a talent for collecting the facts meticulously, which terrified many politicians. On January 8, 2009, he was driving to work when, according to a BBC report, eight unidentified gunmen on motorcycles shot him in the head. He died soon afterward. He was fifty-two.

With an uncanny sense of premonition, the journalist titled his last article "And Then They Came for Me." He wrote, "Electronic and print-media institutions have been burnt, bombed, sealed and coerced. Countless journal-ists have been harassed, threatened and killed. It has been my honor to belong to all those categories and now especially the last." And he added, "When finally I am killed, it will be the government that kills me."[1]

On April 5, 2009, *New York Times* reporter Seth Mydans wrote that the press advocacy group Reporters Without Borders ranked Sri Lanka in 2008 as 165th out of 173 countries in terms of press freedom and called the country the fourth most dangerous for journalists, just trailing Iraq, Somalia, and Pakistan. Mydans went on to discuss the killing of Wickramatunga. Sri Lanka's government has said that it had nothing to do with the murder. But the *New York Times* article makes a convincing case that concerns about the government's brutal actions against the press were well grounded.

In 2001, TI made a posthumous Integrity Award to Georgy Gongadze. This journalist in Ukraine, aged thirty-one, had disappeared in September 2000 and two months later his decapitated body was found in a forest outside of Kiev. It had been sprayed with dioxin and there was evidence that suggested that he had been horribly tortured before being killed. His crime was that as a reporter he investigated the grand theft of public funds by Ukraine's then president, Leonid Kuchma, and his associates. He was fearless in reporting on corruption at all levels of government. His determination was evident in his reporting on television, radio, and on the online opposition publication *Ukrajinska Pravda* (Ukrainian Truth).

Gongadze disappeared after weeks of police surveillance. He faced frequent harassment and intimidation. His death, and the failure of the authorities to engage in a serious investigation, combined with the suppression of peaceful protests in support of Gongadze, contributed to an unprecedented campaign that united civil society and the opposition in Ukraine. This was key to the development of Ukraine's "Orange Revolution" that ousted Kuchma and set the stage for open elections.

Carlos Alberto Cardoso was assassinated only a few weeks after Georgy Gongadze in late November 2000, but on the other side of the world. Cardoso was killed in Mozambique in the middle of an investigation into the largest banking fraud in the country's history. Born in 1952 in Mozambique, Cardoso studied in South Africa and became a student activist against apartheid. He was expelled in 1974 and returned to his home country, where he eventually became a fiercely independent chief news editor of the government-owned Mozambique News Agency. In the following years in various positions he became one of Africa's most prominent investigative reporters. On the day he died, he was being driven through the center of Maputo, the capital, when two vehicles cut off his car. At least two men are said to have opened fire with AK-47 rifles.

It is not governments that are leading the anticorruption charge, rather it is a grand ad hoc coalition of civil society activists, journalists, philanthropists, and scholars. And in the years to come it will continue to be the case that these forces set the agenda, press governments with mounting vigor and impact for reforms, and monitor the measures announced to see that they are effectively implemented.

The leading activists are a breed apart. They seem to have a different kind of blood running through their veins and a level of passion for what they do that is awesome. To sit at a table with Devendra Raj Panday from Nepal, Cobus de Swardt from South Africa, Sion Assidon from Morocco, and Geo Sung-Kim from South Korea is to become swept up in their passion. Each of them is modest, down to earth, and realistic about the anticorruption cause that binds them together and which they lead. Each of them has spent time in prison for their work for human rights and freedom.

These are selfless leaders, willing to risk an enormous amount because they have a deep emotional conviction that their concern is directed at seeking to improve the lot of the world's people and they just do not have a choice, other than to continuously drive ahead. They do not see curbing corruption as an end in itself. They understand from personal experience that corruption is the largest single barrier to the development of decent living for their fellow men and women across most of the world. Their misery is a cause worth fighting for, irrespective of the personal risks.

Thanks to the activists many small steps have been taken in dozens of countries to build civil society anticorruption movements and to raise public awareness of the possibility of curbing corruption. These actions have become increasingly more substantial and more effective and the successes in one country become recognized in many and have an increasingly visible multiplier impact.

It is precisely because of the leadership of the activists in the anticorruption cause that we now stand close to the tipping point—close to that moment where the anticorruption momentum in so many countries becomes so powerful that it starts to force major reforms, so close that we are set to see a rising tide of prosecutions that place the villains on the defensive and on the run.

Elena Panfilova, head of TI-Russia, took her sons shopping in a mall in Moscow one Saturday afternoon and noticed that secret service agents were following her from store to store. Finally, she turned on them and said she would report them. Back at the office she typed a blunt letter of complaint to the head of the Interior Ministry on her computer, but she never sent it. She did not need to. Two days later she got a call from the secret service asking her to explain why she had written a letter of complaint!

Elena is regularly followed, her telephone is tapped, and her computer is hacked. To the question of why she does her work, she simply disarmingly says, "Do I have a choice?"

It was Elena who in June 2009 stood on a public stage next to President Obama in Moscow and decried the curse of corruption that was wrecking her nation. She was well aware that her widely televised statement involved risks; after all, activists in Russia are haunted by the slaying in broad daylight of human rights journalist and worker Anna Politkovskaya in 2006, whose killers have yet to be brought to justice. And in July 2009, Russian human rights activist Natalya Estemirova was murdered in the Caucasus.

You can find Elena on YouTube videos of her press conferences as she demands accountability and transparency in Russian public life. TI-Russia, operating on a threadbare budget and constantly in fear of being closed by the authorities, is pioneering a national Internet network that is encouraging Russians across the nation to speak up and discuss through social media the ways in which their lives are being damaged by corruption. The effort is not to seek broad generalities but rather to make Russians acutely aware of the individual cases and to galvanize action. Despite possible reprisals from the authorities, Russians are speaking up and sharing their stories. Despite the widely voiced view that Russian officials will continue to extort and to abuse their power, irrespective of the volume of complaints, the initiatives being taken by TI-Russia and by other civil society organizations in the country are generating rising public support. And as the impact mounts, the personal risks being taken by the leaders also rise.

Like Elena, Devendra Panday says that his activism is not a matter of personal choice, but the core driver of his life. He could not imagine sitting on his hands and enjoying the restful retirement that he so well deserves after decades in his country's civil service. This former minister of finance has been involved in TI from the start, serving on the inaugural Advisory Council, creating a national chapter in his home country, and later being elected to TI's international board of directors. He is a small and seemingly shy man, but once you get him talking about corruption and injustice in Nepal, he is a firecracker. In late April 2006, I received an e-mail from him from Katmandu, sent just a couple of days after he was released from prison. He wrote in part:

> Dear Frank, I have been free since this Tuesday and I have been in pretty good health and wonderful spirits all along . . . but the victory for democracy is only about 50%. We have to make sure that the reinstated parliament immediately passes a resolution for an election to the constituent assembly so that we can draft a new constitution. . . . Let us hope the experience of Nepal has some lessons for fighting corruption. The King's dictatorship came into being on February 1, 2005 in the name of controlling corruption, among other things. . . . The problem is that we have had the worst corruption and contempt for universal principles of accountability under the King's regime in our history. So, you see, we have to keep at it.

Rueben Lifuka has a smile as wide as the continent of Africa. He seems always to be in good humor, yet he is under constant stress and pressure as he strives to challenge the corrupt elites in Zambia. It was quite a shock, for example, when former Zambian president Frederick Chiluba was finally found not guilty after a marathon corruption trial in 2009. His wife, Regina, was not so lucky and was judged guilty in a separate case for receiving stolen goods (from her husband, no less). Rueben was not overly dejected by the outcome to the Chiluba trial. The major achievement was the trial itself. Thanks to him and many other Zambian activists, a former African head of state was placed on trial for the first time on charges of corruption. People took note across the African continent.

Sion Assidon, a founder of TI-Morocco, and Geo Sung-Kim, a founder of TI-South Korea, were both imprisoned and beaten for human rights activism when their countries had brutal dictators. The memories of those rough times fuel their passionate determination to help establish open and honest societies. Like Rueben, Devendra, Elena, and many others, they know the personal risks that they take, understand the importance in their nations of the leadership roles they have been willing to play, and contribute enormously to the building of a consolidated global anticorruption movement.

Joe Githongo, a Kenyan business accountant, can be especially proud in the anticorruption context of two major achievements: he was one of the original inspirations and founders of TI as a global organization, and he taught his son well. John Githongo started out as a journalist in the early 1990s and seized the opportunity to write about politics, including corruption, when he was given the chance to pen a regular column for the *East African* newspaper. While still a journalist, he started to plan for the establishment of TI-Kenya as a civil society organization, which the government of Kenya opposed, and to convince members of the national parliament to start investigating corruption in the executive branch of the government.

John had significant success on both of his agendas and he participated prior to the 2002 elections in developing policy plans for a future government led by Mwai Kibaki, which the veteran Kenya leader agreed with. When Kibaki won the election, John was offered the senior government anticorruption position in his administration. Friends of John advised him not to take a post because they warned that he would be co-opted by powerful corrupt cronies of the new president. John, however, was confident that he could withstand the pressures and bring about change. He was flattered to be placed in charge of anticorruption in the government with an office in the State House itself.

Initially, he loved his new position and he told me on a visit in 2004 that he was building the resources across the governmental machinery to make a serious attack on widespread corrupt practices. But the initial joy in his office gave way to increasing frustration and concern. Senior cabinet officers were pressing him not to pursue various corruption investigations. He became aware of serious, high-level abuse, but found that his direct complaints to the president fell on deaf ears. He started to receive threats and sensed that his telephone was being tapped.

Many people who found themselves in a similar position would probably resign quietly from the government and keep a low profile. Not John Githongo. As the pressures mounted, he started to secretly record conversations with leading figures in the Kibaki administration. And then, as the death threats became ever more alarming, he boarded an airplane for the United Kingdom, handed in his resignation from the government at the Kenyan High Commission in London, informed several newspaper reporters of his actions, and went into hiding. We met briefly in London at that time and he was certain that he was being followed by agents of Kenya's secret police. He said that he was determined to find a way to blow the whistle on the outrageous theft of public funds that he had seen in the Kenyan government.

Some months later he leaked an extensive dossier, supported by his taped evidence and assorted documents, that revealed extensive grand corruption at the highest levels of the Kenyan government. It forced some resignations, instigated official investigations, unleashed diplomatic protests, and, most importantly, wrecked the "Mr. Clean" reputation of President Kibaki. The full story of John's bravery is detailed in a brilliant book by journalist Michela Wrong, *It's Our Turn to Eat—The Story of a Kenyan Whistle-Blower*.[2] Bookshops in Kenya were scared to put the book on display when it was published in February 2009, but hundreds of copies were quietly and swiftly sold there. It was widely known as a secret bestseller. John returned to Kenya in late 2009, taking great care to avoid the public spotlight, yet working, all the same, to try and bring political change to his country.

Cobus de Swardt is another African who has risk-taking for political causes built into his genes. He starts every day asking himself what he can do that day to strengthen the global corruption fight. Just over twenty years ago he was being beaten up in Cape Town by the agents of the South African apartheid government. His battle scars from those days are now a stimulus to his enormous passion for justice. As the managing director of TI's global secretariat in Berlin, he drives a team of more than 130 highly motivated people to support TI's national chapters in about ninety countries to raise funds for the movement from across the globe, to stimulate global and regional campaigns, and to take advantage of every opportunity to speak truth to power.

SETTING THE STAGE FOR AN ASSAULT ON CORRUPTION

Foreign aid came under mounting criticism in the 1980s. That trio of right-wing leaders in the 1980s—Britain's Margaret Thatcher, Germany's Helmut Kohl, and America's Ronald Reagan—shared a passionate belief in the free enterprise system. They surrounded themselves with advisors who took a highly skeptical view of the policies of aid agencies in making grants and loans to public-sector institutions in foreign countries. Lord Bauer, a British economist and advisor to Thatcher, led the charge in academia against foreign aid, arguing that it undermined the full beneficial development force of private enterprise. When I joined the senior ranks of the World Bank in 1981, a senior Reagan administration Treasury official told me he considered the World Bank to be just a "socialist give-away agency."

The ending of the Cold War represented a major milestone in building public awareness of the evils of corruption (see chapter 11). There was no longer any reason for Western powers to use aid grants to corrupt dictators across the developing world to win their favor in a battle against the Russians. The Berlin Wall was pulled down, the Soviet Union was history, Russians embraced capitalism, and the aid strategies of the United States, the United Kingdom, Germany, and France—key bilateral grant-makers—came under unparalleled review. Parliamentarians from Bonn to Washington, DC, were asking whether foreign aid was effective now in reducing poverty or just a prime source for padding the secret Swiss bank accounts of corrupt African, Asian, and Latin American potentates.

Never before had foreign aid been under such intense attack, nor did corruption in developing countries provide as much fuel for investigative journalists as it started to from the 1980s. Ferdinand Marcos and his wife, Imelda, came to be the poster figures that highlighted public attention around the world to the corruption of Third World leaders. In 1986, the Marcoses were forced to flee into exile from the Philippines to Hawaii amid allegations of massive theft. Within hours of their departure the world's media was full of stories of the extraordinary secret wealth of the Marcoses, right down to the hundreds of high-fashion shoes found in Imelda Marcos's palace closet. For years thereafter, newspaper investigators and public prosecutors sought the allegedly billions of dollars that the Marcoses had stolen. It was colorful stories like these that cemented the image of vastly corrupt leaders of very poor countries who had long enjoyed grand support for Western governments and their aid agencies.

The 1980s also saw the first major global civil society campaigns of any kind against aid agencies. The environmentalists were in the vanguard. A mass movement spreading across many of the leading industrial countries argued that the World Bank and international aid agencies were destroying the environment and creating enormous potential dangers for the world's poorest countries and indeed for the world as a whole. The Environmental Defense Fund in the United States accused the World Bank of destroying the Amazon. Some thirty thousand "green" demonstrators protested the World Bank's annual meeting in Berlin in 1988. The campaigns had a profound impact, and by the late 1980s the leading aid agencies were all hiring environmentalists, creating environment departments, and claiming to be environmental leaders themselves.

CREATING TRANSPARENCY INTERNATIONAL

The rising questioning about the effectiveness of aid and the mounting visibility and success of civil society organizations in campaigning for change at aid agencies had a profound impact on a middle-aged German establishment former lawyer, Peter Eigen, the Nairobi resident World Bank director for East Africa. Peter was frustrated—angry may be a more accurate word. His senior managers at World Bank headquarters in Washington, DC, did not want to hear his complaints that corruption was undermining aid effectiveness in Africa. The official representatives of major bilateral aid agencies and the United Nations with whom he met regularly in official aid discussions in Nairobi were equally deaf.

While the Kenyan government of President Moi stole increasing amounts of public funds, nobody in the international official community was willing to challenge him or cut off aid to Kenya. Moreover, there was no civil society organization around to challenge the corruption problem and do what the environmentalists had done—force the World Bank to listen.

I left the World Bank as its director of information in early 1990 and a few months later the Kenyan government consulted with me to help it establish ways to start communicating more openly with the domestic and international media. I was invited in November to go for talks with senior ministers of the Kenyan administration, which provided an opportunity for fascinating conversations with Peter. Much to my surprise, I learned after my trip that President Moi wanted to see me, so I returned to Nairobi in January 1991 for a bizarre one-on-one chat with the president at his seaside mansion[3] and, far more importantly, for further talks with Peter.

Peter had worked in Africa and in Latin America for many years for the World Bank and he had enormous enthusiasm for the mission of providing resources and expertise to assist development projects that could lift people up from poverty. If his enthusiasm ever flagged, then his wife Jutta, an experienced doctor who spent her days helping the absolute poor in the slums of Nairobi, was always there to encourage him. Now she was encouraging him to make a stand against the World Bank to see that corruption was confronted. Peter was also being encouraged to act by his Kenyan friend, Joe Githongo, as well as others in the Kenyan business community who complained bitterly about the corruption across the Moi administration.

Peter was hesitant and reluctant to be critical of his World Bank colleagues who had long supported his career but were now turning a deaf ear to his complaints about corruption. He understood that the Bank, under its Articles of Agreement, could only provide grants and make loans to governments and that it was owned by governments, and that, as a result, the senior managers considered it politically risky to raise the corruption issue with the institution's funders and borrowers. Peter was rebuffed time and again, and as his frustration mounted, he started to consider an alternative course. If the Bank would not address corruption in development, then perhaps a new civil society organization could raise the flag. His focus was on African development and changing the World Bank. We discussed his idea at length and I offered to help.

In subsequent months he spoke with many people about his idea and none of his meetings were more important than the one that was convened in mid-1991 in a suburb of Frankfurt by then managing director of the German official aid agency GTZ, Hans-Jörg Elshorst. Here Peter found a kindred spirit, a top aid official as angry about corruption as Peter was and keen to encourage Peter to translate his ideas into practice. He received encouragement from many others, including a trio of British experts in business and development, Gerald Parfitt, Laurence Cockcroft, and George Moody-Stuart, as well as US business executives Fritz Heimann and Michael Hershman—each of these early supporters would play important roles in the launch of TI and its future success.

Peter then dug deep into his extensive list of official contacts and struck gold twice as he spoke with then Dutch minister of development Jan Pronk and former World Bank president and former US defense secretary Robert McNamara. Declaring that "the great mistake" he made while at the World Bank was not confronting corruption, McNamara pledged support. He and Pronk co-chaired an official think-tank called the Global Coalition for Africa and they said that they would make a $50,000 grant to an anticorruption organization if Peter believed he could establish one.

By the summer of 1992 Peter had resigned from the World Bank and was on his way to gathering enough support to take planning for the establishment of TI into high gear. A meeting of friends and potential supporters was organized outside of London by Parfitt. It was an event full of enthusiasm and goodwill and at its end Peter, Hans-Jörg, and I drove off for a contemplative afternoon wandering around the colleges of Cambridge University. We chatted about whether we had entirely taken leave of our senses in even thinking we could do anything about corruption. How could a handful of angry middle-aged men make any difference at all?

I think it was that afternoon when the decision was really taken to move ahead as rapidly as possible. Peter needed the assurances of support from Hans-Jörg and he got it. It was not just moral support either. Hans-Jörg indicated that he could arrange for GTZ to provide TI with a line of credit of up to 200,000 Deutschmarks—with this, together with cash from the Global Coalition for Africa, it looked as if TI had the financial base to launch.

Twenty friends met in The Hague in February 1993. Each of them brought their own unique perspectives and determination to the anticorruption cause. While Peter was clearly the leader, he could not translate his vision into practice without the contributions of each of the individuals from a dozen countries that met in Holland at that time. TI's establishment was a collegial effort and in the years ahead, as TI and Peter became well known, the constant, low-key efforts of the original group were of invaluable importance. At the meeting itself, nine members of the group volunteered to serve on the first TI board of directors[4] and they elected Peter as chairman and Hossain and me as the vice chairmen; the three of us constituted TI's "executive."[5] We agreed that TI would have its head office in Berlin and that an inaugural launch conference would take place in May 1993.[6]

Peter became the full-time chair and chief executive officer (CEO) of TI, taking no salary. His energy and charismatic way of talking about the horrendous impact of corruption on economic development and the world's poorest countries proved to be a formula for success, as did his willingness to embrace many ideas from other people and to expand the mission and the objectives of TI.

At first all of our communications between people wishing to become engaged in TI were through expensive faxes and regular telephone lines. Everyone paid their own costs as we had no central TI budget for such expenses. It was not long, however, before the e-mail era dawned and Peter's son, Tobias Eigen, who was at college in Washington, DC, volunteered to teach his father in Berlin and me in Washington how to use e-mail. The development of e-mail hugely multiplied the information flows to and from TI and radically reduced TI's communications costs. Suddenly, or so it seemed, we were communicating with hundreds of journalists, with actual and potential civil society activists across the globe, and with all manner of contacts, new and old, in business and government, with great speed. We should have given Tobias a special prize.

From uncertain beginnings, TI pioneered the nongovernmental organization anticorruption cause. Peter served as chairman for twelve years and then became chairman of TI's International Advisory Council.

TI'S OBJECTIVES

The critical support for TI and the character it assumed in its early years were defined by the inaugural conference in Berlin in May 1993 (which enjoyed a small grant from the German Ministry of Development). We had space for only forty people, but word about the conference had started to spread and we received a range of surprising requests to attend.

McNamara said he would fly to Berlin from Washington, DC, and stay just for one day to ensure the meeting was a success. Devendra Panday said he would come from Nepal. Obasanjo said he would come from Lagos, Nigeria, while the vice president of Ecuador, Alberto Dahik, said that he would also attend. The thoroughly corrupt president of Algeria, Belaid Abdesselam, insisted on coming and informed us that he would bring fifteen cabinet members and a TV crew. We said he could come on his own and that we would allow the TV crew into the meeting briefly. He accepted the terms and used the meeting to tell the people of Algeria that he was at the forefront of a new global movement to end corruption!

Peter and I met McNamara at Berlin's airport and drove into what had been East Berlin and we went for a walk. McNamara told us that he had not been in Berlin since the summer of 1939, when he had made a visit as a student in London. Despite being there on the eve of World War II, America's future secretary of defense said Berlin had been pleasant and he noticed nothing out of the ordinary.

He told us what he wanted us to achieve at the TI meeting. It did not take him long to convince Peter that of all the participants the best leader of a "blue ribbon" TI Advisory Council would be Dahik. He then, in turn, convinced Dahik-on the first evening of the meeting to become the chairman of the new council in return for pledging to ensure that Ecuador would be the first country to open a TI national chapter. McNamara then flew back to the United States. A few years later, swift to escape arrest on charges of corruption (never proven), Dahik fled Ecuador for refuge in Costa Rica.

Obasanjo, Hossain, and Augustine Ruzindana, then Uganda's inspector-general, probably made the most important contributions to the conference. Each of them stressed that corruption was a universal problem and that no country could confront the issue on its own. Some of us had been fearful that our initiative would be seen as an effort by an arrogant Western organization to tell the Third World how to behave.[7] This was one of the reasons we decided not to have the head office in Washington, DC, but rather in Berlin. The interventions by the leaders from the South convinced us that we had nothing to fear. Nevertheless, we also believed that we were right not to place our headquarters in the United States because of an inevitable public perception that we would be close to the US government, and given the previous employment of both Peter and me, too close to the World Bank.

In preparation for the meeting from May 4 to 6, 1993, at the Villa Borsig in Berlin, Laurence Cockcroft, now a member of TI's board of directors, developed a paper that sketched the core objectives of TI. TI saw itself as a coalition builder at the international and national levels with the aim of bringing civil society, governments, and businesses together to find constructive ways to curb corruption. TI would develop and promote standards of conduct for governmental and business institutions; it would raise public awareness of the corruption issue; and it would pursue research on corruption.

The conference endorsed these objectives, but it went much further in highlighting a host of issues that became key to anticorruption strategies for the next two decades. These ranged from the need to campaign for forceful anticorruption laws, to convincing business to adopt meaningful codes of conduct, to reforming the approaches of the foreign aid agencies.

For example, at the outset Dieter Frisch, then director general for development of the at the Commission European Community and later the founder of TI-Belgium and a guiding force on much of TI's development agenda, asserted that human rights, democracy, good governance, accountability, transparency, and the fight against corruption needed to be seen together in a comprehensive effort to enable the world's poorest countries to develop. He argued that the "taboo" of corruption, where the word was never mentioned in official discussions of foreign aid and development, had to be broken. He articulated an agenda for action, mainly by the official aid agencies, which would become an immediate TI priority area and clearly highlighted the culpability of turning a blind eye too often to abuse by aid-recipient governments. Frisch would have a major influence in coming years in reshaping the European Union's (EU) approaches to corruption and seeing that the European Union became a leading supporter of anticorruption efforts in developing countries and in Central and Eastern Europe.

The Villa Borsig meeting concluded on a positive note and we received major encouragement directly thereafter. The international media was generous in its coverage of our young endeavor. While we had neither a permanent office nor staff, we already were being hailed by the press as a new force to be reckoned with. To be sure, the *Economist* called us a Don Quixote and predicted that we would be tilting at windmills and going nowhere fast. But other leading media, including the *Financial Times*, the *New York Times*, Germany's *Der Spiegel*, the news-wires, and the BBC World Service, were more positive. The launch of TI was widely reported across the developing world. The *Bangkok Post* on May 3, 1993, for example, ran a prominent headline: "World watchdog being set up to help fight graft."

The media headlines validated a fundamental assumption that we had made when moving to establish TI: against a background of a post–Cold War era and rising public concerns about corruption, our timing was right.

In the weeks after the launch we found ample proof of this. As the publicity spread, we started to receive telephone calls and faxes from across the world from people who wanted to become involved in TI. A visitor to my Washington, DC, office, for example, introduced himself as a Congolese diplomat and gave me a volume that he said was a secret report on the bribes taken by his government's top officials. He asked me to make sure that TI published the report!

In November 1993, Costa Rican president Oscar Arias Sanchez gave an address in Berlin on the opening of TI's first office. He told a mostly German audience of officials:

> Those that struggle in the name of open and honest government deserve not just our praise, but our active support. Often, leaders of these worthy movements must combat powerful and established elites and they may seem, at first, like powerless Davids confronting Goliaths. But, as events in much of Latin America in recent years have so visibly shown, the power of the people dare not be underestimated for a moment, the Davids can win and, let me stress, their success will be that much more secure if you can get behind them.

BUILDING A MOVEMENT

At the outset, TI could only afford to hire two young—and as it proved, hard-working—assistants, Margit von Hamm and Fredrik Galtung. Margit became the vital administrator of the infant TI, while Fredrik played a host of roles and by the late 1990s pioneered some of TI's most successful research tools. In January 1994, TI had the good fortune to recruit its first managing director in Berlin. Jeremy Pope, who accepted a low salary, is a New Zealander with exceptional human rights credentials and outstanding communication skills. He quit the Commonwealth Secretariat in London, where he had been the General Counsel, and moved at personal financial cost to Berlin in order to become Peter's chief partner. While relieving Peter of a mounting administrative burden, Jeremy started TI's research work, seeking to build a body of knowledge about what actions are effective in different countries in fighting corruption. His successful efforts not only produced books and manuals and developed national workshops in many countries, but also set the ground for TI national chapters in the years ahead to develop their own national integrity reports and use these to engage private- and public-sector leaders in their own countries.

The "TI Source Book" of the mid-1990s, Pope's brainchild, became a blueprint, with chapters on parliamentary oversight, the roles of the judiciary, the need for a free press and for freedom of information laws, the importance for governments to establish general accounting offices to monitor public-sector procurement, and the need for anticorruption commissions to serve as independent forces for reform and for justice. The "TI Source Book" was the first report to clearly develop the concept of "National Integrity Systems," which is now widely used by academics and officials and is an across-the-board approach where no national agency or institution is exempt from over-sight and accountability.

Work on the book taught all of us that there is no single magic bullet to overcome corruption. Rather, there is no alternative to painstaking grassroots efforts on many fronts to make governmental activities transparent, to make public officials accountable to the people they are meant to serve, and to educate, starting in the schools, to establish ethical values when it comes to all aspects of the work of the public sector.

Sitting in Berlin in 1993, the new capital of a now unified Germany, Peter was determined to see anticorruption organizations develop in the former communist countries. In New York in early 1994, Peter and I went to see Aryeh Neier, the former vice chairman of the Fund for Free Expression and former executive director of Human Rights Watch who now was the CEO of George Soros's Open Society Foundation. Hungarian-born Soros, who had made a fortune in the world's financial markets, used his foundation to promote pro-democracy civil society organizations in Central and Eastern Europe. Neier was sympathetic to our cause but argued that he and Soros believed it was more efficient to provide funds directly to civil society groups in the region than to go via an intermediary, such as TI in Berlin. In time, he was to appreciate that TI could be an effective organizer, partner, and monitor of groups in the region and that supporting TI would further the Open Society's goals. For several years in the latter part of the 1990s, TI received grants from this source and Soros's strong support, which was im-portant to building TI national chapters in many countries.

Peter recognized that building anticorruption organizations in Central and Eastern Europe, where people had zero knowledge of what a free press is, what democratic institutions are meant to do, and how to organize grassroots movements, was painfully difficult. All of us engaged in TI came either from the West or from developing countries. We lacked the knowledge to make a real difference in the East.

But, by another stroke of good fortune, Peter heard about Miklos Mars-chall in Washington, DC, and asked me to meet with him. Miklos was the founding executive director of CIVICUS, a global civil society umbrella organization, and he had previously been a deputy mayor of Budapest. He joined TI in Berlin and moved with extraordinary speed and skill to work with a vast array of civil society organizations and activists across Eastern and Central Europe.

What Miklos found everywhere was both a great enthusiasm to establish TI national chapters and to challenge the new leaders of the region, most of whom were widely seen as being corrupt, and concern that the new TI organizations would be infiltrated, or even taken over, by former communists or associates of the current regimes. In this sensitive political environment there was a premium on developing public credibility for new civil society groups engaged in pro-democracy, press freedom, human rights, and anticorruption activities. The 1990s was a period of political and economic turmoil across most of the region, where the combination of massive crime, weak rule of law, and infant democratic institutions were seeing the vast transfer of the wealth of state enterprises into the hands of individuals who, until recently, were low-paid civil servants, were now rising to become some of the world's richest tycoons.

The legacy of communist oppression was a powerful incentive to many people in their twenties and thirties who wanted to open their societies and ensure that individual freedom was secured and that everyone could participate freely in the political process. Miklos, who today is TI's deputy managing director, understood the politics and the dynamics of the former Soviet Union and he found people in one country after another who he recognized as having the political sensitivity, the professional skill, and the total conviction necessary to spearhead the TI movement.

Miklos's tireless work contributed to the growth of more than thirty TI national chapters across the region, from Armenia, Albania, and Azerbaijan, to Georgia, Hungary, and Latvia, to Mongolia, Russia, Ukraine, and across the Balkans.

Crucial to TI's early strategies was building broad public understanding of the problems of corruption. The most effective tool for this purpose became the TI Corruption Perceptions Index (CPI), launched in 1995. There had never been such a league table before. As TI's press spokesman in the 1990s, I was caught off guard by the initial launch of the CPI. The idea of the CPI was that of a young German academic, Johann Graf Lambsdorff, who had proposed it to Peter Eigen and Jeremy Pope. Johann, assisted by TI's Fredrik Galtung, developed several prototypes and then talked to Germany's *Der Spiegel* magazine about it. *Der Spiegel* then published the "TI index," without either Peter or Jeremy Pope knowing that this was about to happen. At first they tried to field a rising tide of press calls while still wondering whether the index was a good idea for TI or not. We agreed to run with it—as Pope said, "The genie was out of the bottle"—and a press release was issued announcing the TI Corruption Index (its original title). We became deluged with press calls. Johann developed the CPI over the next fourteen years and thus made an enormous contribution to raising international awareness of corruption issues.

Governments in many countries were swift to denounce the CPI, and the more they did so, the more the media in their own countries could draw public attention to the index. In Pakistan, Benazir Bhutto was furious in the 1996 elections at finding that at dozens of public campaign rallies she would confront big banners reading "Pakistan: Second Most Corrupt Country in the World."

The rankings in the CPI became pegs for reporters across the world to write about their own countries in terms of corruption. Follow-up stories would compare the home country with the neighboring countries to see which was the most corrupt. As politicians' denunciations of the CPI grew, so did the media and the public's joy in discussing it. Soon, politicians, businessmen, and of course journalists were complaining that the CPI only covered half of the countries in the world and their own country was not ranked—indicating that their country had no corruption! (Today 183 countries are ranked—see appendix 1.)

TI built on the success of the CPI to develop a series of more specialized indices, such as the Bribe Payers' Index (see appendix 2), a TI Barometer to assess in greater depth issues of corruption in a range of countries, and in-depth national integrity reports. These tools, alongside TI's annual "Global Corruption Report," have influenced research in many quarters, influenced evaluations of countries by aid agencies, and, most importantly, influenced the broad public debate about fighting corruption.

The CPI helped greatly to establish TI's influence and profile, which in turn enhanced the young organization's ability to raise funds. Foundations and national aid agencies were approached for money as the infant TI was in fairly dire straits in the mid-1990s. Nancy Boswell, the managing director of TI-USA, played key roles here and worked tirelessly, for example, to convince USAID to support TI. She found a sympathetic ear at the agency in senior official Larry Garber and in time USAID became a major contributor. Its support, in turn, helped to generate support from other official aid agencies.

No achievement by TI compares to that of founding and helping to develop over ninety national chapters across the world. Each has its own agenda, but each adheres to core values of the global movement and each contributes on a consistent basis to strengthening the global organization. Each chapter has its own story of struggle, setbacks in the face of governmental opposition, and successes thanks to the support of the public, the independent media, and partnerships with other civil society groups. The chapters that have built records of success owe much to their founders.

For example, Kamal Hossain, the founder of TI-Bangladesh and one of the fathers of Bangladesh, was arrested during the country's fight for independence from Pakistan in 1971, and in the immediate following years he helped to draft the new country's constitution and held several cabinet portfolios—minister of law, minister of foreign affairs, and minister of petroleum and minerals. Unwillingness to go along with corrupt deals forced him to flee to the United States and into exile for five years, and he has been a bold and outspoken advocate of transparency and accountability in government ever since. His support, courage, and enthusiasm have inspired brilliant young men[8] to take the executive lead in building TI-Bangladesh, which now has over four hundred employees and more than ten thousand volunteers working across the country in its campaigns.

With the continuing engagement of Peter and under the joint leadership of Huguette and Cobus, together with the Berlin staff, increasing numbers of donors are providing funds to the TI secretariat or through it to specific anticorruption programs in different parts of the developing world, or directly to national chapters. The annual revenues secured by TI in Berlin are in excess of $20 million and national chapters around the world raise a similar amount on their own account. For the most part the cash comes from official development-assistance agencies, including the European Union's Commission, and the governments of Australia, Canada, Denmark, Germany, Finland, Ireland, Norway, the Netherlands, Spain, Sweden, Switzerland, Thailand, the United Kingdom, and the United States. Important contributions come from philanthropic foundations—notably, the Bill & Melinda Gates Foundation, TIDES Foundations, and the William and Flora Hewlett Foundation.

TI created a movement that attracted a number of existing national organizations to either establish a formal relationship with TI (for example, Poder Ciudadano became TI-Argentina), while many others forged more informal ties. As TI grew in prominence it influenced many bilateral and multilateral aid agencies to agree to make anticorruption and good governance a priority, which in turn led such organizations to provide funds to dozens of national civil society organizations. Philanthropies, such as the MacArthur Foundation and the Open Society Foundation, also became increasingly active in supporting groups across the developing world that had anticorruption as their mission. Today, there are hundreds of nongovernmental organizations that have anticorruption either as the prime purpose or as one of their major issues.

THE PARTNERSHIP FOR TRANSPARENCY FUND

PTF[9] was created by some of TI's founders and others associated with TI in the late 1990s in order to provide both small grants and advice to civil society organizations in developing countries that have plans to pursue specific anti-corruption projects. It complements the larger policy and public awareness work of TI.

PTF is wholly independent of TI, registered and headquartered in the United States, and has an internationally diverse board of directors chaired by Anabel Cruz from Uruguay, who is the founder and director of ICD, the Communication and Development Institute, in Uruguay and has been the chair of the board of CIVICUS, the global umbrella organization for civil society groups. Indeed, Anabel was recruited to the PTF board in 2002 by then PTF chair Kumi Naidoo, who used to be the executive director of CIVICUS; today Naidoo is the executive director of the organization Greenpeace International.[10]

The growth and development of PTF owes an enormous amount to the zeal, vision, and hard work of Pierre Landell-Mills, a British economist who spent more than thirty years working for the World Bank and, prior to his retirement, was the Bank's country director in Bangladesh. Pierre may legitimately claim to be the first World Bank staff person ever to have raised corruption in a major World Bank report, as he highlighted the issue in a landmark study on economic development in sub-Saharan Africa that he authored and that the World Bank published in 1989.[11] His knowledge of how to make development projects work, combined with his anticorruption passion, resulted in PTF raising funds from a series of official aid agencies; PTF recruiting more than thirty retired former senior World Bank operational managers and others to work on a wholly voluntary basis; and PTF evolving project approaches that have proved to be highly successful according to independent evaluations.

PTF's project grants are usually no more than $30,000. Since its creation in 2000, it has made almost two hundred grants to civil society organizations in forty-four countries on five continents. "The substantial—often dramatic—benefit that can derive swiftly from its small grants is a success story worthy of wider telling," stated the UK government's aid agency review of PTF's work in May 2011.[12]

In late 2010, Daniel Ritchie, a former senior operations director at the World Bank and for a decade a tireless volunteer for PTF, took over for Pierre as the unpaid president and CEO of PTF. In recent times the number of volunteer advisors has expanded significantly, now embracing a range of experts from business and development backgrounds apart from the World

Bank. Together, operating mostly as a virtual organization, the advisors minimize bureaucratic hassle when dealing with civil society organizations applying and then using PTF grants.

The key role of the advisors is to bring their years of development-project experience to the assistance of grant recipients to ensure that the projects happen and meet their key objectives. No aid agency could operate on such a small scale, and small civil society organizations could never afford to pay for the level of expert consulting advice that PTF's advisors provide free of charge. This results in a formidable combination to make inroads in the anticorruption war.

PTF has no shortage of project proposals from Mongolia to Argentina coming across the Internet. It is organizing workshops to bring together civil society leaders to exchange their experiences and knowledge. It is creating regional hubs in Africa and Asia and Latin America, exploring new ways to use its skills to assist civil society organizations to monitor major aid projects involved in governance (see chapter 12) while broadening its range of supporters. In late 2011, it opened its first administrative office in Washington, DC. Some of the projects include the following:

- In India, for example, PTF supported a network of fourteen organizations working at grassroots, mostly seeking to enforce the nation's Right to Information Act. The aim was to help the villagers gain full access to the benefits of a range of public-service programs and to expose officials who might be siphoning off public funds.
- In Moldova, PTF worked with the Institute for Democracy, which established a partnership with the Tiraspol State University, the Institute for Civil Initiatives and Information Development, and the National Institute for Women of Moldova Equality. The goal was to make the financial operations of the university transparent and corruption-free. A key aspect is to establish an Anticorruption Council, which acts as a channel for complaints and monitors developments.
- In the Philippines, a PTF-funded project developed with civil society counters rampant corruption in the conduct of water and irrigation-systems projects in the province of Abra. The problems are due to three interrelated issues that the project addresses: lack of information to the public, low public authority integrity standards, and weak capacity to monitor the operations.

Every PTF project is really about people, mostly very ordinary people who have become empowered to make far-reaching and meaningful changes. In the Philippines, a series of PTF grants contributed to a major effort that came to involve thousands of people across the country to clean up corruption in elementary school book procurement, warehousing, and national distribution.

Government Watch, or G-Watch, is a social accountability action-research program established by the Ateneo School of Government in the Philippines in 2000 as a reaction to the corruption pursued by then president Joseph Estrada. G-Watch deployed fresh college graduates to visit government project sites and collect documents to be used to assess actual government performance in service delivery. In 2002, G-Watch learned that primary-school children were not getting the books that the government had said they should be getting and it started a small pilot program with the Department of Education that it called "Textbook Count." It was not long before they discovered that 40 percent of the books were never delivered. A year later, with the help of a $25,000 PTF grant, G-Watch and the Department of Education launched "Textbook Count 2," which mobilized many organizations in a joint effort to track thirty-seven million textbooks, valued at around $30 million, to 5,500 delivery points.

Publishers and officials had conspired to overprice the books and print fewer of them. Officials and warehouse managers conspired to store fewer books than were paid for and see to the delivery of even less. Thanks to the diligence of G-Watch and a few cooperative public officials, the government rebid publishing, storage, and delivery contracts; new bidding processes were monitored; and printing runs were likewise monitored, as were inventories in warehouses. All the while, G-Watch and many others were directly engaged in seeing that the delivery rate to the schools was improved. In 2004, the Boy and Girl Scouts, as well as Coca-Cola, joined the program to strengthen final deliveries, especially to rural schools. By 2007, G-Watch could report that the delivery rate had reached 95 percent.

KEY ORGANIZATIONS PUSHING THE AGENDA

Activism in the anticorruption arena comes in many forms, from the global awareness and major across-the-board policy and research activities of TI, to the specific project focus of PTF, to building major coalitions to launch specific global campaigns. In this latter area, the London-based Publish What You Pay coalition is making a difference. It has brought together over six hundred organizations under its umbrella to campaign for transparency in the extractive industries. The original founders in June 2002 were mostly based in the United Kingdom and included Global Witness, CAFOD (the UK Catholic aid agency), Oxfam GB, Save the Children UK, TI-UK, and the US-based foundation financed by philanthropist George Soros, the Open Society

Institute (OSI). Today, its members are drawn from more than fifty countries and their focus on securing full transparency in the oil, gas, and mining industries has registered significant successes (see chapter 13).

Working closely with Publish What You Pay is the Revenue Watch Institute, also founded in 2002 and based in New York, which was initially established by OSI. It became an independent organization in 2006, with funding from OSI, the William and Flora Hewlett Foundation, and the Norwegian Oil for Development Fund. It reports on transparency in many oil-producing countries and has been a very effective lobbyist in Washington, DC, in leading efforts to secure new US legislation as part of the Dodd-Frank Financial Reform Act of 2011, which mandates companies in the extractive industries that enter into agreements with foreign governments to report to the US Securities and Exchange Commission on an annual basis on all of their overseas royalty payments to governments. This success story has stimulated European civil society groups to successfully campaign that similar requirements be introduced by the European Union relative to all oil, gas, and mining companies headquartered in the European Union.

The inspiration for these anticorruption efforts in the extractive industries, and also in a host of other areas, is the London-based nongovernmental organization Global Witness. Its focus, like quite a number of other nongovernmental organizations in the anticorruption space, is on investigations. Global Witness was established in 1993 and is run by Patrick Alley, Charmian Gooch, and Simon Taylor. They lead an amazingly brave and prolific team that has exposed corruption and human rights abuse, mostly in Africa and in Asia, with zeal and accuracy.

Global Witness is best known for its work on blood diamonds, which they initiated in 1998, and has been on the leading edge of international efforts to prevent the illicit trade in diamonds that directly funds civil wars and violence in Africa. *Blood Diamond* was a major Hollywood movie in 2006 starring Leonardo DiCaprio, which was based on Global Witness's research. The Global Witness teams have been active in many countries and their amazing work in the Congo, which has received insufficient attention, has highlighted the very close linkages between international corporations doing deals with warlords that are killing and raping tens of thousands of people each year.

Global Witness has also demonstrated that it cannot be co-opted. Successful anticorruption civil society organizations are constantly being befriended by governments and businesses and international official organizations as they attempt to bring them into the establishment fold. Having exposed the trade in "blood diamonds," Global Witness was instrumental in establishing the Kimberly Process (named after the famous diamond-mining town in South Africa) in 2003, which has brought together over seventy participants from government, business, and civil society in a pact to monitor the diamond trade. In December 2011, Global Witness withdrew from the Kimberly Process when the majority of the participants agreed to the export of diamonds from the Marange fields in Zimbabwe. The action was seen not just as giving support to the corrupt government of Robert Mugabe, which has long been supporting the illicit diamond trade, but also as failing to sanction the serious human rights abuses by Zimbabwe's security forces in and around the Marange area.

The success of Global Witness is mirrored in many countries where small investigative organizations and many individual journalists are making the world acutely aware of the crimes of corruption. Ask many of these reporters why they do what they do and many of them smile and say that they simply could not live with themselves if they sought an easier and less challenging life. Ask them why they are so effective and they will note not only that they are independent and obtain funds from many sources without any strings attached, but also that they work closely with civil society organizations to leverage their research in ways that can support reform-promoting initiatives.

The rising numbers of anticorruption organizations now embrace women and men from all walks of life—journalists and academics, lawyers and business executives and public officials. Their skills combine leadership charisma, intellectual knowledge of the challenges that they confront, the political and diplomatic skills to survive, and management and organizational talents that can create growing organizations. Many of these organizations are dynamic and sense that in their towns and countries, as well as regionally and on the global stage—wherever they have their particular focus—they can now achieve far more than in the past. The laws at international, regional, and national levels that have been passed in the last decade reflect their influence. Their current growth, and their mounting impact, is being enhanced by the new age of transparency.

Concern about the victims of corruption is the driver of activism today on so many fronts by so many organizations. All the activists, however, have a clear view as they move ahead with their campaigns and initiatives that they are being confronted by many villains—people who benefit enormously from bribe taking and bribe paying and who, in many cases, will go to extreme lengths to maintain their power and pursue their rotten schemes.

NOTES

1. The full article can be viewed at www.thesundayleader.lk/20090111/editorial-.htm.
2. Michela Wrong, *It's Our Turn to Eat—The Story of a Kenyan Whistle-Blower* (London: Fourth Estate, 2009).

3. President Moi and I sat in lounge chairs on a grand veranda sipping tea and looking out at the ocean. He asked me at length to describe how the White House and the World Bank conducted press relations, but it was unclear whether he had any interest in establishing similar systems himself. Time would show that he did not.

4. Several of the participants felt that their positions in major business organizations and/ or public-sector institutions would represent a conflict of interest if they also joined the TI board. In time, for example, Fritz Heimann, then a senior lawyer at GE in the United States, retired from GE and was elected a TI board director, just as Hans-Jörg Elshorst would retire from the GTZ and become a TI managing director.

5. Governance of TI—a brief note: TI is incorporated as a global not-for-profit organization under German law. Its charter calls for there to be a board of directors, involving an "executive" and members of the association. The board comprises twelve individuals and the "executive" consists of the chair and the vice chair. Board members, including the "executive," are elected for three-year terms and there is an absolute term limit on board membership of twelve years. So far, only Peter Eigen and Frank Vogl, who were part of the original founding "executive," have met this twelve-year term limit. Board directors are elected by the qualified voters in the movement at annual general meetings. Two-thirds of the voters are the designated representatives of national chapters, and one-third are individual members. For example, if there are eighty registered national chapters, then there could be up to forty individual members. Rare among civil society/not-for-profit organizations, the election to the TI board of directors is frequently contested, with there being more candidates than open seats. For example, six members of the board retired or did not seek a further mandate in 2011 and there were eleven candidates for these six seats at the 2011 TI annual meeting. There is secret balloting. TI has established a Membership Accreditation Committee (MAC), with two of its five members appointed by the board and the three others elected directly by the qualified voters at the annual meeting. The MAC regularly reviews the performance, the audits, and the governance of each national chapter and makes recommendations for continued chapter accreditation, or disaccreditation, to the board of directors. This process ensures that each TI chapter respects the TI brand and acts in accordance with the spirit and the rules of the organization, as determined by the board. Individual members are subject to accreditation review by the MAC every three years. These members bring broad experience of anticorruption and civil society engagement to TI, are active volunteers in support of TI's work beyond the activities they may be engaged with in their national chapters, and serve as representatives of TI. While there are no firm rules with regard to the geographic and gender composition of the board of directors or the individual members, these are matters assigned priority by the MAC, the board, and the broader membership. TI has established an International Advisory Council and the board reviews its membership from time to time. The council has no legal powers within TI. Its members are called upon to provide advice, to participate in TI campaigns, and to lend their names, as appropriate, to particular TI initiatives.

6. The founding TI board of directors, formed at the meeting in The Hague in 1993: Chairman Peter Eigen, formerly a World Bank manager (Germany); Vice Chairman Kamal Hossain, former justice and foreign minister (Bangladesh); Vice Chairman Frank Vogl (United Kingdom and United States); and the following directors—Laurence Cockcroft, development economist (United Kingdom); Judge Dolores Espanol (Philippines); Judge Theo Frank (Namibia); Joe Githongo, business auditor (Kenya); Michael Hershman, investigations expert (United States); and Gerry Parfitt, accountant (United Kingdom).

7. The TI co-founders were highly concerned that the organization would not be seen as either another US effort to tell the world's poorer countries how to behave or as a World Bank offshoot. Accordingly, Washington, DC, was ruled out as a head office location. Berlin (especially in 1993, when it was just starting to find its feet as the German capital) had less of this kind of baggage. At the same, it was crucial that at the launch there be strong representation from developing countries and that it be these representatives who underscored support for TI and its mission.

8. For example, Manzoor Hasan, who was a TI-Bangladesh executive director, now heads efforts at promoting investigative journalism and anticorruption training for government officials at BRAC University, part of the world's largest nongovernmental civil society organization. His successor at TI is Iftekhar Zaman, who, like Manzoor, has been a constant thorn in the side of Bangladesh's corrupt government leadership and a constant target of official abuse.

9. The mission of the PTF is to mobilize expertise and resources to provide advice and small grants to civil society organizations to engage citizens in actions to remove corruption in the public sector. PTF strives to support innovative approaches, learn from its work, and share the knowledge gained. The basic premise for creating PTF is that the civil society has an important role to play in the development of anticorruption and good governance programs, and it can play this role more effectively if it is independent, financially, from government or direct bilateral or multilateral funding. See www.PTFund.org.

10. A core strength of PTF is the unique global development experience of its fully engaged small army of volunteers. Its board of directors is representative of the volunteer team: Chair Anabel Cruz, a civil society activist (Uruguay); Vice Chair Frank Vogl (United Kingdom and United States); President Daniel Ritchie, a thirty-year operations veteran of the World Bank (United States); Vinay Bhargava, World Bank veteran and specialist in public-sector governance (India); Peter Eigen, TI Advisory Council chair (Germany); Pierre Landell-Mills, economist and former senior World Bank officer (United Kingdom); Barry Metzger, lawyer and former general counsel, Asian Development Bank (United States); Muthoni Muriu, senior Oxfam executive (Kenya); Ron Points, corporate auditor (United States); Gerry van der Linden, former vice president at the Asian Development Bank (Netherlands); and three former World Bank vice presidents—Fayezul Choudhury (Bangladesh), Christiaan J. Poortman (Netherlands), and Richard Stern (United Kingdom).

11. *Sub-Saharan Africa: From Crisis to Sustainable Growth—A Long-Term Perspective Study*, published by the World Bank in 1989. It was the first book published by any of the multilateral development banks to mention the term "governance."

12. See special publications section of www.PTFund.org for the United Kingdom's DFID mid-term review of its program in support of PTF of May 2011, written by John D. Clark.

Chapter Five

Political Villains

Grand corruption is something that the late George Moody-Stuart, a witty veteran businessman, knew a great deal about, especially in the world's poorer countries in Africa and Asia. He could tell you just how much a prime minister in one country would expect to put in his private bank account on a big deal, or just how much a general in another country could expect to stuff in his pockets on an arms contract.

George would say that a great deal of the small-time corruption in poor countries was due to lowly civil servants not receiving a living wage and feeling forced to use their modest powers to extract small bribes. But George coined the term "grand corruption" and by that he meant the enormous pay-offs to powerful politicians and senior civil servants and military officers—sums that could amount to millions of dollars and that would be often paid into foreign bank accounts.

I first met George in 1990 in the front office of Kenya's minister of finance. The small room was jam-packed with prosperous-looking business-men. Everyone claimed to have an appointment and everyone told the over-whelmed receptionist that their business was of the greatest urgency. I happened to ask George if it was always like this and he smiled and said that it was. I told him that I had just flown into Nairobi at the invitation of the government and he smiled once more and suggested that I go and see another minister. Most of the others, he indicated, were less busy. Indeed, as I was to discover sometime later, the finance minister was one of the president's "bag men"—anyone wanting a government contract had to obtain the personal approval of the minister of finance!

George was a founding member of TI and in January 1994 he authored TI's first publication—"Grand Corruption in Third World Development." Drawing on decades of business experience in Asia and Africa, George noted the following items in this first edition of his work:

- 5 percent of a $200,000 contract may be interesting to a senior official below the top rank.
- 5 percent of $2 million is the permanent secretaries' (director-generals') area.
- 5 percent of $20 million is real money for a minister and a chief of staff.
- 5 percent of $200 million may attract the serious attention of a head of state!

The practitioners of grand corruption are organized and ruthless. They are the leading villains on the corruption stage.

The enormous oil wealth of countries like Equatorial Guinea, Gabon, Nigeria, and Angola should have made the citizens of these countries free of the worst kinds of poverty. They are not. The reason is that the oil wealth has been stolen year after year by national leaders. Late President Abacha of Nigeria, who held power for five years through mid-1998, alone placed an estimated $3 to $5 billion in private European bank accounts. Using 2006 data, this represents 2.6 to 4.3 percent of Nigeria's gross domestic product, or put another way, 20.6 to 34.4 percent of the federal government budget.

In an article in late 1998, J. Brian Atwood, then director of USAID, noted:

> In Nigeria, the late General Sani Abacha and his cronies siphoned billions of dollars out of the oil industry, which is the country's primary source of wealth and accounts for 80 percent of government revenue. Diversion of funds from state coffers led to a marked deterioration in infrastructure and social services and a near-collapse of state-owned oil refineries. The country's per capita income, which was as high as $800 in the 1980s, has now dropped below $300. As this oil-rich country faced a fuel shortage and depression, the government resorted to ever greater repression to stay ensconced in its position of advantage. Only the untimely death of Abacha has provided a possible opening for political and economic reform. [1]

The list of the greatest corrupt thieves is well known. They live in astonishing luxury. They and their families own vast tracts of real estate from Mayfair in London to Monte Carlo in the South of France to Malibu, California. They run Pakistan and Nigeria and Equatorial Guinea, cross the world in private jets, and stash foreign bank accounts full of other people's money.

In Pakistan in the 1990s the people had a choice at election time between two rival villains—Benazir Bhutto on the one side and Navaz Sharif on the other. Each had held power and the families of each of them prospered as a result. To stop the plunder, the military took charge in Pakistan, as it had done before, and General Pervez Musharraf took power in a bloodless coup in October 1999, forcing both Bhutto and Sharif into exile. While initially aggressive in his efforts to clean up domestic corruption, as well as a strong ally of the United States in the "War on Terrorism," he gradually lost his zest for domestic reform and his enthusiasm for his US friends. The internal pressures on Musharraf to tolerate corruption among politicians and the business elite, and duplicity in the intelligence services and the military, lost him US support.

In 2007, the Bush administration, uninterested and/or uncaring about corruption, pressured Musharraf into a power-sharing deal with the then exiled Bhutto. To secure the deal, Pakistan's parliament passed a law giving immunity from prosecution on outstanding corruption charges to Benazir Bhutto and her husband, Azif Zardari, who were living in splendor in Dubai at the time. Soon afterward, Navaz Sharif was also allowed to return to Pakistan from exile in Saudi Arabia.

Ignoring her past corruption, the Bush administration became ever closer to Bhutto and helped her to oust Musharraf. She was assassinated while campaigning in the presidential election in December 2007. Zardari, who is a convicted corruption felon, then was elected president in January 2008, while Sharif headed the political opposition. Pakistanis with extensive political experience suggest that the scale of corruption in very recent years by those at the top of the government exceeds everything that was seen in the 1980s and in the 1990s.

By some estimates the late president Ferdinand Marcos of the Philippines pocketed between $5 billion and $10 billion, while former president Mobutu Sésé Seko of the Congo took between $4 and $6 billion.

Dictators often flaunt their lavish lifestyles and abundant riches. They are impervious to the massive human misery that their greed, arrogance, and criminality create. The more they steal, the more paranoid they tend to become and the harsher they treat all those who they perceive as possibly exposing their crimes. Secrecy related to actual bribe payments and foreign bank accounts are crucial to the corruption process. The most corrupt dictators will go to extraordinary lengths to keep such dealings secret.

Maintaining a corrupt regime and ensuring the loyalty of all subordinates to a dictator is a costly affair. Corrupt leaders need to ensure that some of their spoils are used to pay security services and ensure the support of the armed forces, the police, and the judges. Writing in *Foreign Affairs* in July 2010, Robert I. Rotberg, director of the Harvard Kennedy School of Government's Program on Interstate Conflict, noted that in a November 2009 trip to the United Nations in Rome for a meeting on hunger, Zimbabwe's President Robert Mugabe took an entourage of sixty-six people, and another fifty-nine shortly thereafter, to the Copenhagen summit on climate change. They went, no doubt, to spend their illicit gains and the spoils of their regime's corruption, while millions of their fellow citizens were kept from total starvation solely by the charity of international donor organizations.

Rotberg explained the key to Mugabe's approach in his essay:

> The top brass of the army, the air force, and the police are all slavishly loyal to Mugabe. He has enmeshed the security forces in a dense web of state-sponsored corruption since 1998, when Zimbabwean troops entered the war in the Democratic Republic of the Congo and looted cadmium, cobalt, diamond, and gold as "payment" for their intervention on the side of then Congolese President Laurent Kabila. By intervening there, Mugabe both won the security services' fealty and made them coconspirators in his misrule of Zimbabwe. [2]

Over time the subordinates become more and more greedy, the costs of maintaining power rise for the dictator, and the proclivity to steal from the public purse rises too. Grand corruption pursued by heads of state and their friends creates an ever greater need to steal, which in turn leads to ever greater violations of human rights on basic freedoms and citizen misery. When those who steal the most fear they may be exposed, they engage thugs to intimidate, to torture, and (sometimes) to murder the political opponents, the courageous investigative journalists, the human rights and anticorruption and pro-democracy activists.

The large embedded networks within the bureaucracies have to be fed continuously with more and more illicit cash or more and more opportunities for them to steal and extort. As a result, as we see today, for example, in Mugabe's Zimbabwe, once rich economies become destitute and the conditions that the citizens face become ever harsher.

RANKING THE VILLAINS—THE CPI

We know who many of the perpetrators of grand corruption are. Ever since 1995, TI has published an annual Corruption Perceptions Index (TI-CPI), which ranks countries in terms of how corrupt their governments are perceived to be. It is always controversial (see appendix 1 for the full TI 2011 CPI). [3]

On the publication of the first CPI in 1995, a Malaysian politician asked in his parliament why the country was ranked so poorly. A member of the government responded that this was part of a Western conspiracy against the country. A debate took place and it was agreed that the government would send a team to Berlin to meet with TI and investigate the CPI methodology. This was the first time that corruption in Malaysia had ever been discussed in the parliament. The CPI proved to be an effective catalyst here and in many other countries for triggering public debates about domestic bribe taking.

Sometimes civil society organizations complain about the CPI, arguing that the rankings for some countries are improving too rapidly from one year to another and making it harder to bring meaningful pressures on the governments in these countries. Georgia, to the dismay of civil society in the country, ran an international advertising campaign in 2010 to declare that it is being seen, according to TI, as doing the most among Central and Eastern European countries to fight corruption and that its ranking in the CPI had improved. The aim was to attract foreign investment to the country. Georgia continues, however, to have major corruption problems.

The CPI is an influential instrument. Companies doing political risk analysis for corporate clients reviewing investment opportunities often refer to the CPI. The international ratings agencies often call to check on the CPI. Some foreign aid agencies base some of their grant allocations on the rankings.

Year after year, the Scandinavian countries and New Zealand have topped the list as the countries perceived to have the least corruption in their governments. A long history of clean government and a highly respected system of justice, and broad citizen support for transparent and accountable government, have contributed to this outcome. Meanwhile, a host of developing countries have raced to the bottom of the CPI—countries where the rule of law is either totally in the hands of vicious dictators or ruthlessly enforced by gangs and warlords.

The CPI's scores are derived from thirteen different opinion polls, mostly of business people, undertaken by a variety of organizations, including Gallup, the World Economic Forum, and the World Bank—it is a poll of polls that TI analyzes and publicizes. TI cannot fix the outcomes, which is precisely why the CPI is seen by the media around the world as so credible and why, thousands of times each year, media stories on individual countries include a note on the country's latest CPI ranking. The fact that the vast majority of the world's countries score a lamentable 5.0 or less on a list where 10.0 suggests a country free of corruption and 0.1 signifies massive corruption highlights the continuing scale of the problem.

Remarkably, no other organization has tried to replicate the CPI. The World Bank Institute comes closest with annual publication of highly detailed data on governance conditions across the world. But the World Bank, being owned by governments, is cautious about offending shareholders, especially those countries that are highly corrupt. So the World Bank's excellent governance data does not rank countries as the CPI does. Rather, the Bank provides broad categories in which it places countries from good to weak, which has less appeal than a country ranking for the media.

VILLAINS EVERYWHERE

Chicago

There is nothing subtle or sophisticated in the ways the villains operate, be it in Athens or in Lagos, be it in Kabul or in Chicago. Chicago, once the home of gangster Al Capone, has an almost unrivaled reputation for City Hall corruption. Reporter Evan Osnos, writing in the *New Yorker* about the legacy of Mayor Richard Daley of Chicago, recounted:

> For all the changes that Daley has wrought in his city, he has made scarcely a dent in Chicago's breathtaking capacity for corruption. In 2004, the *Sun Times* (newspaper) investigated the city's Hired Truck program and discovered the Daley administration was spending forty million dollars a year to hire private dump trucks for city work, except that many of the trucks were doing virtually nothing; some were owned by felons or reputed Mob associates like Nick (the Stick) LoCoco, a bookie and juice collector. Among the workers who were taking bribes to dole out trucking contracts was John (Quarters) Boyle, a member of a pro-Daley campaign group who had been hired despite having been convicted for stealing four million dollars—in nickels, dimes, and quarters—while overseeing toll booths. When Quarters was busted for taking bribes—one of forty-seven people eventually convicted in the trucking scandal—he protested, "Everyone else was doing it."[4]

If Chicago has a rival in first world corruption, then it may well be found in Italy. Writing about Prime Minister Silvio Berlusconi in April 2010, Alexander Stille noted, "There were Berlusconi's continuing legal troubles, a sixteen-year saga that has left a long trail of evidence of corruption, bribery, and contacts with organized crime."[5]

However, corruption in many developing countries, as well as in Central and Eastern Europe, tends to be far worse than in the Western mature economies—the villains tend to be richer and far more ruthless. They develop sophisticated systems of state control that mostly protect them from threats and significant risks to their continuous acts of theft. They never act alone. Activists who seek to fight corruption are taking on not just individual powerful public figures but also whole governmental machines designed by their leaders to ensure that the power structure is maintained.

EMBEDDED NETWORKS OF CORRUPTION

Corrupt leaders use strong subordinates to enforce discipline on the lower ranks and to enable the elite to hold power. The leading subordinates, in return for their services, have personal access to the public treasury, or in the case of China, the opportunity to place their wives and their children and their friends in top positions in the governmental structure or in the corporate sector. The leadership groups establish networks of corruption in pyramidal bureaucratic structures across the civil service and the military. In these structures, the people at the helm pocket the highest amounts of cash, while those at lower levels obtain payoffs commensurate with their rank. Often thousands of government workers, both civilian and military, join the illicit payrolls and as their numbers expand, the amounts that have to be stolen to pay them increase. Participants in the pyramid benefit, others in most cases face declining public services and poverty.

Cuba

How the system works is painfully vivid in Cuba. The only people driving modern shiny new cars are members of the governmental and political elites. They enjoy a host of special privileges in a "Communist" country where everyone is meant to be equal. If ordinary Cubans happen to own a car, then it is an American automobile that was imported before 1958!

A few years ago I visited a friend in Cuba and at first she did not answer the door when I rang the bell at her house. I rang again and then once more and eventually she opened up. She said she was scared that it was a local government inspector. The inspectors come to see if she has rented one of the rooms in her house, which the local inspectors claim is illegal. She says she has no option other than to rent a room—how else can she look after her infirm father and support herself and her son at school on a monthly wage of $15 as a senior dentist in a hospital?

Later that day I had dinner at a fine restaurant where the patrons were either tourists or prosperous-looking Cubans (no doubt on the government payrolls), because nobody else can get the special foreign currency coupons needed to enjoy the expensive meals served there. In the embedded networks of corruption there is grand theft at the top and small-time extortion at the bottom and the citizens suffer.

China

In China it is the Communist Party that decides who gets power, who gets good jobs, and who gets rich. Promotions and demotions in the government and in major business enterprises are determined by favors given and favors taken and the networks that individuals develop. Ample opportunity is given to all across the system to take "gifts" for services rendered and to see that the scale of the bribes increases as an individual moves up the ladders to real power. Decisions to investigate individuals for corruption are taken when individuals seek to overreach, become too arrogant, and build too many enemies.

Somehow the system works. I once asked a Chinese scholar how China could secure 10 percent economic growth year after year with such widespread corruption. He responded by saying that one could only imagine how much greater growth would be if the system was efficient and free of all of the nepotism and corruption. He added that the distribution of income would be fairer and better living standards would assuredly be enjoyed by many tens of millions more Chinese.

Much that I had been informally told about corruption in China over many years and a few visits to Beijing and Shanghai going back to 1983 was confirmed in Richard McGregor's book *The Party*.[6]

Almost in hushed tones, foreign reporters that I met over the years would talk about how top Communist Party leaders would place family members in top business positions. Often mentioned was the wife of Wen Jiabo,[7] Zhang Peili, who was vice president of the China Jewelry Association and was said to have major financial interests in the country's biggest jewelry companies. Then Hu Jintao's son, Hu Haifeng, headed a company called Nuctech Co., which was widely reported in 2009 as having allegedly bribed officials in Namibia to win technology contracts.[8]

McGregor noted that Premier Li Peng[9] enjoyed total control over the energy sector where two of his children held powerful jobs; Zhu Rongji had equal influence in the finance sector, where his son secured a top post in China's largest investment bank; Jiang Zemin secured a top position in the private sector in a major technology enterprise; and "[m]ore recently, Zeng Qinghong, together with Zhou Yongkang, from 2007 the Politburo member in charge of the law and state security, have been key players in the so-called petroleum mafia and influential in senior appointments in China's energy sector."[10]

Over many years there have been occasional arrests of senior members of the Communist Party for alleged corruption, followed by trials where they are always found guilty and sentenced usually to long prison terms, and sometimes they are executed. The only thing that has altered over the years, notes McGregor, is the size of the bribes, which now frequently amount to millions of dollars. China has a small but powerful Central Commission for Discipline Inspection that can arrest people suspected of corruption and pursue interrogations for as long as they like. There is no due process. The actions of the investigators are controlled by the Communist Party and decisions to go after very senior officials are taken at the highest levels of the party.

The Communist Party and the Chinese government constantly feel insecure and, as a result, regularly crush all who seek to stand out and challenge the system. This is a characteristic of almost all the world's most corrupt governments. For example, 2010 Nobel Peace Prize winner Liu Xiaobo is a fearless protester who was first jailed for his involvement in Tiananmen Square in 1989. He continued to call publicly for protection of human rights and to try and organize against the Communist Party.

In *The Party*, Richard McGregor writes:

> The Party made its displeasure known by sentencing Liu to eleven years in jail, the longest term ever given someone convicted for state subversion since the offense was drafted in the late nineties. To drive the message home in western governments who had protested against Liu's detention, his trial was held in late December so he could be sentenced on Christmas Day, 2009.

From Internet and press censorship to crackdowns in Tibet, the Chinese authorities seek to create conditions where the actions of top officials can be shrouded in secrecy. The legal machinery is a tool of the Communist Party and, as a leading Beijing University professor told me, "We don't need Western concepts of due process in our courts, the Party knows best." That is precisely the atmosphere in which corruption thrives.

Often, those on the lower ranks of the pyramids are the enforcers: the thugs in the guise of policemen and secret service agents who ensure that critics of the corrupt system are silenced. The police in China can simply pick people off the streets and hurl them into prison for up to three years without formal charges being set.

Singapore

The Chinese have demonstrated that corrupt dictatorships can run hand in hand with rising prosperity. Singapore is an even better example. The country's politics have been dominated since 1959 by the People's Action Party and its leader, Lee Kuan Yew. Lee and his family and many of his closest associates have become enormously rich and the inner workings of how the spoils of power are divided remain their secret. While they decry Western-style democracy and claim it is unsuitable for Asia, and while they censor the press to ensure that criticism of the system is muted, they do not explain how it is that those in power keep in power, become vastly wealthy, and ensure their children inherit political power and fortunes.

Lee and his cronies have been assiduous in controlling the level of plunder and nepotism and establishing economic policy strategies that secured high living standards for the people of Singapore. Without the corruption the citizens might be far freer to express their views, able to participate in honest elections, and perhaps even wealthier.

Lee ensured that public officials are well paid and he believes that this serves as an important counterweight to temptations to accept bribes. Certainly, business people across the globe believe that they can have honest dealings with officials in Singapore, which is a key factor in the excellent showing that Singapore enjoys in the CPI rankings. But it is a precarious system because of its opacity and its domination by very few powerful individuals who are not held publicly accountable.

Singapore is unique. It is not a model that others could try to pursue. The development of Indonesia under Suharto illustrates this.

Indonesia

In Indonesia, for most of the thirty-two years that he held power, Suharto controlled every aspect of politics, the military, and the legal system. He engaged excellent technocrats, many of them graduates from the top American universities, to fill his cabinets and run government departments. The World Bank believed this was a government it could work with. For many years the largest resident office the World Bank had in the world was in Jakarta. Development progress in the country was substantial.

But as Suharto aged, his grip slipped. His family started to take more and more cash out of every government deal. Modest levels of corruption became grand corruption. While the World Bank remained embarrassingly ignorant of the massive malfeasance, increasing numbers of Indonesians saw the Suharto family and its friends looting the government coffers. The 1997/1998 Asia financial crisis revealed much of the corruption mess that Suharto had presided over and his successors have been striving to clean up ever since, while striving in vain to secure the repatriation of the Suharto family's stolen assets that are believed to be in many foreign bank accounts.

Indeed, the villains tend to park their cash overseas. With the connivance of some banking institutions that should ask more questions than they do about the origins of the deposits they take, the villains, using multiple agents, launder their cash through financial-services firms that for years have defied the global regulations governing international finance. From Switzerland to Liechtenstein to Cyprus and Grand Cayman and a host of other so-called "offshore financial centers," numerous secret accounts have been opened for corrupt politicians (see chapter 15 for a discussion of ways to curb money laundering).

Russia

Russia's Communist Party leaders enjoyed enormous privileges and rich lifestyles while their citizens suffered. A different kind of rape of the state's fortunes came soon after the collapse of the Soviet Union and amid fervent demands by Western governments that Moscow privatize its vast state-owned enterprises. This was seen as the path to capitalism and Russian prosperity. It was the view espoused by a considerable number of PhD economists at the International Monetary Fund and the World Bank in Washington, as well as the US Treasury Department, who all had one thing in common—zero experience with Russia.

A small group of Russian civil servants embraced the advice from the West and organized the privatization of oil and gas and metals and manufacturing companies that had all been controlled by the state (for an example, see the introduction to chapter 6). As Marshall I. Goldman reported in September 1998 in *International Economy* magazine, for the first time in that year five Russians made *Forbes* magazine's list of the world's two hundred wealthiest individuals. Ten years earlier none of these Russians had a net worth of as much as $10,000. The rise of the oligarchs, noted Goldman, was all the more impressive given that until 1987 anyone engaging in private enterprise could face prosecution for economic crimes. The new oligarchs, like the American billionaires of an earlier era, were ruthless, but there the comparison ends. The Americans, such as Andrew Carnegie, Henry Ford, and John D. Rockefeller, built vast enterprises, while the Russians acquired the state's properties. Their skill lay in their ability to understand and manipulate the post-Communist system and their access to the country's most powerful new politicians.[11]

Their first actions involved vast transfers of funds from the companies they took control of into foreign bank accounts far beyond the reach of Russia's leaders in the Kremlin. Then they provided funds to those political leaders to assist their election victories in the new democratic system and to build up their own private bank accounts as well.

A major step by the "oligarchs" to consolidate their fortunes was to finance the reelection of President Boris Yeltsin and his cronies in 1996. When Vladimir Putin succeeded Yeltsin, he warned the tycoons that if they challenged him, criticized him, or withheld funds from him and his friends, they would become enemies of the state. A few oligarchs rushed into exile. One multibillionaire indicated he might not toe the line—in 2003, Mikhail Khodorkovsky, the head of the Yukos oil empire, was arrested. He languishes in a Siberian prison today.

Exactly how much cash has entered the private bank accounts of top Russian officials will probably never be known and the ruthless manner in which human rights workers and investigative journalists have been treated in Russia suggests that the country's corrupt leaders will use all of their power to protect their rackets. Top officials have used state enterprises (and, most notably, Gazprom, the world's largest energy company) to increase their power and their fortunes. The chairman of Gazprom is Viktor Zubkov, who was Russia's prime minister when Putin was first president. Dmitry Medvedev, Russia's former president, is a former Gazprom chairman.

Gazprom has been the prime vehicle for corporate domination and corruption used by the Kremlin. The world's largest oil and gas conglomerate has been involved in a wide array of financial dealings that have vastly enriched business people—notably, in Putin's hometown of St. Petersburg. [12] Gazprom has been used to threaten the cut-off of energy to Ukraine, Belarus, and other countries. And its reach has gone deep into Western Europe's power circles.

Within weeks of losing the election of 2005, German Chancellor Gerhard Schröder became involved with setting up a pipeline company to convey fifty-five billion cubic meters of gas annually from Russia to Western Europe. The pipeline had been agreed to by Schröder with Prime Minister Putin when he was still head of the German government. Today, the former German leader holds the title of chairman of the Shareholders' Committee of Nord Stream, a company incorporated in 2006 in the Swiss canton of Zug, which encourages foreign firms because of its vigilant bank secrecy rules and low taxes—Gazprom owns 51 percent of Nord Stream.

Today, the oligarchs have villas in the South of France, mansions in London and New York, outbid all others at major international art auctions, and enjoy tight relationships with Vladimir Putin. Alisher Usmanov and Mikhail Prokhorov are rival oligarchs owning vast metals companies who, among their hobbies, respectively own large interests in the UK Arsenal football club and the New Jersey Nets basketball team. So long as the oligarchs have tough bodyguards and steer far away from serious efforts to oppose Vladimir Putin, they seem to be safe.

POWERFUL WESTERN FRIENDS ADD SUPPORT

The world's most powerful governments (the leading Western industrial nations, plus China and Russia) provide explicit support to many villains and co-conspirators.

At the national level, many of these governments are reluctant to investigate and prosecute corporations headquartered in their own countries that are spreading bribes across the globe. Few leaders of national parliaments have any interest in investigating their own colleagues—"It's not good manners." Rarely have the ethics committees of the US Congress pursued serious and thorough investigations of members of the Senate and the House of Representatives who have allegedly been too close to business interests. And on those rare occasions when investigations have been pursued, the penalties have usually been just a rap on the knuckles.

For years British members of Parliament claimed expenses for homes they did not even own or rent and manipulated the expensing of so-called "second" homes—they all knew what was going on, but nobody was willing to blow the whistle. Of course, all these politicians repeatedly declare in public that they staunchly oppose corruption.

French authorities have gone to great lengths over many years to befriend, protect, and abet the corrupt leaders of former West African colonies that provide vital oil supplies to France. France was not alone in being nice to these crooks. The United States was tolerant as well. A US Senate report in February 2010 noted that President Omar Bongo of Gabon brought $1 million in shrink-wrapped $100 notes into the United States in a suitcase in 2007, while Teodoro Obiang, son of Equatorial Guinea's president, moved "more than $100m in suspect funds through U.S. bank accounts, including $30m to purchase a residence in Malibu."[13]

While an increasing amount of information about abuse is reaching the public domain, little is being done about it, especially by Western European governments. Under the leadership of Senator Carl Levin, a veteran Democrat from Michigan, the US Senate's Permanent Sub-Committee on Investigations has held landmark hearings that have provided both forceful support to US administrations to act while paving the way for major legislation. As a result some of the anti-money-laundering regulations governing US banks are starting to work, and the Swiss and the Liechtenstein tax authorities are starting to cooperate with US authorities to curb tax evasion by Americans. By and large, however, Western governments have not halted corrupt foreign leaders and their families from depositing their stolen funds in Western banks. Swiss authorities only froze the assets in Swiss bank accounts of the former Egyptian and Tunisian leaders after they had been forced out of office.

Even when massive thefts by government leaders have been exposed, Western governments have largely been uncooperative in ensuring that the funds deposited in Western banks are repatriated to the countries where the original thefts took place.

Be it the Swiss or the British or the French authorities, all seem to turn a blind eye most of the time to representations from developing countries for the repatriation of vast stolen assets in Swiss, British, and French banks. European authorities with responsibility to regulate their banks never seem to ask the obvious question: How did people like Obiang, Bongo, Marcos,

Suharto, Abacha, and so many others manage to deposit hundreds of millions, even billions, of dollars in foreign banks accounts when their government salaries were no more than a few thousand dollars a year?

I recall a meeting in which a Swiss diplomat proudly declared that his country had agreed to repatriate several hundred million dollars of deposits in the name of the Abacha family to Nigeria. A top Nigerian official immediately shot back, "And when will you repatriate the one billion dollars of Abacha cash that is still in your bank accounts?" There was no response.

In late 2011, President Joseph Kabila of the Democratic Republic of the Congo held elections. This is a country run by a ruthless and corrupt tyrant, where the nation's vast mineral resources are sold in secret illicit deals on a massive scale, and where the average income of the nation's citizens is among the very lowest in the world. It seems beyond belief that the United Nations, the European Union, and the British government, which provided Kabila with funds to organize the elections, could have imagined for a moment that the elections would be anything other than a charade.

Kabila ran the elections to be able to make fatuous statements at international meetings about being freely elected. The cash he secured from abroad indicated how some foreign governments and the United Nations are comfortable with having this crook in power. The Carter Center, led by President Jimmy Carter, maintained twenty-six teams of international, impartial observers deployed in Kinshasa and the ten provinces for the counting and tabulation of the election results. Its conclusion was blunt: "The Carter Center finds the provisional presidential election results announced by the Independent National Election Commission (CENI) on Dec. 9 in the Democratic Republic of the Congo to lack credibility."[14]

In sum, many of the corrupt leaders in the Third World see governments in major Western capitals as essentially friendly and protective. This, of course, only encourages them to keep on stealing.

And, just like Kabila, many of the corrupt leaders today seek to please their Western government friends by playing the democracy game. They hold elections, but opponents are not tolerated. Critics of elections are jailed. For example, on December 3, 2009, the Associated Press reported, "The government of Equatorial Guinea says the African country's ruler of 30 years has been re-elected with 95.37 percent of votes, while opponents and international human rights groups denounced the electoral process in Africa's No. 3 oil producer as fraudulent. A statement Friday on the government's Web site said President Teodoro Obiang Nguema won 260,462 votes in Nov. 29 elections. Four opponents shared the other votes. The government refused to publish a voters' roll."

THE UNITED NATIONS EXAMPLE

One of the largest international scams of the 1990s involved hundreds of companies and the United Nations. The ambassadors from the major Western governments to the United Nations ignored the stories year after year. They knew that corruption was undermining important policies, but they did not want to rock the boat. Under intense pressure from the Clinton administration, the United Nations most reluctantly appointed an "Independent Inquiry into the United Nations Oil for Food Programme in Iraq" under the leadership of former US central bank chief Paul A. Volcker and with South African lawyer Richard Goldstone and Swiss lawyer and corruption expert Mark Pieth.

Their report is important not only because of the massive scale of corruption that they found and the revelation of the incredible complicity of the United Nations in the malfeasance but also in the fact that such a commission should be established at all. It was a symbol of the new era where not all major governments all of the time were willing to continue to stand idly by as crimes were perpetrated. The UN oil-for-food program for Iraq stretched over seven years and involved more than $100 billion in transactions (over $64 billion in oil sales and approximately $37 billion for food).

The Volcker group concluded that 2,253 companies from sixty-six countries paid bribes totaling $1.8 billion in exchange for contracts under the UN program. In its final press release in September 2005, the commission stressed,

> The Committee's central conclusion is that the United Nations requires stronger executive leadership, thoroughgoing administrative reform, and more reliable controls and auditing. The Programme cannot be laid exclusively at the door of the Secretariat. Members of the Security Council and its 661 Committee must shoulder their share of the blame in providing uneven and wavering direction in the implementation of the Programme.
>
> The Committee's investigation clearly makes the point that as the Programme expanded and continued, Saddam Hussein found ways and means of turning it to his own advantage, primarily through demands for surcharges and kickbacks from companies doing business with the Programme. By the Programme's design, these inspectors were charged only with the inspection of oil and goods that were financed under the Programme. The value of oil smuggled outside of the Programme is estimated by the Committee to be USD 10.99 billion as opposed to an estimated USD 1.8 billion of illicit revenue from Saddam Hussein's manipulation of the Programme.

On the release of the report, Mr. Volcker told a press conference, "The inescapable conclusion from the Committee's work is that the United Nations Organization needs thoroughgoing reform—and it needs it urgently. What is important—what has been recognized by one investigation after another—is that real change must take place, and change over a wide area."

While the commission published voluminous reports, provided the leads to the prosecution of hundreds of companies, and detailed the measures that the United Nations needed to take to ensure that it pursued thorough reform, little happened. There were few prosecutions. The Bush administration was far more interested in waging war in Iraq than prosecuting firms that made money in cahoots with Saddam.

Mark Pieth found himself traveling around the world just to preserve the archive of documents at the United Nations that the commission had assembled and keep a couple of staff members employed to manage the archive and provide information to prosecutors—the UN secretariat said it did not have the cash for this and in time the office was closed.

To be sure, an anticorruption office was established by Secretary-General Kofi Annan, but it was given modest financial and staff resources. When Mr. Annan appointed Tunku Abdul Aziz in 2006 as a special advisor for anticorruption there was hope that the leadership of the UN secretariat was finally going to take the issue seriously. Tunku had been a vice chairman of the international board of directors of TI and, as the founder of TI-Malaysia, a courageous advocate for governance reform in his home country. He was in New York at the United Nations for just one year. The initiative was abandoned by Annan's successor, Ban Ki-moon.

NOTES

1. A special publication called "Economic Perspectives" on the topic of corruption and development, published by the US Agency for International Development in 2008. (In the final sentence of the quote here, the writer says "untimely" death when, perhaps, he meant "unexpected," because on his death in June 1998, at the age of fifty-five, senior Nigerian officials simply announced that he had a "sudden heart attack," and a fuller explanation was never forthcoming.)

2. Robert I. Rotberg, "Mugabe Über Alles—The Tyranny of Unity in Zimbabwe," *Foreign Affairs*, July/August 2010.

3. See www.Transparency.org—Corruption Perceptions Index 2011.

4. Evan Osnos, "The Daley Show—Dynastic Rule in Obama's Political Birthplace," Letter from Chicago, *New Yorker*, March 8, 2010.

5. Alexander Stille, "The Corrupt Reign of Emperor Silvio," *New York Review of Books*, April 8, 2010.

6. Richard McGregor, *The Party: The Secret World of China's Communist Rulers* (New York: HarperCollins, 2010).

7. Wen Jiabo became China's premier in March 2003.

8.   *Daily Telegraph*, July 17, 2009, www.telegraph.co.uk/news/worldnews/asia/china/5851056/Hu-Jintaos-son-linked-to-African-corruption-probe.html. Hu Jintao became president and general secretary of the Communist Party in late 2002.

9.   Li Peng was premier from 1988 to 1998 and then succeeded Jiang Zemin as president until March 2003. Zhu Rongji was premier from 1998 to March 2003.

10.   Zeng Qinghong was a leading member of the Politburo from late 2002 through 2007, and a key leader of the Communist Party. Zhou Yongkang became a member of the Politburo in late 2007. The quote is taken from Richard McGregor's *The Party*, 81.

11.   Marshall I. Goldman (the Kathryn W. Davis Professor of Russian Economics at Wellesley College and associate director of the Davis Center for Russian Studies at Harvard University), "Russian Billionaire's Club," *International Economy*, September/October 1998.

12.   For example, see a lengthy investigative report of Gazprom's financial dealings and financiers based in St. Petersburg in Catherine Belton's "How Gazprom lost control of Gazprombank," *Financial Times*, November 30, 2011.

13.   "Keeping Foreign Corruption Out of the United States: Four Case Histories," a 330-page report published on February 2, 2010, by the US Senate Permanent Sub-Committee on Investigations of the Committee on Homeland Security and Government.

14.   Press release, December 10, 2011, Carter Center, Atlanta, Georgia.

Chapter Six

Business Villains

It takes two to dance the corruption tango: the bribe takers and the bribe payers. The villains on the corruption stage are not just the public-office holders but also the entrepreneurs and business people who constantly seek governmental contracts and an edge over their competitors. Understanding how they operate is key to finding ways to curb corruption across the globe.

OLIGARCH MADNESS

Never before in history have so few acquired so much from the state as swiftly as Russia's oligarchs did in the 1990s.

Communism collapsed and the West supported the new Russian government of President Yeltsin with foreign aid and advice on how to build democratic institutions, privatize industries, and adopt capitalism. Yeltsin and his immediate circle of associates took full advantage to serve themselves, to maintain power, and to privatize the state's industrial base at the expense of the Russian people.

As the Soviet Union fell apart, hundreds of millions of people in Central and Eastern Europe at last had a chance to enjoy freedom. Instead, most of them became the victims of a new dictatorship driven by money and power. Yeltsin was the chief villain, but his ability to stay in power depended on the deals he decided to make with men like Roman Abramovich and Boris Berezovsky.

We know who they were, what they stood for, and how they operated because of an event that no writer of fiction could have invented. The stage is the High Court in London. The time is October and November 2011. The case centers on a suit brought by Berezovsky against Abramovich for over $5 billion (£3.5bn). Berezovsky distrusted the Russian courts, which he viewed as corrupt, and he took his case to where he believed the judiciary was independent and honest: the United Kingdom.

Once partners and now enemies, Berezovsky claimed that Abramovich cheated him out of at least $5 billion. Berezovsky, now living in exile in London after a fight with Russian leader Vladimir Putin, claimed that he was once an equal partner with Abramovich (who still lives in Russia some of the time, has a close relationship with today's Kremlin bosses, and owns several houses in the United Kingdom, as well as Chelsea football club) in the Sibnet oil company. Berezovsky said he was cheated out of his share and pushed out of the company by his former partner with Putin's help. Abramovich claimed that the two were just business associates, never friends or shareholding partners in Sibnet, and that he "hired" Berezovsky to provide political influence and protection from Chechen thugs.

As the trial proceeded the claims and counterclaims became ever more colorful and the stuff of major motion pictures. Berezovsky had been a professor of math and a used car dealer before, quite suddenly, becoming a billionaire. Abramovich had been a car mechanic and then a small-time oil trader before he became even richer than Berezovsky. In 1989, they were both citizens of Communist Russia, where everyone outside of the top governmental ranks was poor. Five years later they met on a Caribbean cruise to form an alliance.

By that time Berezovsky was well entrenched in the Yeltsin inner circle. He had befriended the president's daughter, Tatiana, and became the first businessman to be invited to join the president's tennis club.

The car dealer had become a member of what the London court was told was "the family." Somehow, Berezovsky convinced the president that he could direct the most powerful Russian media organizations to ensure public support and the future reelection of Yeltsin, at which time he obtained shareholding control of leading (and formerly state-owned) TV and print media companies, including the national ORT television group. Much more importantly, he established himself as the man that would-be oligarchs needed to do business with. As was suggested in the court, he could provide "protection," be it against the mafia and thugs or, more important, from the governmental machinery directed by the Russian president himself.

"I never can make millions, ten millions, I can make just billions," Berezovsky told the UK court, according to a report in London's *Daily Telegraph*. "I was one of the first who recognized that if you have political stability, the value of the company will increase enormously and that is reason why I convinced President through my connections to him to take a decision to privatize ORT."[1]

However, seeing that ORT was not a big money-maker, Berezovsky decided that he needed to buy an oil company.

He had met Abramovich, who had suggested the benefits of combining an oil-drilling company and a refinery in Siberia into a new company. Thanks to Berezovsky, Yeltsin and his senior advisors liked the idea and these state-owned assets were put up for auction. The company, Sibnet, could be purchased with loans in exchange for shares (loans to be paid off from the assets of Sibnet once the new owner had control), so the bidders did not have to be rich. Abramovich, backed by Berezovsky, was one of three bidders. The other two, however, were discouraged from proceeding with their efforts—one, apparently, was "bought off" according to testimony in the court, while Berezovsky found that the paperwork of the other bidder was "not in order."

Yeltsin received major support from the media and from the oligarchs for his 1997 reelection bid. Meanwhile, Abramovich managed Sibnet and told Berezovsky, "Boris trust[s] me." A mistake, said Berezovsky, who claimed that he was cheated out of his shares in Sibnet when, in 2000, Abramovich used his influence with Putin and Yeltsin was forced to flee Russia. Berezovsky said in court that Abramovich was part of "black ops" of the Russian security service designed to force him to give up his business interests.

Abramovich denied that Berezovsky was ever a shareholder in Sibnet, but he agreed that he owed Berezovsky for all his help in acquiring Sibnet and securing protection. He said he made a host of payments to Berezovsky, including one transaction for $1.3 billion, which was deposited in a UK bank. Despite UK "know-your-customer" banking laws that call for banks to make full enquiries into the sources of funds deposited, it seems that the Russian had no difficulty in placing vast amounts in the United Kingdom's banking system.

In 2005, Abramovich sold Sibnet to the state-run company Gazprom for more than $13 billion (£8.4bn). At the time, the most powerful and influential member of the Gazprom board of directors was Putin's closest political friend, Dmitry Medvedev, who became Russia's president in 2008.

The fortunes that the oligarchs made were due entirely to their conspiracies with the top political leaders of Russia. The assets that the oligarchs acquired from the state were bought with borrowed funds, plundered on a massive scale, and to this day we know very little about who exactly received how much and where the villains placed their stolen cash. The dealings and the ways decisions are taken between the Kremlin leadership and the Russian tycoons remain opaque—there is neither transparency nor public accountability.

THE CORPORATE BRIBE PAYERS

Multinational corporations have been paying bribes for years. The taking of bribes by public officials is illegal in many developing countries, but laws are not enforced. The payment by corporations of bribes to foreign government officials only became a crime in the United States in 1977 and in the other leading industrial countries in 1998 (see chapters 10 and 11). The Russian government said it would enact such a law in 2011.

There is no defense for acts of corporate bribe paying. When, as is sometimes the case, corporate executives claim that they had to pay bribes to win contracts because their rivals were actively bribing, then these executives have lost their moral compass.

The public official/political villains on the great corruption stage know exactly what they are doing and why, and so do the business people who pay them bribes. Neither the bribe takers nor the bribe payers have respect for the law. The scale of the fortunes that corrupt leaders amass results in large part from collaboration with crooked giant corporations. Enterprises engaged in infrastructure engineering; real estate development; arms sales; oil, gas, and mining; and pharmaceuticals are often found to be at the forefront of international bribery.

From time to time a national scandal erupts, often thanks to courageous public prosecutors. In France, investigating judge Eva Joly took personal risks that in the end were to terminate her career. Joly, a member of the European parliament today who stood in the 2012 French presidential elections as the candidate of the "Europe Ecologie-Les Verts Green Party," shot into the headlines in the 1990s as the determined examining magistrate in France in pursuit of some of the biggest names in French business and politics related to corruption at one of Europe's largest oil companies, Elf Aquitaine. She refused to buckle under political pressures from the French establishment or cease her investigations as a result of threats on her life. She is one of the heroes of the fight against corruption.

On the basis of researching what she has described as some ten cubic meters of evidence,[2] she prosecuted thirty-seven people involved in a case where she proved that more than $400 million of Elf's funds related to Middle Eastern and African oil contracts were not accounted for. She charged the company's leaders with bribery, kickbacks, and fraud. She prosecuted a cast of characters that included former politicians, and none was more prominent than former foreign minister Roland Dumas. Top officials were jailed. After the trials, Joly quit her job and France and went to the safety of Norway, where she was born, to work with the Norwegian aid agency on anticorruption issues. In 2009, she was asked by the government of Iceland to act as a special investigator and look into banking corruption in the wake of the global financial crisis.

Joly was horrified by what she found in Iceland. The banks had been allowed to run riot, to take massive gambles across the world yielding huge commissions for individual bankers, and providing the public at large with a totally delusionary sense of their wealth. Striving to understand just what happened, author Michael Lewis went to Iceland and in October 2008, just after the country "went bust" (to use his phrase), he discussed the situation with an official of the International Monetary Fund, who explained, "Iceland is no longer a country, it is a hedge fund."[3]

The banking booms and the housing bubbles it created from Spain to the United States were built on the greed of sales people in finance with the express permission of governmental regulators. When some of the top bankers were forced to resign as their firms plunged into near-bankruptcy, they triggered their employment contracts and walked away with millions of dollars in compensation. This was the bluntest signal of their arrogance.

But the seemingly systemic corruption in finance that Joly and Lewis have highlighted mirrored widespread bribe paying by many multinational corporations over many years. In the late 1990s, Fredrik Galtung, then TI's senior research advisor—and back in 1993, the first full-time staff member of TI—pioneered the TI Bribe Payers' Index (BPI) to rank the world's most corrupt multinational corporations (Galtung was also responsible for creating the TI Global Corruption Barometer). While Galtung concluded that it was not possible to develop a credible methodology that would list by name individual firms, he worked with Gallup International to run an international survey based on perceptions of people with expert knowledge around the globe of the countries that served as the headquarters for corrupt companies. The focus was on the countries whose enterprises accounted for significant shares of global trade.

Until 2009, TI had published three BPIs and while each had merits and each added to the general stock of knowledge, each also had weaknesses that forced the TI team to go back to the drawing board. In 2011, TI released a new BPI based on a stronger methodology and its findings are insightful (see appendix 2 for the TI 2011 BPI). Companies from Russia and China that invested US $120 billion overseas in 2010 are seen as those most likely to pay bribes abroad. Companies from the Netherlands and Switzerland are seen as least likely to bribe.

The two giant global corporations that have paid the heaviest fines for bribing foreign government officials are Siemens of Germany and Halliburton/KBR of the United States. Their activities illustrate the mindset and the schemes that determined corrupt executives pursue.

SIEMENS

Siemens AG is Europe's largest electronics manufacturer and its top former executives had no remorse about the global-scale bribery in which they engaged. They said they felt they had to get under the covers with crooked politicians in a dozen countries in order to beat their rivals in a nasty, competitive world. They established dummy bank accounts in assorted countries to hide the bribe payments, they fiddled the company accounts as part of the cover up, and they never thought they would be caught.

The Siemens leaders were caught and prosecuted and forced to pay the largest-ever fines for corporate international bribery in history, amounting to more than $1.6 billion. Significantly, that settlement included guilty pleas by Siemens AG and its subsidiary, Siemens S.A. (Siemens Argentina), to criminal violations of the US Foreign Corrupt Practices Act (FCPA) and a plea agreement in which Siemens AG and Siemens Argentina agreed to pay fines of $448.5 million and $500,000, respectively. The US authorities saw this as an important milestone on their path of their investigations, not the end of the journey.

The company, under new management leadership, pledged to introduce a state-of-the-art anticorruption code for all its employees, rigorously enforce it, and pursue anticorruption through staff-training programs. Siemens also launched a major global public relations campaign involving the disbursement of millions of dollars to anticorruption civil society organizations and research centers to officially demonstrate sympathy with the cause and to restore its battered image. Many people in TI national chapters viewed this initiative as too brazen and too self-serving for Siemens and they refused to apply for grants from a company that remains as the single largest corporate payer of bribes to foreign government officials ever to have been prosecuted.

On December 13, 2011, the US Department of Justice announced that "eight former executives and agents of Siemens AG and its subsidiaries have been charged for allegedly engaging in a decade-long scheme to bribe senior Argentine government officials to secure, implement and enforce a $1 billion contract with the Argentine government to produce national identity cards."[4]

To its credit, the management of Siemens did cooperate with the US investigators into the Argentina case, but the details of the case and its scale are a reminder of the misdeeds that Siemens perpetrated in the past. Moreover, the details are yet one more example of just how the giant multinationals sometimes operate.

The indictment charged Siemens executives, along with agents and conduits for the company, with committing to pay more than $100 million in bribes to high-level Argentine officials in two successive administrations. The payments were allegedly made during and up to a bidding contest that ended with a contract to Siemens in 1998 as the Argentine government sought to replace an existing system of manually created national identity booklets with state-of-the-art national identity cards. The Justice Department said that during the conspiracy some of the bribes were placed in German bank accounts, then cash was taken over the border and deposited in Swiss bank accounts, then some of the cash went into New York banks, and seventeen offshore shell companies were also used as well as fake consulting contracts—all to hide the ill-gotten gains of the bribed officials.

However, at the turn of the century and in the midst of Argentina's worst financial crisis, the contract was suspended, and so when a new government came to power, Siemens allegedly sought to restore the deal by offering new bribes. Amazingly, when this did not work, Siemens allegedly paid more bribes to hush up its past bribery while it decided to sue the Argentine government for $500 million for breaking the original contract. Failing in the local courts, the company then sought international arbitration and in February 2007 it was awarded nearly $220 million plus interest in Washington. However, after finalizing all of its various bribery cases with the US and German authorities in August 2009, the Justice Department noted, "New management of Siemens caused Siemens AG to forego its right to receive the award and, as a result, the company never claimed the award money."

The lengths to which Siemens went reminded me of a bizarre telephone call I once received from someone who most earnestly wanted to know if I had contacts that could help him to recover a bribe he had paid a government official that had, nevertheless, failed to produce the desired contract. My caller was angry at having lost his cash!

HALLIBURTON-KBR

The case of how KBR bribed Nigerian officials over several years serves as a good example of many of the facets of international bribery by giant corporations. The bribery took place while Sani Abacha was Nigeria's president; he was notorious for striving to set a global record in terms of the scale of his plunder of the nation's treasury. Any corporation negotiating a multibillion dollar contract with Nigeria at that time must have been highly alert to the risks of being asked to pay bribes.

At the outset it is useful to note that in the 1990s, when KBR was paying many of its bribes, it was a wholly owned subsidiary of Halliburton of Texas. Halliburton's chairman and CEO for much of this period was Richard Cheney, later to become vice president of the United States. He was never mentioned in any of the reams of documents related to this case that were compiled by the US Department of Justice and the US Securities and Exchange

Commission (SEC). The cases against Halliburton and KBR and KBR's former CEO were brought by the US authorities at the time when Cheney was the nation's vice president.

Albert Jackson Stanley surely never imagined that as the highly successful and prominent head of KBR he would celebrate his seventieth birthday in prison, let alone ever be charged with a crime. He was a pillar of Houston's big business community. However, after years of uncertainty over his eventual sentencing, he had to accept a thirty-month prison stretch. After finally cooperating with prosecutors, Stanley was handed down his prison term in February 2012, four years after he was first interrogated by US federal prosecutors. His downfall was due to a tip from French official investigators to the US Justice Department.

Stanley was a Cheney subordinate, serving as the chief executive of KBR from 1995 to 2000. In the course of the 1990s KBR, alongside France's Technip SA and Snamprogetti Netherlands B.V., an affiliate of Italy's ENI SpA, paid $180 million in bribes to Nigerian government officials to obtain $6 billion of construction contracts.

The US-French-Italian consortium agreed to make payments to high-ranking Nigerian government officials through a lawyer in London, who would act as an agent. In late 1994, the consortium signed a Memorandum of Understanding with the Nigerian government on a $2.2 billion deal that was formally approved in late 1995 with construction starting in 1996. And in the first quarter of 1995, $60 million went to the Nigerian officials via the UK agent. In March 1999, another deal for $1.3 billion was done with KBR and its partners and soon thereafter the UK agent sent the officials a further $32.5 million.

Stanley visited Nigeria several times and in 2001 another deal was discussed, this one worth $1.6 billion; a further $51 million went to the officials through the UK agent. Discussions then proceeded on a $935 million contract, finalized in 2004, with a payment made in 2002 of $23 million through the UK agent to the officials. However, between 1996 and 2002, Stanley and his partners also agreed to make payments to other Nigerian officials of $50 million and this time they used a Japanese agent. All the bribes, amounting to a total of $182 million, were described in KBR documents as legitimate expenses.

The bribe payments were transferred via agents in London and Tokyo through bank accounts in Gibraltar, London, Tokyo, Amsterdam, New York, and possibly other cities as well, with most of the proceeds ending up in bank accounts in Switzerland.

Halliburton and KBR agreed in 2009 to settle cases being brought against them by the US Justice Department and the SEC by paying total fines of $579 million. These are the highest fines ever paid by a US company for charges of violating the FCPA, which makes it a crime to bribe foreign government officials.

Who were the victims of KBR's crimes?

To be sure, competitor companies suffered as the bribery agreements were forged. But the major victims were the people of Nigeria. They were cheated by their own crooked public officials and their own government, which probably paid far more to the KBR consortium than was necessary, wasting public funds that could have been used for roads and hospitals and all manner of other necessary public services. Halliburton's shareholders were also punished for the crimes perpetrated by KBR's leaders.

The corruption villains, be they individual government dictators or the individual business people who pay them or multinational corporations that develop large-scale corruption strategies, are rarely punished. As mass public engagement against corruption increases, the villains face a more difficult time ahead. As the new information technologies uncover hard evidence of bribery, the bribe payers and the bribe takers have ever fewer places to hide. Transparency is gradually prevailing over secrecy.

NOTES

1. Report by Duncan Gardham, security correspondent, *Daily Telegraph*, October 6, 2011.

2. Eva Joly, *Justice under Siege: One Woman's Battle Against a European Oil Company* (London: Arcadia Books, 2006).

3. See Michael Lewis, *Boomerang: Travels in the New Third World* (New York: Norton, 2011).

4. US Department of Justice press release, December 13, 2011.

Chapter Seven

Global Security

Major Western governments shoulder a portion of the blame for the scale of global corruption. Their actions are not motivated by the self-enrichment of leaders, nor do they entail abuses of law or criminal behavior. Yet, by supporting corrupt regimes in the developing world with military and economic aid that is often poorly audited, by peddling a soft line on money laundering and on the repatriation of stolen assets, they have collaborated in what amounts to corruption conspiracies. The gravest consequence of such Western governmental complicity relates to international security.

To an increasing degree, opacity in approaches to international arms sales and contracts with governments for natural resources that have been pursued by Russian and Chinese authorities and state-controlled enterprises have followed models long undertaken by Western governmental authorities. This further complicates the effort to curb international corruption.

Old habits are hard to end. In the Cold War era the game was to convince Third World leaders to be the West's devils rather than the Soviet's devils. Through foreign aid and military aid and other government funds, the Western powers made many African, Latin American, and Asian leaders rich so that they would be "on our side." Today, the funds of many Western taxpayers continue to enrich wretched dictators. This does not make the world safer. Quite the contrary.

In this new age of transparency the publics at large across the world see their own corrupt leaders in bed with Western leaders and they resent the Western powers as a result. From Iraq to Egypt, Afghanistan, and Pakistan, the United States, which has poured tens of billions of dollars into these countries, is widely despised.

For years the United States told the Egyptian people that it supported democracy and human rights and was directly assisting in the nation's economic growth. The US Agency for International Development (USAID) had been working closely with the regime of President Mubarak for three decades, sending billions of dollars of US taxpayer cash to the Egyptian government, as had the World Bank, the world's largest multilateral aid agency (whose largest single shareholder is the United States). Egyptians had long been deeply skeptical about the motives behind US aid. Many did not believe it had anything to do with poverty alleviation and the economy's success. Rather than seeing the American aid as benefiting the people, they saw it as a crude payoff to the top elite of the regime in return for compliance with US strategic policies, including support for Israel.

The United States has not been alone in propping up corrupt dictators. The recent records of France and the United Kingdom have been terrible:

- As the scale of the protests mounted in Tunisia in January 2011, the French government continued to assure President Zine el-Abidine Ben Ali, seventy-four, of its support. Just twenty-four hours before the president fled abroad, the French Foreign Ministry was offering to send him French troops. At the time, French Foreign Minister Michele Alliot-Marie had been vacationing in Tunisia and had spoken to Ben Ali about continuing French support, and it also emerged that her family had close business interests with Tunisians associated with the Ben Ali family.
- In 2009, the British government headed by Prime Minister Gordon Brown did a deal that it refused to explain fully with Libya's Colonel Qadhafi that saw the release from a Scottish prison of Abdel Baset al-Megrah, who had been involved in the "Lockerbie bombing" that killed 270 people aboard Pan Am Flight 103 in 1988—a terrorist act directed by the Qadhafi regime. The Brown administration claimed the decision had been taken entirely by the Scottish authorities and that the prisoner was released because he was at death's door (he was still alive three years later). At about the same time, the UK-headquartered global oil company BP finalized a new oil agreement with the Libyan government.

Peace and security will be enhanced when the most powerful Western governments confront the realities of this new age of transparency in which people everywhere are both better informed about the abuses of power of their governments and more willing than ever before to take a stand against such abuses. Placing international relations on a more honest and transparent stage than has hitherto been the case is a challenge to the West's strategic policymakers. If the issues are confronted, then the world will become a safer place. Continuing to see powerful Western governments support vicious dictatorships across the world is a recipe for further international instability.

One of the largest obstacles is the legacy of Cold War approaches that seem to still pervade much strategic foreign policy thinking. Some examples underscore the past and present approaches that do so much damage:

- Throughout the Cold War the competition to secure the support of poorer nations prompted lavish payments by Moscow and Washington to leaders across the South. Western powers knew, for example, about the massive looting of public funds by President Mobutu in Zaire, but they never sought to confront him—he was seen as a valuable Cold War "friend." To this day, the Western powers have treated the leaders of the Democratic Republic of Congo (DRC) with kid gloves because of the interests of international companies to purchase minerals, despite the massive corruption, rape, and murder in the DRC.
- The French, British, and Chinese governments know that the government leaders of many oil-producing countries are stashing vast sums of oil payments from French, British, and Chinese companies in their own pockets. Former prime minister Tony Blair quashed a Serious Fraud Squad investigation into billions of dollars' worth of arms sales to Saudi Arabia by the United Kingdom's BAE Systems, Europe's largest merchant of weapons systems, to avoid a clash with the oil-pumping Saudis. Chinese companies have signed oil-supply deals with the corrupt regimes in Sudan and Angola and none of the details have been publicly disclosed.
- The crooked leaders from African oil-producing countries deposit their cash, at least in part, in bank accounts in Zurich, Paris, and London, safe in the knowledge that the authorities will ask no questions about how the fortunes were acquired and provide no meaningful support to citizens of these African countries who seek the repatriation of these stolen funds.
- The World Bank has at times been pressed by its largest shareholder, the United States, to lend to corrupt foreign regimes that serve American strategic interests. President Bush secured the appointment of former deputy US secretary of defense Paul Wolfowitz to become president of the World Bank in 2005 and it was not long before he was pushing hard for a significant expansion of the Bank's support for the government in Iraq. Wolfowitz sought to use the Bank to promote the strategic policies that he had so forcefully advocated while at the Pentagon. In this case his efforts were foiled by one courageous individual—then World Bank vice president for the Middle East, Chrik Portman, who resigned in protest and subsequently became a senior manager at TI and a board director of PTF.

Ending such dealings and confronting the complexities of the issues involved with security and corruption is overdue. The importance of corruption within key discussions of global security in Western governments and "think-tanks" is largely overlooked. There is too little investigation and research in this area. One of the few people striving to raise public awareness and connect the dots between terrorism, crime, corruption, and international security is Professor Louise Shelley, director of the Terrorism, Transnational Crime, and Corruption Center at the School of Public Policy at George Mason University in the United States.

The United States and its Western allies have been doomed to failure in their wars in Afghanistan and Iraq (as illustrated later in this chapter) in part because they repeatedly ignored the seriousness of corruption. Thousands of soldiers have died and hundreds of billions of dollars have been lost in these countries. Both countries rank today among those perceived to be the most corrupt in the world.

Civil society anticorruption organizations, including TI, have largely avoided the global strategic issues that are paramount in this context (see the section on proposals for the defense sector in chapter 14). This needs to change. The issues that this chapter highlights are important.

TERRORISM

Corruption threatens our global security in a variety of ways, from bribes paid to nuclear scientists to get them to share top secret information to the international trade in arms and weapons systems that is riddled with bribery. The constant quest by nations and companies to secure oil, gas, and mineral reserves produces a whole array of illicit and corrupt transactions and agreements. Not infrequently in developing countries the bribe payer is a Western government—using foreign aid, military aid, or funds from an intelligence agency.

Bribery plays a vast role in all aspects of terrorism. The terrorist organizations bribe constantly to secure weapons, to obtain counterfeit documents, to engage in international criminal cartels,[1] to launder the cash they raise from supporters and transfer it across the world. And, importantly, many of the payments by Western taxpayers to foreign governments, which end in part in the pockets of top government officials, are made explicitly as part of Western antiterrorism strategies.

The payment of small bribes can do staggering damage. With passion, Elena Panfilova, director of TI-Russia, describes how on August 27, 2004, two women from Chechnya bribed a Moscow airport official a total of just US$140 to sell them tickets on two commercial flights. The terrorists were able to get through the first security points and then paid a further $25 to another official to let them board commercial flights. The two women carried explosives, which they detonated after take-off, destroying both planes and killing a total of eighty-nine passengers and crew. Elena protests that it is not just massive corruption involving vast fortunes at the top of government and industry, but also small-time corruption, that can lead to mass murder. "Imagine, for just a bribe of a few dollars, so many people were killed," she says.

There are no accurate estimates of the cash resources available, for example, to the Taliban or the amounts of weapons that terrorist organizations across the world obtain. Bribes grease the operations of terrorists at every turn: bribes to arms manufacturers and their agents; bribes to suppliers of transportation and telecommunications; bribes to local leaders to provide safe refuges and places to hide caches of arms; bribes to obtain airline tickets, and so on.

In order to fund such bribery, the terrorist organizations need to use sophisticated cross-border money-laundering devices. They need to be able to secure the services of establishment lawyers and agents to open secret numbered bank accounts for them in the many offshore financial havens that do not report who the real owners of these bank accounts are. From the Cayman Islands to Cyprus, from Jersey to Dubai, the terrorists join the mafia and the drug dealers and the corrupt politicians in placing their cash abroad. Smash the offshore havens and you strike a major blow at the funding of bribes that can cause massive violence. So far, the havens remain busy and the bribes keep flowing.

The US taxpayers supported the transfer of hundreds of billions of dollars into Iraq in the name of ridding the world of a dictator that the Bush administration falsely claimed had ties to the terrorists that blew up the World Trade Center on 9/11. The US command in Iraq, however, took scant interest in supporting efforts to build a strong system of justice and anticorruption in Iraq; after all, if effective, it might have gone after the same senior politicians who were viewed by the White House as invaluable allies.

Judge Radhi Hamza al-Radhi was appointed in June 2004 to lead Iraq's Anti-Corruption Commission. Under his determined efforts, the commission filed 541 cases in its first eighteen months, including forty-two that involved government ministers. Speaking before a committee of the US Congress in 2008, the judge said that the cost of corruption across all ministries in Iraq was an estimated $18 billion.

The judge's key message went far beyond the waste of US taxpayer cash by officials in Baghdad. He said that he was unable to do his work. Between 2004 and 2007, thirty-one of the commission's employees were assassinated and twelve family members were murdered. Judge al-Radhi lived under constant threat and ultimately had to flee, seeking political asylum in the United States in August 2007.

In Kenya, it is Western concerns about terrorism that once again hurl aside issues of corruption as the West provides the government and the Kenyan military with substantial amounts of economic and military aid and as the intelligence services operate in Kenya. Corruption at the top levels of the Kenyan government has been a major problem for over three decades, but Western geopolitical strategists have not been interested. Their prime concern has been ensuring the full support of Kenyan authorities in cooperating to prevent the infiltration of Al Qaeda operatives from Somalia into Kenya and to protect the Kenyan port of Mombasa from terrorists. These are seen as overriding strategic priorities in the "War on Terrorism."

In Pakistan, where terrorism is widespread and corruption is endemic, the Central Intelligence Agency (CIA) has close, albeit tense, relationships with a wide swath of senior politicians, military leaders, and intelligence-services leaders. The motives and tactical actions that the CIA and the Pakistani intelligence and military powers pursue are often difficult to decipher. The US killing of Osama bin Laden in Pakistan was an acute embarrassment to the Pakistanis, while Pakistan's occasional support of the Taliban has been deeply troubling to the Americans. Nevertheless, Pakistan receives billions of dollars in US aid and some of it slips into the pockets of top officials, but to whom and how much is a secret. It is likely that the way Pakistani officials abuse their office is well known to the CIA and could be severely curtailed if the United States were to use its intelligence knowledge for this purpose. But it chooses not to do so. Pakistan, with its nuclear weapons, is potentially the most dangerous nation on the planet. Friendship with Pakistan's governing elite, however, is seen by US policymakers as key to America's regional strategic goals, irrespective of how corrupt leaders in Pakistan may be.

NUCLEAR SECRETS

The worst nightmare is the thought of terrorists or rogue states obtaining nuclear weapons. One thing is certain: the path to such a situation involves corruption.

How did North Korea, Libya, and Iran obtain their top secret nuclear technology?

They paid bribes.

They bribed powerful people in Pakistan and for many years the central figure in the conspiracy was seen to be Dr. Abdul Qadeer Khan, the celebrity scientist known as the "father of the Islamic bomb." In 2004, he was arrested and after an interrogation he confessed and was placed under house arrest. Then Pakistani president Pervez Musharraf argued for leniency, noting that Khan was a national hero. The Pakistani High Court freed Khan in February 2009, and he has recanted his confession since then, claiming that he was pressured by his government to admit to bribery that he never was a part of.

There has also been speculation, fueled in part by Khan himself, that Musharraf was well aware that Khan had been, perhaps, no more than a pawn in a far larger bribery scheme involving senior politicians and officials over many years. There have been media reports, most notably in various publications by researcher Simon Henderson, suggesting that Khan could never have gotten away with such sensitive sales on his own; the evidence, published in both the *New York Times* and the *Washington Post* in July 2011, has supported his assertions.[2] Whatever the truth, the Khan affair underscores the extraordinary dangers that bribery can create in a nuclear age.

Reports providing information on just what secrets and what equipment were sold by Pakistan continue to emerge. For example, the Associated Press reported in September 2011 that the International Atomic Energy Agency (IAEA), headquartered in Vienna, Austria, had developed an internal report that confirmed that North Korea's nuclear facilities were "broadly consistent" with designs sold by a "clandestine supply network." The confidential report made available to the Associated Press seems to allude to the black market suppliers led by Dr. Khan. That group provided Iran with the backbone of what was a clandestine nuclear program before it was revealed eight years ago. Khan, it is alleged, was the main supplier of centrifuges used to enrich uranium before his operation was disrupted in 2003. Enrichment can create reactor fuel of the fissile core of nuclear weapons.

We may never learn the full truth about Pakistan's nuclear dealings. The story first broke in 2003 when a shipment of nuclear equipment from Pakistan to Libya was discovered in the Italian port of Taranto. Swiss government investigators have been on the trail ever since in the belief that several Swiss citizens played key roles as agents in organizing the Pakistan–Libya deals.

The greater the nuclear proliferation, the greater the risk that officials will be bribed to provide secrets that can have massive destructive power.

ARMS SALES

There is corruption both in the formal international sales of weapons systems pursued by major multinational corporations and in the foggy world of arms supplies to rebel and terrorist groups. Let us start with the more formal, big business operations.

World military expenditure is estimated to have been $1,630 billion in 2010.[3] Total arms sales of the "SIPRI Top 100" of the world's largest arms-producing companies were $401 billion in 2010.[4] According to research published by the Stockholm International Peace Research Institute (SIPRI):

Studies suggest that corruption in the arms trade contributes roughly 40 per cent to all corruption in global transactions. This corruption exacts a heavy toll on purchasing and selling countries, undermining democratic institutions of accountability and diverting valuable resources away from pressing social needs towards corrupt ends.

A number of systemic features of the arms trade encourage corruption, of which two are particularly important. First, its deep and abiding link to matters of national security obscures many deals from oversight and accountability. Second, the rubric of national security facilitates the emergence of a small coterie of brokers, dealers and officials with appropriate security clearances. These close relationships blur the lines between the state and the industry, fostering an attitude that relegates legal concerns to the background.[5]

No area of the corruption story is as full of intrigue and shrouded in secrecy than international trade in arms and weapons systems. Corruption in this sector may be even greater than that in the extractive industries. It is not just that firms develop special ties to the military and to governments, as is well illustrated by the investigations into corruption in Iraq. It is also, and more pervasively, that so much of the relationship between an arms supplier and a government purchaser of arms is considered by the purchasing government to be a matter of "national security." Under this heading the government can shroud the deals in total secrecy, thus providing the cover for bribe taking and paying. Chapter 14 discusses diverse approaches to curbing corruption in the arms industry. Progress is vital, yet it is unlikely to be swift.

Almost every aspect of international sales of weapons systems to governments involves collusion, shrouded in secrecy, between the manufacturers and their home governments. Many deals result in substantial payments to military and civilian government officials on the buying end and, of course, lucrative contracts for the suppliers and their agents. Governments work hand in glove with defense contractors and have a greater say in how international deals are developed and concluded in this business sector than in any other. Governments are more concerned with export earnings from their defense sales and with geopolitical strategic goals when it comes to allowing the export of weapons systems than with bribe paying.

It is difficult to quantify the volume of arms sold through black markets to support rebels, terrorists, and civil wars. Few people have investigated this areas as fully as Andrew Feinstein, author of *The Shadow World: Inside the Global Arms Trade* (2011). He paints a picture of a shadowy world where sometimes major Western governments find it convenient to use international agents who buy, ship, and sell weapons to anyone and everyone who seemingly wants the arms and has the cash. He describes situations where massive shipments of arms from Eastern Europe flood into the hands of Africans waging civil wars.

The costs of these wars in Africa total billions of dollars each year. 2011 Nobel Peace Prize winner Ellen Johnson-Sirleaf, president of Liberia, wrote in August 2007:

> This is money Africa can ill afford to lose. The sums are appalling: the price that Africa is paying could cover the cost of solving the HIV and AIDS crisis in Africa, or provide education, water and prevention and treatment for TB and malaria. Literally thousands of hospitals, schools, and roads could have been built, positively affecting millions of people. Not only do the people of Africa suffer the physical horrors of violence, but armed conflict also undermines their efforts to escape poverty.

These comments come from the foreword of a joint report by IANSA, Oxfam, and Safeworld published in 2008, which estimated that Africa loses around $18 billion per year due to wars, civil wars, and insurgencies. It added, "The real costs of armed violence to Africans could be much, much higher," going on to note the following:

> The evidence also suggests that at least 95 per cent of Africa's most commonly used conflict weapons come from outside the continent. The most common weapon is the Kalashnikov assault rifle, the most well-known type being the AK-47, almost none of which are made in Africa. A steady supply of ammunition is required to keep arms deadly, but little military ammunition is manufactured in Africa. Although it is impossible to demonstrate precisely, our research suggests that the vast majority of ammunition has to be imported from outside Africa.[6]

For many years, nongovernmental organizations have been making slow but sure progress to secure the approval at the United Nations of an international Arms Trade Treaty (ATT). Gradually, the major Western powers have indicated their support, but it may be a long time before there is a substantial ATT that is effectively enforced. The arms trade is very big business and too many governments, directly or illicitly, find it in their strategic and financial interests to support it.

On November 2, 2011, the *Washington Post* ran the following headline: "Arms dealer Viktor Bout convicted." Bout, sometimes known as the "Merchant of Death," is a former Russian military officer who over many years has been involved in many shipments of arms to all manner of terrorist and rebel groups. He was found guilty in a New York court of selling anti-aircraft weapons and other arms to Colombian rebels to kill Americans. He has been involved in the sale of arms from Russia—some experts suggest the weapons have been stolen on a massive scale by Russian military officers—to groups in Latin America, Asia, and in Africa. Bout is certainly one of the most notorious global arms merchants, but there are many others who evade justice, buy stolen arms, bribe customs officials to ensure they can be exported and imported across the globe, and fuel civil conflicts at huge costs.

So far, despite the occasional criminal prosecution and the speeches by diplomats in support of ATT, very little is being done to stop this rotten trade.

For seventeen years, Global Witness has been the leader in uncovering massive corruption and human rights abuses related to natural resources. Often, the Global Witness reports suggest that the proceeds of corruption in this area are directly used to buy arms on black markets to be used in civil wars. The connections between corruption in the extractive industries and in the arms game are compelling. Global Witness has made the case repeatedly in its investigations in such countries as Cambodia, DRC, Sierra Leone, Angola, and Zimbabwe.

NATION BUILDING

Western governments have engaged in diverse forms of what best can be described as nation building over several decades. They have used foreign and military aid to assist developing countries to address critical issues of poverty, security, and governance. No area of the stage of corruption and global security is more complex than that related to nation building. In both Iraq and Afghanistan, corruption has played significant roles and the results are not just demeaning for the United States and wasteful of US taxpayer dollars, but have also seriously undermined US strategic interests.

How the United States in coming years redefines its strategic international approaches as it seeks to continue to assist governments in developing countries to build their nations is important. If this can be done in ways that finally eliminate the use of bribes, then the world may be a safer place and respect for the United States in the world might increase. Developments in Iraq and Afghanistan may prove to be crucial in building support for a fundamental rethinking by Western governments of the use of bribery in geopolitical efforts to support nation building in developing countries.

Iraq

The misuse of taxpayer funds by America's "friends" abroad reached its zenith as the United States invaded and then deployed in Iraq from 2003 to 2008. The extensive reporting in the media and in reports to Congress of the misuse of billions of US dollars in Iraq should have prepared members of Congress for the repeat performances that were to play out in Afghanistan.

Chapter and verse of the waste, fraud, and corruption in Iraq was routine-ly provided to the US Congress in reports and public testimony by the Office of the US Special Inspector General for Iraq. The courageous incumbent, whom the Bush administration at one point sought to fire, was Stuart W. Bowen Jr., who brought all of his findings, covering about $50 billion in US funds appropriated by the US Congress for Iraq between 2004 and late 2008, together in a book that has received far too little attention and was published just after President Obama entered the White House in January 2009.

Under the title of *HARD LESSONS: The Iraq Reconstruction Experience*, Bowen pointed out that from the start of the American invasion no considera-tion was given by the White House or the Defense Department to contract monitoring and oversight. He noted that the overuse of cost-plus contracts, high contractor overhead expenses, excessive contractor award fees, and un-acceptable program and project delays all contributed to a significant waste of taxpayer dollars.

In every facet of the invasion and subsequent deployment there were American business contractors, often with Iraqi partners, who were, in effect, plundering the vast flow of taxpayer cash. Bowen pointed out:

> In the absence of effective management by government officials, contractors in Iraq were often left in dangerous circumstances to carry out insufficiently defined contracts written by inexperienced contracting officers who lacked situational awareness. In this chaotic environment, it was, at times, difficult to differentiate between reliable contractors who would carry out good work and those whose ad hoc operations and lack of experience pointed to failure. [7]

At the outset of the invasion Under-Secretary of Defense Douglas Feith recognized that a key priority was revitalizing Iraq's oil sector. With little hesitation KBR, a wholly owned subsidiary at the time of the Halliburton engineering company in Houston, Texas, was awarded the first significant contract under Iraq reconstruction. The award was made as KBR was being investigated by the US Justice Department for paying bribes in Nigeria, but the Pentagon was not interested in such matters.

KBR had links to Vice President Richard Cheney, a leading architect of the US invasion who had been the chairman and CEO of Halliburton in the years directly before he was elected vice president. The potential appearance of a conflict of interest for Cheney and KBR concerned some officials at the Pentagon and, according to Bowen, they insisted on raising the matter with the Office of the Vice President. Bowen wrote, "White House officials said the mission took priority over whatever political fallout might occur from granting a sole-source contract to KBR."

President Bush, Vice President Cheney, Secretary of Defense Donald Rumsfeld, and Deputy Secretary of Defense Paul Wolfowitz displayed scant interest in transparency and conflicts of interest, or even auditing and procurement monitoring, in regard to the disbursement of US taxpayer money in Iraq. The corruption involving taxpayer money in Iraq is part of their historic legacy.

Bowen described rampant "mismanagement, fraud and corruption" in contracting. He provided examples of one contract after another, from engineering deals to public-works projects, where substantial sums disappeared and contract overruns were charged and paid for without the work being done. Ignoring every aspect of auditing, and managing the vast sums of cash that the United States poured into Iraq, enabled grand corruption. Not until the special inspector general of Iraq started to deploy in Baghdad in March 2004 did the United States start to build an auditing and investigating capacity on the ground. From 2006 to 2008, some US funds were spent explicitly on assisting the Iraqi government to fight corruption, but the amounts were modest. In fact, there was no coordinated leadership on rule-of-law initiatives and a paucity of personnel engaged in this.

There was no place in the Pentagon of Rumsfeld and Wolfowitz for ensuring that the rule of law was clearly, transparently, and swiftly established. Business people with ties to the US government's contracting operations in Iraq enjoyed a bonanza.

The issue only reached the agenda of America's top diplomats in Baghdad two years after the invasion. Bowen noted:

> A succession of contracting and program management offices suffered under varying sets of complex contracting regulations, divergent chains of authority, changing program requirements and shifting reconstruction priorities. A shortage of qualified contracting officers, continuous staff turnover, and poor program management practices, particularly regarding quality assurance programs, weakened oversight of reconstruction projects. Finally, contracting officers did not have adequate information systems to track contract activity. [8]

The leaders of the Bush administration took no interest in the fact that vast sums of American cash went for a walk in Iraq. It is probable that much of the cash lined the pockets of politicians that the administration helped to gain power. In 2004, then US ambassador to Iraq, Paul "Jerry" Bremer III, established an anticorruption commission, but it lacked meaningful authority. It was constantly threatened by the very politicians that the United States increasingly trusted to run the country. Many of those politicians are still in charge. The 2011 CPI underscores the horrendous scale of corruption in Iraq and places the country among the ten most corrupt of the 183 nations in the rankings.

Afghanistan

In Afghanistan, the Bush administration installed Hamid Karzai as president of the country in 2004 and treated him as royalty thereafter. Karzai placed his relatives and friends in important governmental positions and they, in turn, installed their allies in new pyramids of power. In an article about Karzai in the *New York Times* magazine in August 2009, reporter Elizabeth Rubin interviewed one of his political opponents, Ashaf Ghani, who ran in the presidential election that month. Said Ghani, "I judge a president by his record and his company. We ranked 117 on Transparency International [Global Corruption Perceptions Index] in 2005. Now we rank 176, the fifth-most-corrupt country on earth. It happened under his watch."[9]

(In its 2011 CPI, Afghanistan's position had slipped to 180th position, just ahead of the absolutely worst-ranked countries—Myanmar, North Korea, and Somalia.)

The Bush administration learned nothing about corruption from its experiences in Iraq and it, and the international community more generally, ignored critically important governance issues as taxpayer cash, running into tens of billions of dollars, financed the war in Afghanistan. Writing in *Foreign Affairs* magazine in January 2011, Paul D. Miller, assistant professor of international security studies at the National Defense University in the United States, concluded that donors to Afghanistan "neglected governance programs."

Miller described how the international aid donors, led by the United States, pledged a miserly $200 million per year between 2001 and 2006 for governance and rule-of-law programs and disbursed about half this amount. He noted that relatively small amounts of donor aid were allocated to establishing a Civil Service Commission and instituting training and a merit-based career system. After five years of operations, the Afghan government could only boast that 7,500 civil servants had actually been recruited under the merit-based criteria out of a total of 240,000 government employees. Miller said that so little was really done by the donors to support good governance that "the international community was effectively asking Afghans with no shoes to lift themselves up by their bootstraps."[10]

New York Times, November 2, 2009
Obama Warns Karzai to Focus on Tackling Corruption
By Helene Cooper and Jeff Zeleney
WASHINGTON—President Obama on Monday admonished President Hamid Karzai of Afghanistan that he must take on what American officials have said he avoided during his first term: the rampant corruption and drug trade that have fueled the resurgence of the Taliban.

President Obama was probably familiar with the reports of corruption in Iraq and Afghanistan, but we can mark November 1, 2009, as the date when he gave voice to his sense of outrage. Never before had a US leader so bluntly chastised a foreign allied leader in a time of war as Obama rebuked Karzai. He was troubled about the open election fraud that Karzai perpetrated in the fall of 2009 to secure his reelection. President Obama was angry that the Karzai regime, far from acting to counter corruption, was a central part of massive corruption scams.

President Obama's concerns were explained before the US Senate's Foreign Relations Committee on December 3, 2009, by Secretary of State Hillary Clinton. Her comments were again unprecedented for their clarity and directness. She stated in part:

> We have to do a better job in the international side to coordinate our aid, to get more accountability for what we spend in Afghanistan. But much of the corruption is fueled by money that has poured into that country over the last eight years. And it is corruption at every step along the way, not just in Kabul.
>
> You know, when we are so dependent upon long supply lines, as in Afghanistan, where everything has to be imported, it's much more difficult than it was in Iraq, where we had Kuwait as a staging ground to go into Iraq. You offload a ship in Karachi and by the time whatever it is—you know, muffins for our soldiers' breakfasts or anti-IED equipment—gets to where we're headed, it goes through a lot of hands. And one of the major sources of funding for the Taliban is the protection money.

President Obama and Secretary Clinton had considerable evidence at hand about the negative attitudes of the Afghan people toward the Karzai government because of grand corruption, and bitterness toward the United States because it supported Karzai politically and with lavish amounts of cash. The hostility to the United States by ordinary Afghans was most helpful to opponents of Karzai, including the Taliban, in gaining public support.

In the run-up to the 2009 Afghan elections, surveys conducted by the Pentagon across Afghanistan showed weak support for Karzai. Several months later, just before Karzai visited Washington, DC, in May 2010, the Pentagon ran a new survey and found that his government enjoyed public support in only 29 of 121 districts that the US military considered to be strategically important. Corruption was widely seen as the key issue of concern.

Interviewed by *Rolling Stone* in June 2009, academic Andrew Wilder of Tufts University noted that the scale of funds that the United States was pouring into Afghanistan was dangerous. He said, "A tsunami of cash fuels corruption, delegitimizes the government and creates an environment where we're picking winners and losers—a process that fuels resentment and hostility among the civilian population."[11]

Perceptions of corruption in Afghanistan, by Afghans and people around the world in this new age of transparency, have been fostered by major investigative reports by leading international journalists. To my mind, two journalists have led the reporting—Matthew Rosenberg in his reports first for the *Wall Street Journal* and more recently for the *New York Times*, and Dexter Filkins, formerly with the *New York Times* (now at the *New Yorker*)—and many others have not been far behind. Their energies have repeatedly underscored the scale of the corruption, the disgust of the Afghan people with the crooks they see running the country, and the tensions between the US authorities and President Karzai. Their stories have highlighted what an utter mess can be made of Western strategic objectives when corruption is allowed to thrive, fueled by Western governments.

Rosenberg reported in the *Wall Street Journal* on August 12, 2010:

> Corruption in the Afghan government and business establishment has become a major source of tension between Mr. Karzai and the U.S. government, threatening to derail the U.S.-led coalition's counterinsurgency strategy. U.S. officials say it is crucial to restore the trust of ordinary Afghans in their own government, which has been shaken by pervasive commercial and government graft.[12]

President Obama's public statements about corruption involving a "friendly government" probably shocked Hamid Karzai while setting off alarm bells in the luxurious palaces that are homes to the thoroughly corrupt presidents of Pakistan, Egypt, Kenya, and many other countries whose wealth came directly from the United States in return for their political loyalty to the goals of America's Department of State, Department of Defense, and CIA.

OBAMA SPEAKS OUT

The public statements that President Obama and Secretary Clinton have made about corruption augur well for stimulating the necessary major public policy discussion on the issues of corruption and security. So far, the foreign policy establishment has applauded politely and then gone ahead with its old ways, skeptical that anything can be done about corruption and with a mindset that bribery is just a standard part of the strategic policy toolkit.

To be sure, there have been crises in very recent times where the United States has looked as if it is understanding the full meaning of the Arab Spring and the new age of transparency. President Mubarak of Egypt might have expected the United States to provide him with strong support as the 2011 protests started and assure him that it would enable him to retain power. But

President Obama understood that this was no longer an option. The best he could do for an old friend was to send him a special envoy with the message that if he left the country quickly and quietly, his safety would be assured. Mubarak rejected the offer, and so the White House told him publicly to resign.

Just as the US president had criticized Karzai in late 2009 and been even blunter with Mubarak fourteen months later, it was inevitable that he would be even more direct in his resignation demands to the leaders of Libya and Syria. With each of these public pronouncements, Obama made it ever clearer that the United States understood that it has a choice to make in the way it pursues foreign policy—it can side with oppressed peoples craving opportunities to escape poverty, to be free and determine the course of their own lives and restore their dignity, or it can continue to support corrupt despots.

If Obama and Clinton appear to have become bolder in their public condemnation of corruption in allied governments, then this is in part due to the findings of US congressional investigations of vast sums of stolen American cash in Afghanistan.

The congressional work underlines the importance of the new age of transparency in which the corrupt ways of governments are now being uncovered on a scale and in a degree of detail that has rarely been seen before. Speaking at the 2011 annual dinner of Global Financial Integrity [13] in Washington, Senator Carl Levin noted that new technologies have given enormous assistance to complicated investigations. Investigations pursued by the US Senate's Permanent Sub-Committee on Investigations, which he chairs, have at times produced millions of pages of documents. New technologies that enable effective word search can unlock what he called the "golden nuggets of evidence" that can be decisive.

Never before has there been so much information—be it produced by investigative reporters, by witnesses under oath before US congressional committees, or in the form that Levin spoke about—to shed light on politics and corruption. For example, on July 28, 2010, a congressional committee cross-examined senior US administration officials about the spectacle of vast sums of cash being filmed and photographed as it was being loaded at Kabul airport for shipment to Dubai. The cash had a one-way ticket. It would never return to Afghanistan. Some of it was used to buy apartments in Dubai by Afghan government officials and their relatives, who just happen to regularly win government contracts. (Dubai real estate has been a favorite investment for many politicians and business people from Pakistan and Afghanistan.) After the hearing and the decision to delay special further funding for Afghanistan, Congresswoman Nita Lowey from New York said,

I am pleased the Committee's action has already helped to spur increased scrutiny of funds, including an investigation by Afghanistan's top anticorruption agency of the billions in cash that has left the country, the Afghan Ministry of Finance's announcement of a joint international investigation into the country's hawala network, and the creation of a US government task force to review contracting practices.[14]

The scale of the theft and all of the details on how much is involved and where it goes are so staggering that neither the Congress nor the White House could ignore the abuse.[15] The *Financial Times,* for example, reported on March 19, 2012, that Afghanistan's central bank revealed that the amount of cash that flew abroad through Kabul airport in 2011 doubled from the previous year to $4.6 billion—almost the same size as the country's national budget. Most of the cash went in the form of large bricks of $100 bills and the prime destination was Dubai. It amounted to over $150 per Afghan citizen. This is the official tally and far more may well have left the country without being reported. The cash almost certainly represents two major sources of income to Afghans: the proceeds of the opium trade and related crimes and the theft of vast amounts of foreign aid, mainly provided by the United States.

In mid-June 2010, the US House of Representatives' Subcommittee on National Security and Foreign Affairs published a revealing report, *Warlord, Inc.: Extortion and Corruption along the US Supply Chain in Afghanistan.* It was the product of a six-month investigation. The chairman of the subcommittee, Congressman John F. Tierney, wrote in the introduction:

> The report exposes the circumstances surrounding the Department of Defense's outsourcing of security on the supply chain in Afghanistan to questionable providers, including warlords. The findings of this report range from sobering to shocking. In short, the Department of Defense designed a contract that put responsibility for the security of vital U.S. supplies on contractors and their unaccountable security providers. This arrangement has fueled a vast protection racket run by a shadowy network of warlords, strongmen, commanders, corrupt Afghan officials, and perhaps others. . . . The "fog of war" still requires a direct line of sight on contractors.

It is one thing for politicians in Washington to recognize the abuse; it is another to translate such a finding into new policies and strategic action. This is difficult and yet vital in a dangerous world—all the more so because of the complexities involved in issues of corruption impacting global security in two crucial industrial sectors: weapons systems, including nuclear weapons, and natural resources, especially oil, gas, and other minerals.

Global security is impacted by the risks of terrorists and rogue states paying bribes to obtain nuclear secrets, by the abundant bribery involved today in international arms sales, and by the corruption related to the competition, led by companies from the world's largest economies, to secure oil, gas, and other vital minerals. In each of these areas the policies of powerful governments toward corruption play key roles. Certainly, in these areas the enhancement of our global security rests to no small degree on the determination of a handful of key powers—notably, the United States, China, and Russia, as well as the United Kingdom and France—to adopt anticorruption policies. Each of these countries has pledged to do so in broad anticorruption statements made within the forum of the Group of 20—notably, at the G-20 summit in Cannes in November 2011.

NATURAL RESOURCES

For decades, Western governments, operating hand in glove with major oil, gas, and mining companies, forged deep ties with the governments of resource-rich nations, from Libya to Nigeria, from Indonesia to Saudi Arabia. The companies secured exploration and then production rights in these countries in return for agreed royalty payments. They did not ask what the host governments did with the massive revenues that they obtained. If the leaders of these countries wanted to deposit the funds in their own personal bank accounts (or those of their families) in London or Zurich, then they found no objections from the British or Swiss governments or from the bankers who took the deposits.

Many of the greediest practitioners of grand corruption—past and present—hold sway in countries that have been endowed with enormous natural resources (see discussion on how to reduce corruption in the extractive industries in chapter 13). More than five million people have died in the DRC in recent years as warlords and public officials have illicitly claimed control of vast quantities of minerals. They have then sold the minerals to foreign companies for their personal benefit and, set against a host of ethnic rivalries, they have claimed, in the words of the title of a book on Kenyan corruption by Michela Wrong, "It's Our Turn to Eat."[16]

For decades, oil companies have had cozy and secret ties to the governments in whose countries they operate, from Russia and Central Asia, across Asia and through the Middle East and into sub-Saharan Africa. It is with intense frustration that anticorruption activists watch the dealings between major global oil companies and a host of African countries that have vast oil reserves, such as Nigeria, Angola, Equatorial Guinea, Chad, and others. Given their oil resources the living standards of the peoples of these countries should be high. Instead, living standards are among the very lowest in the world.

The royalties that Exxon, BP, Chevron, and other giant firms pay to the host governments in order to have the right to extract oil should be going into new schools and hospitals and public infrastructure, but they are not. Oil royalties are among the world's single largest source of corrupt spoils for a relatively small number of governments in countries where general living conditions are appalling. Exposure of these royalties is now, after many years of campaigning by civil society, likely to become a reality (see chapter 14).

France, for example, has ensured that its oil companies have access to the substantial oil of former West African colonies. The royalty payments by these French companies have been the source of the incredible fortune of President Teodoro Obiang Nguema Mbasogo of Equatorial Guinea, who has been in power since 1979. The Obiangs own real estate from Beverly Hills, California (paid for in part through phony shell corporations with names like Unlimited Horizon and Beautiful Vision), to Cannes in the South of France. Their assets have been investigated by a US congressional committee and are under investigation by a French judge. Obiang no doubt feels confident that he is secure and can continue to pocket the nation's formidable oil revenues, because France needs his oil.

The same holds true for the Bongo family in nearby Gabon. French president Nicolas Sarkozy and his predecessor, Jacques Chirac, both paid tribute to one of Africa's most corrupt ruling families when they attended the funeral, in June 2009, of Omar Bongo, who had been Gabon's president for forty-two years and who was succeeded by his son, Ali-Ben Bongo.

US and UK oil companies (including Shell, which is a joint UK-Dutch company) have been the prime sources of enormous royalty payments to the governments of Nigeria and Indonesia, whose former leaders Abacha and Suharto are among the past giants of grand corruption. There is also zero transparency related to the oil deals that are done by President Omar Al-Bashir of Sudan—who is wanted under an arrest warrant from the International Criminal Court for perpetrating genocide in Darfur.

What makes the issue of corruption in natural resources far more complicated from a global security perspective is that Western interests are increasingly colliding with Chinese and Russian interests. As the Russians strive to build global corporations in the extractive industries they have no national laws to worry about that suggest they could be prosecuted for bribing foreign officials and they have the strong strategic backing of the Russian government. Chinese state-owned enterprises are investing on a massive scale across sub-Saharan Africa to add to China's own resource security. The deals that the Chinese do with host African governments are secret.

The Chinese have not joined any international initiatives to raise transparency in extractive industries and curb corruption. Yes, they have joined Group of 20 summit pledges to support the United Nations Convention against Corruption, but they have given no indication of implementing its provisions. Confronting them and seeking to convince them that an open, competitive trading and investing world is in everyone's economic and political interest is a challenge that Western governments have, so far, shied away from.

The quest by all countries that are dependent on imports of natural resources to strengthen the security of supply of such resources plays directly into the hands of corrupt governments, from Russia to Nigeria to Saudi Arabia, that control vast resources. Somewhere along the line, Western governments are likely to compromise on public stands against corruption. They will continue to facilitate arrangements by major multinational oil and mining companies that enable them to do deals with corrupt foreign governments where all aspects of the contracts are hidden from public inspection; they will continue to fall short on public pledges against money laundering where the regimes of minerals-exporting countries are concerned; and they will continue to place obstacles in the paths of efforts to repatriate assets held in Western banks by the families of corrupt leaders to the people who are the legitimate owners of such assets.

What thoroughly confuses the situation today is the appearance of Western governmental hypocrisy in which public rhetoric is all against corruption and money laundering while governmental actions continue along well-trodden paths as if the public statements never existed. US congressional hearings and investigations take place and senators and congressmen huff and puff, but at the end of the day little changes when it comes to all of the corruption associated with weapons systems and natural resources. UK and French authorities are not going to get out in front of the Americans, and the conflicts of interests in the United States paralyze action.

The United States has by far the largest defense budget in the world and it is the largest national oil-importing country in the world. American manufacturers of weapons systems dwarf almost all rivals and receive massive research subsidies through the Pentagon that enhance their competitiveness. Foreign companies, such as BAE Systems in the United Kingdom and Thales in France, have major US subsidiaries and walk and talk just like their US rivals for the very good reason that their survival also depends first and foremost on Pentagon contracts. Almost all of the non-state-owned major oil and minerals companies outside of Russia are highly dependent on the US capital markets and on partnerships of diverse kinds with US companies.

Indeed, the US authorities have enormous power to control the major companies in the arms and extractive industries if they like. But, as of right now, they are not taking the lead in these areas when it comes to corruption. Final policy decisions seem to rest with the foreign-policy establishment and the intelligence communities, which appear to continue to view corruption as a necessary evil that they cannot, and should not, do anything about.

The diverse aspects of the issue of corruption and global security are only a part of the landscape of corruption issues that burden our planet today. Like so many of the other corruption-related issues, those concerned with security are now coming under greater public scrutiny than ever before. It is unclear whether this will force a sufficiently deep review of all aspects of the uses of bribery in international strategic relations. It should.

NOTES

1. For example, see the *New York Times*, December 14, 2011, front-page article by reporter Jo Becker: "Beirut Bank Seen as a Hub of Hezbollah's Financing—Evidence of Money-Laundering Network in Inquiries that Point to Drug Trade."

2. See R. Jeffrey Smith, "Pakistan's Nuclear-Bomb Maker Says North Korea Paid Bribes for Know-How," *Washington Post*, July 6, 2011; David Sanger, "Pakistani Army Linked, in Letter, to Nuclear Sale," *New York Times*, July 7, 2011.

3. Estimate from the Stockholm International Peace Research Institute (SIPRI).

4. SIPRI press release, February 2011.

5. *SIPRI Year Book 2011* (Oxford: Oxford University Press, 2011), chapter 1 summary, "Corruption and the Arms Trade: Sins of Commission," by Andrew Feinstein, Paul Holden, and Barnaby Pace.

6. Oxfam Briefing Papers, "Africa's Milling Billions—International Arms Flows and the Costs of Conflicts," report published on October 11, 2007, edited by Debbie Hillier and jointly published by Oxfam International, Safer World, and the International Action Network on Small Arms.

7. Stuart Bowen Jr.,*HARD LESSONS: The Iraq Reconstruction Experience* (Washington, DC: US Government Printing Office, 2009).

8. Bowen, *HARD LESSONS*.

9. Elizabeth Rubin, "Karzai in His Labyrinth," *New York Times*, August 4, 2009.

10. Paul D. Miller (assistant professor of international security studies at the National Defense University and a former director for Afghanistan in the US National Security Council from September 2007 to September 2009), "Finish the Job—How the War in Afghanistan Can be Won," *Foreign Affairs*, January/February 2011.

11. Michael Hastings, "Stanley McChrystal: The Runaway General. Obama's Top Commander in Afghanistan Never Takes His Eye Off Real Enemy," *Rolling Stone* 1108/1109, July 8–22, 2010.

12. Matthew Rosenberg, "Afghanistan Money Probe Hits Close to the President," *Wall Street Journal*, August 12, 2010.

13. December 14, 2011. Senator Levin was the recipient of Global Financial Integrity's annual award.

14. Statement by Representative Nita Lowey (D-NY), former chair of the State and Foreign Operations Subcommittee of the Appropriations Committee of the US House of Representatives, following hearings on corruption in Afghanistan by her committee, July 19, 2010.

15. On August 12, 2010, Matthew Rosenberg reported in the *Wall Street Journal* that special Afghan teams of anticorruption investigators had raided the headquarters of Afghanistan's largest "hawala" money-transfer business, the New Ansari Exchange. Documents they found were said to include links to money transfers, often through physical shipments of cash by plane from Kabul to Dubai, for "some of the most powerful political and business figures in the country, including relatives of Mr. Karzai." The documents indicated that $3.18 billion of cash was flown out of the country between the start of 2007 and February 2010.

16. Michela Wrong, *It's Our Turn to Eat—The Story of a Kenyan Whistle-Blower* (London: Fourth Estate, 2009).

Part 2

Action

Chapter Eight

The New Age of Transparency — Media and Research

Thomas Friedman, author and *New York Times* columnist, has written at length about the impact of new information technologies and globalization. Apart from reporting over several years on technological innovation, he also stood in Tahrir Square to see the birth of the Arab Spring. He has recognized that the prices that consumers have to pay to acquire new technology are declining to the point where their mass availability is growing rapidly and set to grow still more rapidly. In a *New York Times* column on November 12, 2011, he described a new Indian tablet computer that could sell for as little as $50 and wrote:

> We're at the start of a nonlinear move in innovation thanks to the hypercon-
> necting of the world—through social media, mobile/wireless devices and
> cloud computing—which is putting cheap innovation devices into the hands of
> so many more people, enabling them to collaborate on invention in so many
> new ways. This Great Inflection will be an opportunity and a challenge for
> every worker and company because we're going to see more and more product
> "price points" broken in big ways. [1]

The increasing availability of very low-cost communications devices of all kinds will further propel the successes of many civil society organizations. The new age of transparency, in which more people than ever before can learn all manner of things from all manner of places at minimal cost and with amazing speed, is transformative: a relatively narrow path peopled with academics and members of the establishment concerned with anticorruption is now giving way to a vast boulevard named mass public engagement. The swift growth of TI and of many other civil society organizations in recent years owes much to the Internet. It has and it is

- enabling civil society groups within countries and across national borders to share information—TI and many other global civil society movements would never have grown so fast and so efficiently in the last fifteen years, and especially in the last five years, had it not been for the Internet;
- hugely assisting national civil society organizations to secure grassroots support across their countries at a speed and on a scale that has no precedent (see ALACs in the next chapter);
- enabling people to find the fuel for common languages of protest and action thanks to Twitter and Facebook and an increasing plethora of social media tools;
- providing prosecutors with powerful tools to gather compelling evidence via the hard drives of computers, traces on e-mails, and new telecom tapping devices—in trial after trial the smoking guns have been e-mails that the villains wish they had never sent;
- ensuring, of course, along with other new information technologies, that the general public in scores of countries is better informed about the corruption that abounds in so many areas of government in so many countries.

The massive dissemination across the globe via the web of news and information about corruption owes a great deal to the significant rise in media coverage in recent years of governmental and corporate crime. Gross theft by government leaders, for example in Afghanistan, Nigeria, and Peru, and their efforts to hide their cash abroad have increasingly been the substance of investigations and lengthy media reports. As noted in an earlier chapter, US congressional investigations have often been triggered by outstanding reporting by the mainstream media, which in turn has generated increased media coverage.

The media's focus on corruption has been just as great on the governmental activities in the leading industrial countries as in the developing ones. It was investigative work by London's *Daily Telegraph* in 2009 that revealed that two hundred UK members of Parliament had fiddled their expenses. The US media has given bold front-page coverage to the prosecutions of leading New York and Illinois politicians caught in recent years with their hands in the public till. The opposition media has spared no effort in Italy in recent times to reveal every allegation for corruption that could be found about former prime minister Silvio Berlusconi. And the more people in the "North" learn about the corruption in their own backyards, the more they can feel a bond with all those in the "South" whose lives are ruined by the corrupt practices of their own governments.

Editors have increased their attention to business crime as a result of the extraordinary greed at major corporations that was exposed in the first decade of the new century. The early years of this century saw corporate scandals involving Enron and its auditors Arthur Andersen, Adelphia, Hollinger, Tyco, WorldCom, and numerous others in the United States and overseas. Top executives were sent to prison for long stretches. They used their enterprises as personal piggy banks, spending massively on ever more personal luxuries at the expense of their shareholders and then playing games with the corporate balance sheets to hide their malfeasance. Those outrages created the background for the even more damaging scandals that came to the fore as the world's financial system started to melt down. Bernie Madoff in New York was exposed as the greatest swindler of all time, stealing $50 billion from people who trusted him; Lehman Brothers collapsed in the largest bankruptcy of any financial institution in modern times.

The scandals had a major impact on the way many media reporters viewed corporate behavior. For many years there was an inclination in the powerful US press to accept self-serving claims by the public relations departments of giant enterprises, which would dismiss the occasional cases of fraud and bribery as just the work of rogue individual employees. The major corporations proudly talked about their ethics codes, their attention to corporate social responsibility, and pride in their corporate philanthropy. Enron's CEO Kenneth Lay pontificated on his company's state-of-the-art ethics code at the January 2001 World Economic Forum in Davos, Switzerland—by the end of that year, Enron had collapsed and Lay was the center of investigations.

Furthermore, the media has given increasing attention to public attitudes to corporate and public-sector governance, so that words like "accountability" and "transparency" have come into everyday usage in this context across the globe.

Middle classes are building in scores of nations that never had them before and their impact on anticorruption efforts is formidable. They not only see the virtues of democracy and open societies, the advantages of fair market competitiveness, and the benefits of globalization, but they also want to participate in building appropriate institutions in their countries.

The world of the twenty-first century is seeing increasing numbers of young leaders in scores of countries that share common values of how governments should serve the public interest and within those values there is no place for corruption. These young leaders are winning media attention, ensuring that their views spread widely.

To be sure, the media is not totally on the side of the angels when it comes to corruption. There is corruption within the media: journalists pay bribes and take bribes in many countries. Many media organizations claiming to be objective in their reporting have firm agendas dictated by their owners. The alleged payments by reporters at News Corporation's former major UK newspaper, the *News of the World*, to UK policemen sparked a major British scandal in 2011 and underscored the dark side of the reporting trade.

CENSORSHIP

Such scandals provide ammunition to those wielding political power who seek to muzzle the media. Indeed, the greatest threat to further progress in enhancing the reach of all forms of media rests in continuing approaches by governments to impose censorship. In 1994, at a seminar in Budapest on corruption, Lee Tucker, a fellow at the Human Rights Watch Fund for Free Expression, summed matters up:

> A free media can have tremendous impact in combating corruption. Where media shelter their government out of choice or necessity, corruption flourishes. When the press acts as a watchdog, however, corruption becomes a risk to government officials. Their illegal acts are more likely to be discovered and disseminated to the public, leaving them vulnerable to public outrage, demands for investigations and prosecutions, and ejections from office. Corrupt governments are correct to fear a free and curious press. [2]

Many countries continue to have official secret acts of one kind or another that enable governments to declare that certain issues cannot be published in the media on grounds of national security. More often than not this is a means for governments to hide actual and potential matters that enable corruption, such as the procurement of military equipment. Many countries, such as the United Kingdom, have the kinds of libel laws in place that enable powerful people to ruin financially those who write and publish negative articles about them. This is a form of censorship, of course.

Censorship also exists through quasi-monopolistic control of the media. In China, almost all print media, radio, and television is controlled by the state. In Russia, many of the most powerful media organizations are either state owned or controlled by business people whose wealth depends entirely on the deals they strike with the nation's political masters. In Western countries, the lack of rigid antitrust controls enables vast media networks with enormous influence, such as Rupert Murdoch's News Corporation, to be run by a single individual, whose decisions as to what his many publications and television channels report (and how they report) may have a lot more to do with his business interests and his prejudices than with exposing the truth.

Reporters and editors have been struggling with censors since the first days of journalism. The mantra of those campaigning against censorship is anchored in the First Amendment to the US Constitution, which states in part:

> Congress shall make no law respecting the establishment of religion, or prohibiting the free exercise thereof; or abridging the freedom of speech, or of the press; or the rights of people peaceably to assemble, and to petition the Government for redress of grievances.

Many books have been written about press freedom, but this is not the place to examine the issue in depth. Suffice it to say, however, that without the determined zeal of so many people in the media (or associated in one form or another with the media) to expand the boundaries of press freedom, the prospects of rooting out corruption would be far bleaker.

In 2000, the World Press Freedom Committee published a book of more than one hundred short letters and essays by media activists, editors, and reporters about "What a free press means to me." In their very different styles and forms of expressing themselves, they each underscored the importance to a democracy of a free press. They all stressed the need to keep up the political pressure to set the media free in so many countries where the governmental censors, and often the media barons who conspire with them, limit press freedom.

In one of the final essays in that volume, dated February 17, 2000, Ann Cooper, then executive director of the Committee to Protect Journalists, wrote in part:

> Every year the Committee to Protect Journalists documents hundreds of attacks on the media worldwide: journalists killed, thrown in prison, physically assaulted or harassed, because the words they write expose incriminating or embarrassing information. We defend these journalists because without a free press that can investigate corruption or wrongdoing, a nation's freedom of speech is jeopardized, and so are its hopes for democracy.[3]

The battle for press freedom will continue to be crucial for the broader war against corruption. Finding ways around new efforts by governments to censor the worldwide web will pose new and vital challenges. I believe that over time the impact of the censors will decline and the force of the globalization of instant information and new technologies will be overpowering. Indeed, I believe that the power of the new age of transparency continues to be widely underestimated by many of those who take a dim view of the prospects of curbing corruption. They fail to recognize the sheer force and dynamic of new technological developments.

INVESTIGATIVE REPORTING

It is sometimes argued that the financial problems of many newspapers are forcing cuts in investigative journalism that will have disastrous consequences. There is no question that amateur bloggers and website pontificators are no substitute for the tough, determined, professional reporters who dig deep to find reliable sources and hard evidence and can piece difficult stories together. But today we are seeing two phenomena in particular, almost at different ends of the media spectrum, that are most encouraging. First, an increasing number of highly educated and professional journalists in developing countries are willing to work with very small financial resources to investigate corruption and find courageous people to publish their reports, be it in print or on the web. Second, not-for-profit organizations that use professional and experienced journalists and focus on corruption are growing and doing outstanding work.

Charles Lewis, a former US television news producer, established the Center for Public Integrity in Washington, DC, in 1989. Time and again the center, now led by former National Public Radio veteran Bill Buzenberg, has broken major stories on abuse in America's political system. It is a fiercely independent watchdog and a pioneer in its field. It is funded by individual donations and an array of foundations and its mission is "to reveal abuses of power, corruption and dereliction of duty by powerful public and private institutions in order to cause them to operate with honesty, integrity, accountability and to put the public interest."[4]

One of Lewis's researchers in the late 1990s was Nathaniel Heller, who started a conversation with Lewis about the possibility of doing at the international level what the center was doing nationally. Another colleague, political scientist Marianne Camerer, based in Cape Town, South Africa, was thinking similar thoughts. They pioneered a novel approach of finding journalists and academics in many different countries who could report on corruption in their countries. In 2002, they secured funding for a twenty-five-country pilot project, and the growth of the project led them to decide to establish an independent not-for-profit organization, Global Integrity, in Washington, DC, in 2005.

With Heller as executive director and Camerer as international director, Global Integrity today engages more than twelve hundred in-country experts in more than one hundred countries. Its continuous work into evaluating progress on the fight against corruption across most of the developing world and in Central and Eastern Europe represents outstanding journalism and an enormous contribution to the extensive research on anticorruption that now abounds.

A relative newcomer to the field of not-for-profit anticorruption journalism outside the framework of a traditional media organization is ProPublica in New York, which is directed by one of America's most thoughtful journalists, Paul Steiger. Paul, a former *Los Angeles Times* reporter who joined the *Wall Street Journal* and became its managing editor, has been at the forefront over the last two decades in building award-winning teams of investigative journalists. From 2005 until June 2011, he was chairman of the Committee to Protect Journalists. He brought his experience of managing investigative journalism and his passion for justice to ProPublica, which he started to plan in 2007 on his retirement from the *Journal*. Steiger met Los Angeles entrepreneurs and philanthropists Herbert and Marion Sandler, who had built a major financial services firm in California and then established the Sandler Foundation, which agreed to provide ProPublica with an annual budget of $10 million.

Steiger has demonstrated that the money is well invested. With a team of more than thirty investigative reporters, the organization has broken one story of political and financial corruption after another in the United States. In 2010, it was the first web-based media organization to win a Pulitzer Prize, the most prestigious award in US journalism, and then in 2011 it won another, as well as a slew of other prizes.

RESEARCH

The work of civil society organizations, journalism groups like those run by Heller and Steiger, and exceptional investigative reporting of corruption by individual reporters in many countries all combine to make the corruption story very big news. This, in turn, has been a stimulus for two decades now of rapidly rising academic interest and research in this area.

In the mid-1990s, the World Bank viewed corruption as taboo, but by 2010 the World Bank Institute had become one of the global leaders in surveys, data, and analysis of corruption across the developing world. The Brookings Institution and the American Enterprise Institute in the United States, which had never considered corruption as an issue in the 1990s, had scholars devoted to the topic a decade later. The Institute for Development Studies in the United Kingdom is a major center for key research in this area now.

Such leading US corruption scholars as Susan Rose-Ackermann at Yale University, Michael Johnston at Colgate University, Robert Klitgaard at Claremont Graduate University, and Louise Shelley at George Mason University, who have been writing about corruption for many years, have now been joined by hundreds of other academic researchers in the expanding field of corruption studies.

They have pursued research into every corner of the corruption edifice, from its impact on political campaign finance to its undermining of progress on climate change. They have created surveys and indexes to measure corruption. They have contributed enormously to the understanding of many aspects of the issues by both the civil society activists themselves and, importantly, rising numbers of people in business, the law, and the multilateral and bilateral aid institutions, as well as politicians.

The Anti-Corruption Research Network (ACRN), organized by TI, was engaging around five thousand academics across the world by late 2011. This web-based forum has enabled academics to share their research widely, to "blog" about research, to meet other academics online, and to strengthen the overall impact of research on policy. ACRN has a team of contributing editors in a number of major universities who keep the conversation going and keep prodding for new research among the registered worldwide ACRN membership.

Conferences on anticorruption were few and far between in the first half of the 1990s; now there are a plethora of them. The topics of corruption and governance have become the height of fashion in many academic quarters. All of this is good news, of course, in terms of raising public awareness, pressuring politicians to promote reforms, and gauging the level of success that is being attained.

Rising media coverage of corruption and the impact of the new age of transparency, plus growing research and the enormous growth of civil society organizations active in the anticorruption war, all have combined to place exceptional pressures on governments and international institutions. They are adding enormous substantive knowledge to all corruption issues. They are also combining, as the following chapters highlight, to change the way the establishment thinks and acts when it comes to the abuse of public office for personal gain.

Former World Bank president Robert Zoellick sees one of his major accomplishments at the Bank as increasing significantly the public's access to the Bank's data resources. He said at a Washington, DC, conference in May 2012, shortly before he retired from the World Bank, that access to the enormous volume of the Bank's data provides the public with the opportunity to learn a great deal, to strengthen research into the Bank's work, and to enable civil society to monitor the implementation of World Bank–funded projects and programs.

NOTES

1. Thomas L. Friedman, "The Last Person," op-ed article, *New York Times*, November 12, 2011.

2. "Corruption & Democracy," Institute for Constitutional and Legislative Policy, affiliated with Open Society Institute, report of a seminar in Budapest in 1994. Lee Tucker's contribution at the conference was based on a detailed discussion of censorship related to corruption titled "Off Limits: Censorship and Corruption," published by Human Rights Watch, July 1991.

3. Dana Bullen, ed., *Voices of Freedom 2000: What A Free Press Means to Me* (Reston, VA: World Press Freedom Committee, 2000).

4. iWatch News, the Center for Public Integrity, www.iwatchnews.org.

Chapter Nine

Justice and Democracy

In December 2009, just before his ninetieth birthday and his retirement after thirty-five years as the Manhattan district attorney, Robert M. Morgenthau came down to Washington, DC, for a dinner in his honor hosted by Raymond Baker, director of the Institute of Global Financial Integrity. The evening was especially memorable because Morgenthau could surprise once again, this time by completing another sensational prosecution of a giant corporation. Nobody has had a record as long and as successful at prosecuting establishment titans for white collar crimes, corruption, money laundering, and tax evasion as Morgenthau, and here he was, in the final hours of his tenure on New York's payroll, once again pulling a rabbit out of a hat.

Not an ordinary rabbit by any means. For several years, Morgenthau had taken a close interest in the international financial dealings of the government of Iran. He was convinced that they laundered huge sums through international financial institutions, but he lacked proof. Just a couple of months before that December dinner, he had come down to Washington to give a talk at the Brookings Institution about his concerns that the government of Venezuela was working closely with the Iranians to obtain their technological skills in building major munitions factories in Venezuela. He suggested that considerable amounts of Iranian cash were flowing into secret bank accounts in New York from Venezuela. The United States had sanctions against the involvement of any US banks, or banks operating in the United States, taking Iranian deposits.

On the eve of the Washington dinner, Morgenthau announced that he had won an agreement from one of the world's largest banks, Credit Suisse, to pay a fine of $536 million. The Swiss financial giant was charged with assisting Iranian, Libyan, and Sudanese clients to violate US sanctions and,

141

by means of false documentation, place funds in the American financial markets. This was vintage Morgenthau—the fine was huge and the rogue was a veritable pillar of the global corporate establishment.

Robert Morris Morgenthau was born in 1919 in New York City into one of the great American political families of the first half of the twentieth century—his grandfather, Henry S. Morgenthau, had been an important US ambassador, while his father, Henry Morgenthau Jr., had been US Treasury secretary in the administration of President Franklin D. Roosevelt. Robert dedicated himself to the cause of justice and spent most of his professional life in public service, assuming his last full-time post as the elected New York district attorney in 1975 and repeatedly winning elections to this position for a record thirty-five years.

Morgenthau is the model tough and ethical public prosecutor. Nobody could bribe him or shake his determined efforts to fight crime. He went after the mafia bosses in New York and the corporate tycoons. In 2002, for example, he charged the leaders of Tyco International, chief executive officer Dennis Kozlowski, and chief financial officer Mark Swartz with enriching themselves to the tune of over $600 million by plundering Tyco's finances. They are now serving long prison terms.

He was passionate about exposing money laundering and corruption and set a new high standard in this area when he led investigations in 1985 into the international activities of the Bank for Credit and Commerce International (BCCI). Controlled by a group of Pakistani individuals, BCCI became a global operation with major businesses in Asia, in Europe through the United Kingdom and Luxembourg, and into the United States. BVCI went bankrupt, leaving thousands of cheated depositors, and while the European authorities stumbled around seeking to find ways to discover what had happened, Morgenthau followed the cash, which took him to secret accounts in the Caribbean. His investigations led to criminal prosecutions and the first successful major international offensive against financial institutions engaged in large-scale money laundering.

Fast-forward to Washington, DC, in December 2009 as Morgenthau commented on his brand-new case against Credit Suisse. He noted that it was unprecedented for a Swiss bank and the Swiss government to provide the kind of access to data and records that they did as soon as it became clear that his investigations were serious and that he was amassing evidence that could lead to a major prosecution:

> The standards of transparency have come a long way since I first began investigating financial crime in the 1960s. From secret Swiss and Liechtenstein accounts then, to the conduct of BCCI in the 1980s, to this year's actions involving Iranian banks, the standards of transparency have risen, and we expect more from international financial institutions today than ever before.

Credit Suisse's transgressions in this regard were severe—they intentionally hid the involvement of Iranian banks for almost two billion dollars in U.S. dollar transactions. But, to their credit, from the time we contacted them they gave us excellent cooperation and a high degree of transparency, as well as detailed analysis from their internal investigation. The message to other banks involved in similar practices should be clear: if you are engaged in sanction-busting misconduct, you should self-report, clean up your shop, and give us a full accounting. That is what we should expect and demand from major international banks.[1]

Curbing corruption demands the full force of a legal system that is ethical, widely respected, and headed by people as fearless and as skilled as Robert Morgenthau. That may well be a great deal to ask. Yet one can take heart both from the real progress that Morgenthau reported and from the fact that in an increasing number of countries we are seeing remarkable judges and public prosecutors come to the fore with a ruthless determination to combat corruption.

CORRUPTION AND JUSTICE

The number-one priority in the fight against corruption rests in the rule of law. Where the legal systems fail to enjoy public respect, fail to be seen by the general public as honest and fair, and where it is seen as a mere pawn of corrupt political leaders, then prospects for curbing corruption are bleak.

The World Justice Project's "Rule of Law Index 2011," directed by Alejandro Ponce, is a remarkably innovative research project that assesses the state of justice in dozens of countries around the world. As used by the World Justice Project, the rule of law refers to a rules-based system in which the following four universal principles are upheld:

- The government and its officials and agents are accountable under the law.
- The laws are clear, publicized, stable, and fair, and protect fundamental rights, including the security of persons and property.
- The process by which the laws are enacted, administered, and enforced is accessible, fair, and efficient.
- Access to justice is provided by competent, independent, and ethical adjudicators, attorneys, or representatives, and judicial officers who are of sufficient number, have adequate resources, and reflect the makeup of the communities.

The question that needs to be asked is this: Do people believe that they get treated fairly and honestly by the judiciary and the police?

When the answer is yes, then corruption is either at manageable levels or can be brought within such levels. As TI stressed in its *2007 Global Corruption Report*:

> Transparency relating to the judiciary serves to increase public knowledge about the judicial system, provides recourse for redress when problems occur and decreases the opportunities for corrupt practices. It is vital that appointments, complaints and disciplinary processes are transparent and objective, and that the public has a means of challenging decisions where they are unreasonable or improper. Transparency also bolsters judicial independence. A diligent judge, for example, can demonstrate that they are acting in accordance with the law. In addition, information on judicial conduct and discipline enables the public and civil society to act as a check against arbitrary executive interference.[2]

An effective legal system is one that is as free as possible from political pressure and interference. With a background running from Aristotle through Aquinas, Locke, Hume, and Rousseau, the architects of the US Constitution and Bill of Rights were acutely aware of the tendency of politicians, if given the chance, to abuse their offices. They understood that all in government needed to ultimately be accountable to those they should serve. They saw the need for the judiciary to play a separate and equal role in the balance of political power.

At times, governments and even aid agency officials suggest that cultures and traditions are very different from those based on the wisdom of the "social contract" and the United States' separation of powers and that, therefore, alternatives to Western concepts of democracy are legitimate. This can take one down a slippery path to even suggesting that there can be "benign dictators." Absent the checks and the balances, however, the verity of Lord Acton's dictum is all too evident: "Power tends to corrupt and absolute power corrupts absolutely."

AN INDEPENDENT JUDICIARY

Politicians have much to fear when the judiciary is independent, including the fear that their abuse of office will be investigated, prosecuted, and, if the facts add up, also punished. It took fantastic skill and amazing courage for a small team of public prosecutors and honest judges in Peru a few years ago to bring corruption charges against the country's two most powerful leaders and to see that they received long prison terms for their crimes.

The jailing of General Vladimiro Montesinos and President Alberto Fujimori was a victory for the rule of law. It sent shockwaves across Latin America, especially as Fujimori's efforts to dodge the law were rebuffed when the government of Chile agreed to extradite him to Peru for trial. This was the first such extradition of a former head of state by one Latin country to another. It demonstrated that the anticorruption forces were gaining ground.

The crucial importance of the rule of law and of honest judges in the anticorruption context is all the greater because it impacts not only top officials, but all citizens. Kamal Hossain, former minister of law and minister of foreign affairs in Bangladesh, brings the point home. Writing in the TI *2007 Global Corruption Report*, Kamal noted with regard to judicial corruption and the suffering of ordinary people that

> this resonates particularly strongly for me, coming from Bangladesh where the executive controls the appointment, promotion, posting, transfer and discipline of all judges in the lower tiers of the judiciary. This defies both the constitution and public demands that these powers should be the sole prerogative of the Supreme Court, thereby ensuring the separation of political power and the impartial delivery of justice. Without formal separation of the executive and the judicial branches of government, systemic corruption threatens to swamp the courthouse. A household survey conducted by TI-Bangladesh in 2005 found two thirds of respondents who had used the lower tiers of courts in the preceding year paid average bribes of around $108 per case. That amounts to about a quarter of the annual average income in one of the world's poorest countries. Such courts have been reduced to the status of bartering shops, with the lowest bidder risking his or her rights to property, status, or worse, liberty.[3]

The challenge for the anticorruption movement in most countries is to ensure that anticorruption laws are enforced and that legal redress for injustice can be secured through a functioning judicial system. As Kamal Hossain has noted, "In my country the executive controls the appointment, promotion, posting, transfer and discipline of all judges in the lower tiers of the judiciary. This defies both the constitution and public demands that these powers should be the sole prerogative of the Supreme Court, thereby ensuring the separation of political power from the impartial delivery of justice."[4]

Corruption in the judiciary, which is commonplace in many countries, goes beyond bribe-taking judges. Often, court staff members are bribed to lose cases or slow down judicial processes. Bribery can help to make the court systems inefficient, which plays into the hands of corrupt officials awaiting trial. I recall a meeting some fifteen years ago with a group of Russian judges who had been invited to Washington, DC, by the US Department of State. They were being trained by experts from the American Bar Association. They confided, however, that they were very poorly paid and their court staff was even worse off. It was difficult, lamented one of the judges, to effectively prosecute a rich tycoon for tax evasion when he was willing to use bribes amounting to a tiny fraction of his tax liabilities to ensure that his case was "misplaced" in the court's administrative files!

Creating and sustaining an independent and well-resourced judiciary may seem unrealistic in many countries. But determination can overcome the naysayers. Pakistan is one of the most corrupt countries in the world. For many years the political leaders of the country have waged war on the Supreme Court and the lawyers that support an independent judicial system. In recent times, the lawyers have fought back.

The decline in public support that President Pervez Musharraf confronted in Pakistan in 2007 and 2008 was due in large part to his actions to place Supreme Court leaders under arrest and appoint men on whom he could count. His attempt to introduce a state of emergency and thus sideline the courts backfired and contributed to his resignation in August 2008.

As Musharraf moved on the Supreme Court, respectable lawyers in formal suits and stiff collars and ties took to the streets and clashed with the police and protested. Having played so important a role in ousting Musharraf, the lawyers were in no mood to give his successors an easy time. To his dismay, President Zardari had no choice other than to reinstate the former Supreme Court chief justice Iftikhar Muhammad Chaudhry and his senior colleagues in 2009. The Supreme Court demonstrated its independence by goading the parliament into lifting the amnesty against prosecution for corruption that had earlier paved the way for Zardari's return to Pakistan from exile.

Individual situations from Pakistan to Peru of independent judges and prosecutors taking on formidable politicians and winning are encouraging anticorruption activists everywhere. News of such victories travels fast through the worldwide web. Moreover, rising support for strengthening the judiciary in developing countries has been one of the positive aspects of Western aid in support of governance reforms in recent years. Pioneering work in training judges, for example, has been undertaken in many countries by the International Development Law Organization, based in Rome.

A major effort pursued by civil society organizations in many countries is to make the existing judicial system more transparent. The more the public understands how the legal system works, what rights the citizen can enjoy, and what recourse to mistreatment is available, the greater becomes the public pressure on governments and the courts to build a publicly accountable system of justice.

COURAGEOUS PUBLIC PROSECUTORS

Crucial to the effective anticorruption work in this area is support for a strong set of public prosecutors. They need to have the protection of independent judges and the stature and resources to confront intimidation by organized crime and powerful politicians alike. Such powerful offices of public prosecutors exist in far too few countries today. The prosecutions of former President Fujimori in Peru and former President Chiluba in Zambia were important in building public respect among ordinary citizens for their own national legal system. Nonpolitically driven prosecutions (unlike Chinese-type and Russian-style show trials) of a few prominent public figures from time to time can have a vital role in establishing public confidence in the legal system and send the message that nobody is above the law.

Cases have to be carefully selected and excellently prepared if public respect and confidence in the legal system is to be increased. When rogues go free because prosecutors have mismanaged their briefs, then corrupt government officials and those who bribe them can feel emboldened. For example, US Department of Justice prosecutors bungled the prosecution on assorted corruption charges of the late senator Ted Stevens of Alaska, who, as the former chairman of the Senate's Appropriations Committee, was one of the most powerful politicians in the country. He was found guilty by a jury in his trial, but before he was even sentenced the judge dismissed the whole case when an internal Justice Department investigation revealed serious misconduct with regard to the evidence by the prosecutors themselves. By the end of 2009, there were some thirty ethics cases pending before the ethics committees of the US Congress—there was no action on most of them. No wonder Americans take a skeptical view of the idea of political integrity.

The reputation of the US Justice Department was modestly repaired with the prosecution some months after the Stevens case of former congressman William Jefferson of Louisiana. In November 2009, he was sentenced to thirteen years in prison on corruption charges. It was not just the most severe sentence for corruption ever imposed on a US congressman but also the first time that any US politician had been indicted for violating the FCPA, having allegedly been involved in various bribery schemes with African politicians. He was found guilty of eleven counts of bribery, racketeering, and money laundering.

The public anger with corruption in politics in the United States has been the major influence on the work of many public prosecutors across the country. As the public sees the blatant influence of special interests on politics and the vast sums spent by these interests on election campaigns, the ill smell of political ethics rises. Public prosecutors have responded. In Illinois, Florida,

Louisiana, New York, and New Jersey, the number of arrests of officials and local politicians for bribery and kickbacks, mostly related to public contracts, has increased significantly.

No public prosecutor in the United States has a more powerful record of going after top politicians than Patrick Fitzgerald. Based in Chicago, Illinois, he was a federal prosecutor for fifteen years until his retirement from government service in June 2012. In a stint as a special prosecutor he investigated the White House (specifically, the Office of the Vice President) and successfully prosecuted Vice President Richard Cheney's chief of staff and special advisor to President George W. Bush, Lewis "Scooter" Libby for perjury. Libby was sentenced to prison in January 2007.

Governor George Ryan of Illinois was found guilty in 2006 of multiple charges of illegal sales of government licenses, contracts, and leases. He is now serving a six-and-a-half-year prison sentence, as are dozens of other officials from his administration who were all successfully investigated and prosecuted by Fitzgerald and his associates. Then Fitzgerald went after Ryan's successor, Rod Blagojevich, who is now starting a fourteen-year prison stretch for corruption.

There are other US prospectors who have been just as prominent as Fitzgerald in recent times. Former New York attorney general Eliot Spitzer made headlines as he went after corrupt New York State politicians, as well as crooked tycoons. His successor and now New York state governor, Andrew Cuomo, has been ruthless and successful in exposing major corruption among some of the state's most powerful politicians and civil servants.

Just as persistent are the prosecutors in Italy. For years they went after the mafia and some of the country's most prominent politicians, and the investigations of extensive corruption changed the Italian political map. In late March 1995, TI held its annual meeting in Milan and I shall never forget the comments made there by Gerardo Colombo, the Milan public prosecutor. He noted that 7,800 people were under investigation after five hundred had been put on trial and most were convicted. Despite the numbers, what stunned me was his candor in saying that

> there was still a long way to go. The magistrates had discovered only a small part of a very big picture. So it was that people were continuing to pay bribes into the present, notwithstanding the examples being made under the Clean Hands operation. Public servants and politicians were continuing to receive kickbacks.

Colombo and his associates continued the fight. They exposed corruption at the highest levels of the major political parties and the government. They traced key links between major enterprises and politicians and organized crime. They faced threats and public denigration by the very politicians who were the most corrupt. They persevered. Did they clean up Italian politics?

The result of their efforts in part was the creation of new political parties and the rise of Silvio Berlusconi, who first became Italy's prime minister from 1994 to 1995, then again from 2001 to 2006, and then again from 2008 until late 2011. Throughout his political life he has been dogged by investigations by Italian prosecutors of corruption.

The tussle between justice and Berlusconi highlights the best and the worst situations. For two decades the most powerful political forces in the country have been doing combat with a relatively small group of effective and courageous public prosecutors, whose license to investigate has been supported by an equally courageous group of judges. Berlusconi has sought to both intimidate the state lawyers and humiliate them in the media (he owns much of the most popular press and TV in Italy), as well as using his power to convince parliament to grant him immunity from prosecution. But the prosecutors and the judges keep coming back with ever greater determination.

Remarkable public prosecutors in developing countries have come to the fore in recent years whose courage and example are a shining light to prosecutors everywhere.

Dr. Ana Cecilia Magallanes Cortez was seriously ill when she traveled from Peru to Guatemala to a TI conference to receive the 2006 TI Integrity Award. She came because she wanted the world community to understand the struggle that a government prosecutor must face to bring the most powerful political and military figures in a country to justice when they abuse the public trust for their personal gain. She wanted people to understand that her fight and those of her courageous colleagues—notably, Peruvian prosecutor José Ugaz—had to be fought and was worth all the personal hardships it involved.

Ana Cecilia, who died in 2007, played key roles along with Ugaz in the successful prosecution of former Peruvian president Alberto Fujimori and his chief collaborator, military leader Vladimiro Montesinos. Both are now serving long prison terms.

As secret tapes of the bribe paying became public in Peru, Fujimori fled to Japan, which had no extradition treaty with Peru. The first task of the prosecutors was to bring him back to face justice. The Japanese gradually became quite unhappy about being seen across Latin America as harboring a fugitive, while Fujimori became convinced that he could make a grand political comeback. He moved to Chile to plan his return to political victory in

Peru. But the Peruvian prosecutors kept pushing and pushing for justice, and to Fujimori's amazement, the Chileans agreed to extradite him so that he could stand trial in Peru. It marked a milestone in ending impunity, says José.

The initial investigations into the grand corruption perpetrated by Fujimori and Montesinos involved enormous personal risks. Each of them had ruthless networks of associates. José and Ana Cecilia and their small group persevered. Late in the battle the heat became so great that José moved to Washington, DC, for a time. The prosecutors were swift to understand that if their work was to have a real impact, then they had to do more than go after the corrupt bosses; they had to map the entire embedded network of corruption across the government bureaucracy and use the law to dismantle it.

In the end, apart from jailing the two major leaders of the grand Peruvian corruption, the courts succeeded in prosecuting fourteen generals from the armed forces and police, the former president of Congress, the former federal public prosecutor (their boss), Supreme Court justices, and judges and prosecutors at various levels along with media owners. The work of the prosecution team saw the recovery of over $250 million in stolen funds.

Argentina has also produced courageous prosecutors who have left their mark on reforming the legal system and using it to hold government abusers accountable. I first met Luis Moreno Ocampo in the early 1990s when he headed Poder Ciudadano, which he had established in 1989 and which became the TI national chapter of Argentina. He displayed amazing courage in the 1980s as a young lawyer in playing leading roles in the prosecution of the generals that had tyrannized his country. Investigating their horrendous crimes left a deep impact. As he pursued investigations and trials in the public interest, he became convinced that one of the gravest plagues in his country was corruption. His dedication to the cause of anticorruption would place him repeatedly under political pressures and win him many enemies.

Luis, for example, had been a candidate for a very prominent international legal position some years ago, but his prospective United Nations employers could not get Argentina's political leaders at the time to agree. Only a change of government ensured that he would be able to accept the post as the first chief prosecutor of the International Criminal Court (ICC) when he was elected in early 2003.

At Poder Ciudadano, Luis would pursue detailed investigations of corruption in many parts of the public sector. They would, for example, investigate the charges that municipal hospitals would make for medications and assorted services and compare these and highlight often massive differences between closely proximate hospitals. He would ensure, as he continued to do at the ICC, that the harsh facts were publicized and told their own story.

From the courts of Milan in Italy to those of Lima, Peru, courageous prosecutors, backed by honest judges, have withstood enormous personal pressures and threats to lead investigations and trials into corruption by powerful top government officials. Their work goes hand in hand with the activism seen in civil society organizations. It is no coincidence that some of those courageous prosecutors from developing countries have been active in TI—Ocampo was highly active prior to his ICC appointment, while Ugaz was elected to the TI global board of directors in October 2011.

Public prosecutors need public support to persevere in the face of the kind of intimidation that a Berlusconi can unleash. Their ability to win is getting stronger because of the new tools at their disposal, and this is very good news for the anticorruption fight.

Increasingly, it is the hard drives of computers that are providing key pieces of evidence. E-mails recovered by prosecutors have become the smoking guns at trials. Strengthened cooperation between prosecutors in different national or international jurisdictions—notably, in sharing e-mails between bribe payers and bribe takers—is enhancing the ability of prosecutors to win complex corruption cases.

ENDEMIC POLICE GRAFT

While this is very good news and augurs well for the future, the successes of the judges and prosecutors are to no small degree dependent on the effectiveness of the police. Here the news is discouraging.

Police corruption affects nearly every Nigerian, though it disproportionately impacts Nigeria's poor. Those in precarious economic situations, scraping out a living day to day, are more susceptible to police extortion because of the profound effects that unlawful detention, or the mere threat of arbitrary arrest, have on their livelihoods . . . criminal acts by the police, coupled with their failure to perform many of their most basic functions, severely undermine the rule of law in Nigeria. The police routinely extort money from victims to investigate a given criminal case, which leaves those who refuse or are unable to pay without access to justice. Meanwhile, criminal suspects with money can simply bribe the police to avoid arrest, detention, or prosecution, to influence the outcome of a criminal investigation, or to turn the investigation against the victim. Ordinary Nigerians are further denied equal protection under the law due to a widespread practice whereby senior police officers sell for their own personal enrichment police protection to Nigeria's wealthy elite. By the inspector general of police's own account, in 2009 at least 100,000 police officers were working as personal guards for the wealthy, at the expense of the majority. In addition, the abject failure of the police to provide for the security of ordinary citizens has led some communities to turn for protection to armed vigilante groups who often operate outside the law and commit further abuses.[5]

According to TI's Global Corruption Barometer in 2010, 34 percent of survey respondents with lower incomes said they bribed the police, while the rate among higher-income people was 27 percent on average. Sean Rayment, the defense correspondent of the London *Daily Telegraph*, has repeatedly reported on police corruption, especially in Afghanistan, as he sees this corruption as one of the main problems in controlling the opium trade there. For example, on May 20, 2012, he reported that among "the Afghan National Police . . . many of their officers were drug addicts and the organization as a whole was riddled with corruption."[6]

In many of the poorer countries of the world the police are paid so badly, often at levels below a living wage, that extorting cash from the public at large is seen by the police as a necessity. Most Nigerian policemen, for example, earn less than $200 a month and many have to pay for their own fuel and telephones. In a story in the *Wall Street Journal*[7] it was reported that according to a study by the International Society for Civil Liberties and the Rule of Law in Nigeria, bribe-seeking police in the small state of Anambra alone in 2008 collected $4.5 million from some seventy checkpoints.

Routine extortion of the poor is easiest because the poor have the fewest means of filing effective complaints and resisting police pressures. Better training and emphasis on integrity and good values no doubt can greatly help with raising the self-respect of policemen and strengthening an anticorruption culture within the police. Projects launched in Uganda by civil society organizations in conjunction with the police in these areas have been promising. Yet the key to reform rests to no small degree on pay.

The international development agencies have done very little to examine this issue and to strongly encourage the governments that they assist to make major priority initiatives to strengthen the cultural training and the pay of the police. Absent major reforms in this area, the prospects of reducing police corruption are low. This is particularly tragic because the police are the most frequent and common face of the legal system that citizens routinely encounter, and if the police are totally corrupt, then the public will have a cynical view of the integrity of the legal system as a whole, irrespective of courageous efforts by some judges and public prosecutors.

Almost every effort to establish systems of transparent, accountable, and honest justice in countries has been either initiated by the establishment or from international pressures, such as those pushed by aid agencies. Anticorruption commissions have been created in many countries as a result, but very few of them have had more than a token impact. Where they have been a success, such as in Hong Kong and in Singapore, it is because they could rely on strong support from noncorrupt judiciaries.

One light at the end of a dark tunnel of corrupted legal systems today is coming from the grassroots. In a rising number of countries people are becoming engaged in efforts that are having a growing impact to voice their complaints, to share their experiences as victims of corruption, and to seek broad support for their efforts to secure justice (see chapter 12). The catalysts for these positive efforts are civil society organizations in more than fifty countries that are building Advocacy and Legal Advice Centers (ALACs) and commanding attention from national governments.

ESTABLISHING DEMOCRACY

Ultimately, the success of efforts to curb corruption on a sustainable basis—nationally and internationally—will depend on the existence of strong and independent legal systems that can enforce laws that criminalize the abuse of public office for private gain. This can only evolve if countries have strong democratic institutions that ensure the checks and balances between branches of the government and include effective nongovernmental watchdogs, from the media to civil society organizations and independent academic institutions.

In the foreword to the *TI Source Book 2000*, Nobel Peace Prize winner Oscar Arias Sanchez from Costa Rica noted:

> Under totalitarian regimes, corruption is often directly linked to human rights violations. In Latin America, many dictators justified their governments for years by pointing the finger at corrupt regimes in the recent past. These same dictatorships were often fronts for thieves and embezzlers. And in each of these cases, citizens and journalists were deprived of the legal resources necessary to expose the presumptuousness and corruptness of their government to a competent and credible judicial system. But, at the same time, corruption is best exposed, and best attacked, in a democracy. Corruption can only be examined and eradicated in an environment of pluralism, tolerance, freedom of expression, and individual security—an environment that only democracy can guarantee.[8]

For many activists the fight to curb corruption is a vital, if not sufficient, ingredient in the challenge to build sustainable and vibrant democracy. The conviction to tread this path can burn so deep that activists have and do take great personal risks. Devendra Panday, a former minister of finance in Nepal, the founder of TI-Nepal, and a veteran of public protests and time in Nepalese prisons, has often stressed to me that the ties between justice, anticorruption, and fighting for democracy are inseparable. He has had to try and deal on the one side with a corrupt monarch and on the other with Maoist rebels and has sought time and again to assert that core principles of transparency and governmental accountability need to be paramount.

Devendra is acutely aware that democracy is by no means immune from corruption and that too often countries race to embrace democracy by calling elections without having carefully considered what democracy needs to entail. Rushed, multiparty elections absent rules of the democratic game that the public at large views as fair and balanced may well prove to be counterproductive.

The first free elections in the Palestine territories in January 2006 saw Hamas win a decisive majority in the Palestinian Legislative Council. The key issue in the elections was the conviction of most Palestinians that the Fatah party was riddled with corruption. Hamas had brought basic services to people and its officers did not extort bribes from ordinary citizens. Following the election, Hamas had the opportunity to build on its gains, to become a major legitimate voice by renouncing violence and the destruction of Israel. It chose not to do this, nor to respect the continuing Fatah rule in Gaza. Soon, Hamas and Fatah were on a collision path that would end violently with Hamas seizing control of Gaza, arresting Fatah leaders there and critics of its administration.

In 1998, in Venezuela, the people voted for an unknown young soldier who had come to power at first in a coup, Hugo Chavez, for the sole reason that they were disgusted with the old establishment governments that for years had been enriching the elite of Venezuela while doing nothing in this oil-rich nation for the poor. Chavez appeared to be the youthful antidote to corruption. Chavez has proved, however, that he cares little for democracy; he hounds opponents and he and his cronies have gained great wealth from their powerful government positions.

Many people engaged in the anticorruption fight see a seamless connection to working to build democratic institutions. They share with so many other activists in civil society a passion for truth, liberty, and justice. They work for increased transparency across the activities of government and for increased accountability by the public sector to the people at large.

Delia Ferreira Rubio has brought knowledge and experience about political systems in her country of Argentina to the fight against corruption and helped to secure major changes. Her impact has resulted in international organizations lining up to convince her to visit hosts of countries and share her research and her wisdom. Over the last twenty years, Delia has published books, lectured at universities, worked with politicians and the Argentine Congress, served as president of Poder Ciudadano (TI's national chapter), and been twice elected to TI's international board of directors. She admits, even with a smile, "My mother worries about me. My telephone is tapped and 'friends' call me to advise me not to go on a TV program or make publicity. But, you know, my grandfather was a politician, and I come from a politically active family, so I must be engaged."

Delia is concerned that corruption in party political funding and in the financing of election campaigns is a major source of instability and grand corruption in many countries. During an interview, she told me, "The challenges of money and politics are huge in Latin America. Not so long ago, we did not have the laws to end the opacity in political finance in our country. Now, the situation has improved. We have also developed Internet-based systems to monitor election finance and to share the information with the press, which makes people aware. For me, the issues of opacity in election funding and the building of democratic institutions are intertwined. We need to be very concerned with the substance of democracy. This relates to investigations that I have done into abuse of power and to the prevalence of the use of decrees by the president. To secure change you need passion and courage."

Delia notes that tools to be used to reduce the influence of money in politics and to increase transparency have to be applied to local conditions; there is no toolkit that everyone can just use. In dozens of countries today civil society organizations are striving to end what Delia calls the "opacity in political finance." They are pushing forward with investigative work, public-awareness campaigns, and broad-based efforts to secure transparency and accountability changes across the political board. It was a revelation to the Kremlin, and particularly Prime Minister Putin, to discover the scale of public outrage over his efforts to rig the 2011 parliamentary elections. The massive protests by tens of thousands of Russians reflected the effectiveness of many civil society organizations and determined individuals to raise public awareness about the need for honest and open democratic systems and clean politics.

In late 1999, TI's first managing director, Jeremy Pope, sought to take stock of all that the eight-year-old movement had learned about fighting corruption from literally scores of workshops and research reports that TI had been engaged with. The detailed results, articulated in the form of a large number of essays on specific approaches to curbing corruption in many different areas of government and business, were published in *TI Source Book 2000*, which can be found online. Pope's conclusions are as valid and central today as they were a decade ago when he first compiled them. The elements of a serious and concerted anticorruption reform effort need to include the following:

1. A clear commitment by political leaders to combat corruption wherever it occurs and to submit themselves to scrutiny (revisiting the need for immunities and privileges which may shield some from legal process)
2. Primary emphasis on prevention of future corruption and on changing systems (rather than indulging in witch-hunts)

3. The adoption of comprehensive anticorruption legislation implemented by agencies of manifest integrity (including investigators, prosecutors, and adjudicators)
4. The identification of those government activities most prone to corruption and a review of both substantive law and administrative procedures
5. A program to ensure that salaries of civil servants and political leaders
   adequately reflect the responsibilities of their posts and are as compar-
   able as possible with those in the private sector
6. A study of legal and administrative remedies to be sure that they
   provide adequate deterrence
7. The creation of a partnership between government and civil society
   (including the private sector, professions, and religious organizations)
8. Making corruption a "high-risk" and "low-profit" undertaking (i.e.,
   increasing both the risk of being detected and the likelihood of appropriate punishment thereafter)
9. Developing a "change management scenario" that minimizes the risks
   to those who may have been involved in "petty" corruption and that
   wins the support of key political players (whose participation may be
   crucial) yet which is seen by the public as fair and reasonable in all the
   circumstances (blanket amnesties can trigger riots in the streets; equally, a blanket imposition of legal penalties can lead into the quicksands
   of political oblivion)

It is the combination of each of these key points that can create the open
societies where justice is fair and independent and respected, where justice
can combat abuses of power in the name of the public at large and meaningful democracy can blossom. In the long term, this task demands reaching
beyond institutional arrangements to build a culture of integrity across all
aspects of public life. Governments need to set about instilling an anticorruption culture across all layers of the public sector and reach beyond so that
young people can learn to look up to public servants, respect good government, and see honesty in government as a badge of honor.

Geo-Sung Kim, a veteran human rights advocate in South Korea and for
several years a member of the TI international board of directors, has been a
leading advocate of involving young people in anticorruption programs. He
has had a significant influence in a number of Asian countries in starting to
strengthen awareness of how vital youth programs can be to the long-term
development of governmental integrity cultures and practices.

Creating a strong integrity national culture is not easy, but New Zealand,
Sweden, Finland, and Norway are fine models worthy of emulation everywhere. Year after year, these countries have been ranked at the very top of
the TI Corruption Perceptions Index, as being seen across the globe as the

cleanest of all nations. And nations that can develop such a culture and embed it into their institutions of power, from government to business to civil society, including organized labor and religious institutions, will be best positioned to enjoy the full fruits of democracy.

Few people engaged in the war on corruption would disagree with the wisdom of Professor Michael Johnston of Colgate University in the United States, who has argued:

> A look at societies where corruption is under control, or is moderate in scope at most, makes it clear that citizen participation, honest competitive elections, mechanisms of accountability, and a strong, active civil society are essential parts of the anti-corruption package. Where citizens participate as partners, demanding good government and rewarding those who provide it, political will is backed up and rewarded by significant incentives. Accountability works because major interests in state and society share an interest in it. Bad or corrupt governments are punished at the polls while those who govern well have the opportunity to take credit for their accomplishments. Legal punishments are augmented by social sanctions ranging from widespread public disapproval of corrupt officials and their private partners to more specific kinds of penalties imposed by trade and professional associations. The law itself enjoys a legitimacy and broad-based support that grows, not out of fear of punishment alone, but out of a general sense that people live better and economies are more likely to flourish where the rule of law is secure.[9]

NOTES

1. Speech by Robert Morgenthau at a Global Financial Integrity dinner in his honor in Washington, DC; notes by the author. Also see full details in the December 15, 2009, press release issued by the Office of the District Attorney of New York County, "District Attorney Morgenthau Announces Deferred Prosecution Agreement with Credit Suisse," http://manhattanda.org/press-release/district-attorney-morgenthau-announces-deferred-prosecution-agreement-credit-suisse.

2. Transparency International, *Global Corruption Report 2007—Corruption in Judicial Systems* (Cambridge: Cambridge University Press, 2007).

3. Kamal Hossain, "Foreword," *Global Corruption Report 2007—Corruption in Judicial Systems* (Cambridge: Cambridge University Press, 2007).

4. Hossain, "Foreword."

5. From "Everyone's In On the Game: Corruption and Human Rights Abuses by the Nigeria Police Force," a 102-page Human Rights Watch report (New York: Human Rights Watch, 2010).

6. Sean Rayment, "Why Britain's Pledge to End Afghanistan's Deadly Heroin Trade Has Failed," *Daily Telegraph*, May 20, 2012.

7. Will Connors, "In Nigeria, a Cop Takes on Cops," *Wall Street Journal*, September 29, 2011.

8. *TI Source Book 2000* (Berlin: Transparency International, 2000).

9. Michael Johnston, ed., *Civil Society and Corruption—Mobilizing for Reform* (Lanham, MD: University Press of America, 2005).

Chapter Ten

Criminalizing Bribe Paying—It Started with Watergate

The single most important development in changing the anticorruption land-scape—indeed in initiating the international anticorruption effort—was due to Richard Milhous Nixon, the thirty-seventh president of the United States. It is an event that came well before all the other developments highlighted in this book and was crucial in setting the stage and telling giant corporations in no uncertain terms that the time had come for them to stop bribing foreign government officials.

What is remarkable is that actions taken in the 1970s in the United States to address corruption were not replicated in any form overseas until the 1990s. The US actions were totally due to one of the largest political scandals in the country's history. Watergate was seen overseas as a unique US event, as were all the legislative actions that followed it, from meaningful efforts to introduce transparency in political campaign financing to criminalizing the payment of bribes by corporations to foreign government officials.

The enactment of the US Foreign Corrupt Practices Act (FCPA), which was the first national law anywhere to make bribe paying by corporations to foreign government officials a criminal offense, was due, above all, to two men, Frank Church and Stanley Sporkin. President Jimmy Carter signed the FCPA into law in 1977. It created the template, a generation later, for the Organisation for Economic Co-operation and Development (OECD) Anti-Corruption Convention, the most recent signatory of which is Russia.

In the mid-1970s, Senator Church, a Democrat from Idaho, and Stanley Sporkin, the director of enforcement at the Securities Exchange Commission (SEC), joined forces to bring giant enterprises to their knees and expose their huge foreign bribe payments that would rock governments from Belgium to Japan. Their success in building cases against some of the most powerful multinational corporations in the world owed much to Nixon, whose "Watergate" crimes involved the illegal solicitation of funds from major corporations.

Until 1977 there was nothing in US law to prevent corporations from bribing foreign government officials to win contracts. Even after the United States enacted legislation in 1977 to change this, it took a further twenty years before any other country adopted similar legislation. For example, until the late 1990s, German companies could not only bribe foreign politicians and officials to win business without fear of any form of German prosecution but also deduct the costs of their bribe payments from their German taxes.

The number of cases brought in 2010 by the US Justice Department against US firms that paid bribes to foreign officials was eighty-three—a record. This does not suggest that the volume of bribe paying is rising. Rather, it highlights a major increase in the focus of the US authorities on the crime of foreign bribe paying, combined with an unprecedented level of international cooperation between public prosecutors in sharing evidence of corporate wrongdoing. The fines imposed on firms are at a record level and the risks that firms face of being detected are mounting (see chapter 15). Given the mood of opposing all business regulation in some US political quarters in 2011/2012, it is not altogether surprising that the US Chamber of Commerce should have launched a lobbying campaign to curb the FCPA-enforcement zeal of the US Justice Department. Memory of the scale of abuses that first led to legislating the FCPA has dimmed.

The Watergate scandal, which led to President Nixon's resignation in August 1974, resulted in part from investigative reporting as journalists discovered who had hired the burglars who broke into the headquarters of the Democratic Party in Washington's Watergate office building and where the money came from to pay them. "Follow the money" is a key dictum for every investigative reporter and in this case the trail led to a host of major US corporations that were secretly funding the Nixon reelection. Some of these companies, it subsequently transpired, also won major international contracts by bribing foreign government officials.

The sprawling Watergate hotel, apartment, and office complex on the banks of Washington's Potomac River was originally financed by an Italian controlled group, Societeà Generale Immobiliere, with links to both the Vatican and to major Italian criminal groups. One of the high-profile executives involved with the firm was an Italian banker, Michelle Sindona, who had a long history of dealings with the Vatican Bank in the 1960s and who, in the early 1970s, took control of the Franklin National Bank in New York. Franklin went into bankruptcy a couple of years later and the FBI started taking an interest in Sindona's diverse international dealings. In 1980, he was convicted in New York on sixty-five counts of fraud and perjury and other crimes and in 1984 the Italian government sought his extradition. He had not been long in an Italian prison before he died of cyanide poisoning. Put another way, the Watergate building had a few criminal scars to its name from the day its original foundations were being set.

The Democratic National Committee (DNC), preparing for the 1972 US presidential election, rented office space at the Watergate. President Nixon's associates recruited a bungling bunch of burglars to break into the DNC to obtain election campaign plans. The "Plumbers," as they were called, were caught and an odyssey started that by August 1974 led to Nixon's forced resignation. I came to Washington, DC, in March 1974 as the US economics correspondent of the *Times* of London and found myself in the immediate months and years thereafter reporting on the corporate involvements in financing the Committee for the Re-Election of the President, widely known as CREEP, and the subsequent investigations led by Church and Sporkin. It was on July 14, 1974, just three weeks before Nixon's resignation, that the US Senate's Select Committee on Presidential Campaign Activities revealed that offshore subsidiaries of major US corporations had been used to hide payments to CREEP.

American Airlines, for example, was reported to have made a $55,000 contribution to the Nixon campaign by channeling cash through a New York bank to a Swiss bank account of a Lebanese agent. The company booked the payment as a special commission in connection with used aircraft sales to Middle East Airlines. To take another example, Ashland Oil used an affiliate in Gabon in Africa to channel a $100,000 contribution via a Geneva bank. Goodyear Tire and Rubber also made use of Swiss banks to contribute a similar amount. Then, Gulf Oil made its $125,000 contribution through a subsidiary registered in the Bahamas. More importantly, there were ever noisier rumblings around the US Senate and the austere offices of the SEC that efforts were under way to expose far larger corporate bribery scandals.

The illicit payments that some of these American corporations had made to CREEP were a fraction of the total volume of bribe payments that they made overseas to government officials.

Washington in the mid-1970s was in a state of shock. People had lost confidence in the government. While Washington insiders in the press and in the corridors of Congress claimed that the system had won and that not even the president could cheat the American people, most ordinary citizens were less confident. In fact, the American political system was on the verge of a nervous breakdown. Nixon left the White House and Vice President Gerald Ford moved in. Within a month Ford had pardoned Nixon, which undermined hopes of a swift restoration of public confidence in the ethics of the nation's leaders.

This was also the time, lest we forget, when the Vietnam War was winding down with citizens across the nation despairing at the massive loss of American life in a war that growing numbers of Americans had come to view as wrong-headed. Memories were still fresh of the assassination just a few years earlier of Martin Luther King and the race riots that gripped major cities as a result—central Washington, DC, remained a place where middle-class people did not wander after dark. The Organization of Petroleum Exporting Countries (OPEC), driven by Saudi Arabia, unleashed in 1973 a vast boost to oil prices, demonstrating its monopolistic power and leading to endless lines of cars at gas stations as fuel was in short supply. The US economy was in a mess and set to get worse with inflation rising to record levels.

In the midst of this deeply depressing environment Sporkin and Church decided that this was the right time to expose the systemic corruption that drove the international strategies of the world's most powerful corporations. Perhaps, had the overall political environment not been as tested and depressed, the efforts of Church and Sporkin might have gained less traction. But if ever there was a time for a good government moral crusade, then this was it and the two leaders proved to be as determined as the most ardent crusaders had ever been.

Senator Church entered the Senate in 1957 at the age of thirty-four and was one of the first members of that legislative body to protest America's rising engagement in the Vietnam War in the early 1960s. He became a member of the Foreign Relations Committee and headed its Sub-Committee on Multinational Corporations, the vehicle he used to shine a starkly embarrassing spotlight on the likes of Exxon, Mobil, Gulf Oil, Ashland Oil, and numerous others—most notably, the Lockheed aircraft company.

The short, pudgy Sporkin was often depicted in the media as the toughest cop on Wall Street. Had Sporkin's SEC successors in recent years been half as tough as he was, and half as intelligent and as driven by a solid sense of integrity, then many of the worst scandals that have taken place may well have been detected far earlier and a swindler like Bernie Madoff, whose schemes robbed investors of up to $50 billion over the last decade, would have been caught far sooner. Many of Sporkin's successors used their SEC positions to befriend the biggest law firms and banks on Wall Street, and then jumped from the government to join one of those enterprises at many times their SEC income. Sporkin could not be bought. Following an extraordinary career at the SEC, he became the General Counsel of the CIA and then a judge.

EXPOSING CORPORATE BRIBERY

Sporkin's Enforcement Division at the SEC knew from their studies of corporate balance sheets that major American companies were using bribes, which they reported as business expenses, to win foreign deals and he hated it. But there was no specific anticorruption law that he could use to nail them. He told me in a conversation at that time that he believed that shareholders had a right to know the full details of what their companies termed as expenses and that he wanted to bring the malfeasance into the sunlight. But, as one of Sporkin's SEC colleagues also told me, it would be difficult to bring charges against firms for covering up the bribes that they were reporting as expenses and that the SEC probably would not support such actions. The law was just too fuzzy. What was required was clarity about what kinds of expenses needed to be fully and publicly reported. Sporkin was never short of finding alternative courses to attain his goals. If he could not use the SEC's powers in full, then why not use those of the US Congress instead?

Sporkin set out to publicly humiliate the bribe-paying giant corporations in order to set the stage for a future corporate antibribery law. Enter Senator Church on the scene. Sporkin's staff started to collect information on foreign bribes and quietly pass it to members of Senator Church's staff, who started to prepare public hearings. As they examined the books of major companies and cross-examined executives, they discovered at one firm after another that bribing foreign officials was widely seen as routine. Church's impact in the months that followed and through many public hearings was all the greater because of the strong support he received from other members of his Senate Committee on Multinational Corporations.

The lead Republican was Senator Clifford Case of New Jersey and next to him was Senator Charles Percy of Illinois, a former chief of a major corporation, Bell and Howell. One of the more junior members of the committee, but constantly vocal in decrying corporate bribery, was then US senator Joe Biden of Delaware, now the vice president. I was to find as a reporter that, at times when Church's staff was somewhat shy with the press, Case's staff would be helpful in leaking documents. The members of the committee knew that powerful and consistent publicity about corporate foreign bribery would, over time, help to create a broad sense of public disgust that would translate into support for tough legislation.

Gulf Oil Corporation, a major international oil company then, was in the hot seat in one of Church's early hearings in May 1975. I remember the mostly empty room and how very few journalists were in attendance to hear Gulf CEO and chairman B. R. Dorsey admit under cross-examination to a host of bribes paid to foreign leaders, including $4 million to the ruling party of South Korea. He declared that the bribes were made under intense pressure, and he noted, "This left little to the imagination as to what would occur if the company would chose to turn its back on the request."

Senator Church wagged his finger at Dorsey and declared, "This has been a dismal story that you have told. We know it and you know it." Then Senator Percy fulminated, "Corruption is the dry rot of the capitalistic system or any other system for that matter."[1]

The law as it stood had no means to punish Gulf and the company's shareholders did not appear to be greatly concerned about the ethics used to win deals. Sporkin was convinced that getting big firms to stop paying bribes demanded public humiliation and that the public had to be brought gradually to the understanding that the abuse was rampant and unacceptable. Gulf's story of bribe paying was to be just the modest opening act in the drama that he was orchestrating, but it was enough to alert editors around Washington that Church's rather obscure committee was entering the news-making business.

Next up before the committee was United Brands, which at the time was one of the largest food-processing companies in the world. The SEC charged it with hiding $750,000 of payments to Italian politicians and a further $2.5 million to General Oswaldo Lopez, then the president of Honduras. Staff on Church's committee leaked the news that investigations were mounting, embracing some of the largest US firms and spreading into Venezuela, Peru, Bolivia, Ecuador, and Italy.

At the next round of hearings, one month later, the hearing room was packed and a battery of TV cameras was in place. Executives from Ashland Oil admitted that the company had made more than $800,000 of secret payments through offshore subsidiaries to top politicians in Gabon, Nigeria, Libya, and the Dominican Republic. And so the stage was now ready for the humiliation of Exxon, at the time the world's largest corporation. In mid-July 1975, Senator Church opened a hearing by declaring, "A cancer is eating away at the vitals of Western society and that cancer is corruption."[2]

For many companies, such as Exxon, demands by host politicians for campaign contributions and other personal payments were a sordid necessity of building supply and retail networks in foreign countries. Italy, for example, was no exception. The Church hearing that honed in on Exxon produced a mass of detail on just how the company went about paying $51 million to Italian politicians through tax evasion, falsification of records, and (as Senator Church noted) "by fraud on the Italian Government." Exxon controller Archie Monroe admitted that some of the payments could well have been outright bribes. My editors back in London were getting nervous that the *Times* would be sued for libel by Exxon and others. My colleague and bureau chief, the tenacious Fred Emery, backed me to the hilt, but only the provision to the newspaper's lawyers of the actual documents from the Multinationals Committee—often provided to me ahead of the hearings by cooperative US Senate staff—would smooth the way to getting my reports published.

Directly after Exxon had faced the Senate's music, on July 16, 1975, it was the turn of its largest competitor, Mobil Oil. It had made at least $2 million of secret political payments in Italy. Grilling the Mobil executives that day was frustrating for the senators. The firm had gone to great lengths through dummy companies to hide the payments while at the same time arguing that there was nothing illegal. "We have to find a way to put an end to this epidemic of corruption," rasped Church. The next day, the Internal Revenue Service revealed that it was investigating 111 US companies for possible tax evasion related to secret overseas payments!

Soon thereafter I received a telephone call from a senior member on Senator Case's staff; "Stay tuned to what we do next—it's the big one," she declared. Sporkin and the Multinationals Sub-Committee were choreographing the final dramatic act of their play. It would involve shocking bribes by Lockheed to foreign governments.

Lockheed of California was one of the largest aerospace companies in the world. It had long been a leading contractor to the US Pentagon and to foreign governments seeking weapons systems. Its chairman in the 1960s and early 1970, Douglas Haughton, had huge ambitions. He was a gruff and blunt character who was fearless in challenging giant commercial aircraft manufacturers McDonnell Douglas and Boeing. The great opportunity, he believed (as did his rivals), lay in building long-distance, wide-body planes that could carry more people than ever before. Haughton negotiated a deal with Rolls Royce of the United Kingdom to provide the engines for just such an aircraft, the Lockheed Tristar.

But Haughton had to confront the sales forces of his rivals as they launched direct competitors, the Boeing 747 and the McDonnell Douglas DC-10. The hard fact, as each manufacturer was to discover, was that the global market was not big enough for three rivals. The pressure was greatest on Lockheed, which lacked a strong record in commercial aircraft sales. So Haughton and his colleagues resorted to bribery.

At the opening hearing Haughton challenged Senator Church by declaring that bribery was part of global business. It was the way things got done. He admitted that his firm had made foreign payments to politicians in the previous four and a half years of around $22 million. Republican Senator John Tower of Texas added that it was unfair to demand that American companies stop making bribes if foreign rivals engage in such practices.

Tower was reflecting a widespread view in US business, but it was not a universal one. William E. Simon had made a personal fortune on Wall Street, became "energy czar" under Richard Nixon during the 1973 OPEC oil crisis, and then was appointed US Treasury secretary by President Ford. He rebuffed the business apologists and memorably told the Church Committee, "To argue that bribes to foreign officials are necessary for effective competition is contrary to every principle under the free market system."[3]

Simon carried great weight. He was a conservative Republican and he spoke for many in his party who fervently believed that the illicit activities pursued by major corporations was an arrow at the heart of free market capitalism. The arguments that were being made in the Church hearings by both leading Republicans and Democrats would be repeated over the next two decades in many countries as governments struggled to determine whether foreign bribe paying by their companies should be criminalized or whether bribes should just be accepted as part of the global way of doing business.

What Haughton refused to disclose on that first day when he confronted the Church Committee was to whom the Lockheed payments had gone. But Sporkin knew. He also knew that when ready to disclose all the facts, they would blow right out of the water all the defenders in US business and politics of foreign corporate bribery. But Lockheed was determined to keep the names secret and with the assistance of its chief lawyer, William Rogers, Nixon's first secretary of state, pressures were brought to bear on the current secretary of state, Henry Kissinger, to claim that disclosures would damage America's national security interests. The SEC was being mugged. But this goaded Sporkin and Church to use the committee to circumvent the lobbies.

By mid-September 1975, evidence was released that Lockheed had used agents to make major payments to win sales from the governments of the Philippines, Iran, and Saudi Arabia. Some payments went to associates of the Shah of Iran. Major "commissions" went to a Saudi agent, Adnan Khashoggi, via Swiss and Liechtenstein bank accounts that would go on to Saudi officials who placed orders for Lockheed aircraft. Khashoggi would argue that his way of doing business was perfectly legal in the Middle East. In fact, the use of agents like Khashoggi to represent multinational corporations and fix deals with foreign governments in ways that could always be kept secret and that could easily contain payoffs to officials that would never see the light of day were commonplace. The practice remains widespread today.

The Lockheed story was the first detailed account of how foreign agents of multinational corporations operated and were used to facilitate bribe payments. In later years, issues of how to curb these activities by agents would become a major concern for both law enforcement and companies that wanted to avoid bribe paying. It led, for example, to the creation in the United States of a not-for-profit organization called Trace International that pioneered anticorruption training programs for agents, the building of registers of credible agents for use by corporations, and the development of anticorruption compliance programs in big companies that involve foreign agents.

LOCKHEED AND JAPAN

In February 1976, Sporkin and Church were ready for the showdown with Lockheed. The senator released a report accusing Lockheed of paying millions of dollars of bribes to officials in Japan, Italy, West Germany, Turkey, Switzerland, and Scandinavia, plus more than $1 million to "a high" government official in Holland (soon thereafter Dutch officials vigorously denied press reports that the recipient of over $1 million of what Lockheed liked to call "gifts" was Prince Bernhard, but a special investigation by a Dutch government commission subsequently cast doubts on the initial denials).

Soon afterward I got word that the climax was near and I called Sporkin. Usually, he was polite and even provided me with a tip or two, but this time he gruffly said, "No comment." I asked some of his staff investigators and while none of them gave me any details, none of them would deny that something big was brewing. In a vast pile of documents assembled by the Church Committee was the disclosure that Lockheed had made political payments of around $12 million in Japan to secure sales of its Tristar to Japan Airlines. It was clear that Prime Minister Kakuei Tanaka was involved in the secret payments. A political scandal erupted in Japan.

As the scandal unfolded, it appeared that there was greater "loss of face" due to the fact that the disclosures had been made public than from the bribe taking itself. Tanaka retained his seat in the Japanese parliament, the Diet, but the once most powerful politician in Japan was undone. He faced criminal prosecution and, upon being found guilty, was sentenced to four years in prison. He repeatedly appealed and while the High Court in Japan a decade later denied his appeal, it was ill health that saved him from prison.

Meanwhile, the never repentant Daniel Haughton was forced to retire from Lockheed, as was the company's vice chairman and president Carl Kotchian. Two decades later in 1995, when Lockheed was about to be bought by the Marietta Company of Maryland, the latter insisted that Lockheed first settle yet another huge bribery case involving Egypt. The new joint enterprise paid a fine to the US authorities of $24 million. At that time, the Marrietta Company's CEO and chairman was Norman Augustine, a towering leader for excellence in corporate governance and business ethics.

In the months that followed the Tanaka revelations a series of reports from the US government and statements by an array of companies, such as ITT and Northrop, confirmed the sense across the power corridors of Washington that legislation was needed.

Despite the forceful condemnation of corporate bribery by Democrats and Republicans alike in the Congress, the FCPA was widely seen in US business as unfair. It was depicted as placing US firms at a competitive disadvantage to foreign bribe-paying rivals. In the early 1980s, as the Reagan administration took office with strong pro-business policies, major US firms sought to quietly have the FCPA either repealed in its entirety or watered down. They won a modification in the law to permit "facilitating payments," but they failed to get the law repealed. The memories of the Church Committee hearings, especially the Lockheed scandal, were too strong.

Ever practical, in the course of the 1980s, US business gradually started to change its tactics. Firms started to lobby the government to press for international agreements that would take the FCPA global and, according to business lawyers, create a level playing field where all multinationals faced criminal charges if they bribed foreign government officials. The effort was never a major priority for US business because it was clear that the Reagan administration did not share any of the Carter administration's zeal when it came to going after bribe-paying US corporations.

The 1980s saw very few US prosecutions under the FCPA. The Department of Justice and the SEC both complained that they were understaffed, that this was not a Reagan administration priority, and, importantly, that they could not get cooperation overseas to build solid cases.

Giant US oil companies, despite having been exposed for bribery in the Church Committee hearings of the 1970s, were secretive about the deals they made in the Middle East and Africa to secure oil concessions. And nobody appeared to be pressing them for information. Across Africa, Latin America, the Middle East, and Asia, assorted national political leaders (notably in oil-rich countries) accumulated staggering personal fortunes.

INTERNATIONAL SILENCE

The United Nations was silent on the subject of corruption, as was the world's largest and most powerful development assistance agency, the World Bank. The media was also not interested. (I served from 1981 to 1990 as the World Bank's chief press spokesman and as its director of information, and I cannot recall receiving questions from the Washington press about global bribery.) It was as if the Church hearings had never taken place.

As the Cold War continued, both Washington and Moscow found themselves in a seemingly never-ending struggle to win Third World friends. In that effort the powerful Kremlin and White House politicians cared not at all about corruption. The beneficiaries were men of extraordinary greed from Suharto in Indonesia to Mobutu in Congo.

Mobutu Sésé Seko, who died peacefully just before his sixty-seventh birthday in 1997, was widely known by his people in the country he called Zaire as "the Leopard." His vast country in the heart of Africa is home to staggeringly large and valuable minerals of all kinds. It has long been the focus of determined international mining companies that have used whatever means were and are necessary, mostly with the backing of their governments, to grab or buy some of Zaire's resources. The determination of the West to ensure that access to these resources remained outside of Soviet hands in the Cold War made "the Leopard" the beneficiary of great Western largesse, irrespective of the massacres that he perpetrated against his own people and the extraordinary lengths he went to plunder his government's coffers.

In the introduction to her book *In the Footsteps of Mr. Kurtz—Living on the Brink of Disaster in Mobutu's Congo,* author Michela Wrong[4] says that the longer she stayed in Zaire, "The more fascinated I became with the man hailed as the inventor of modern kleptocracy, or government by theft. His personal fortune was said to be so immense that he could personally wipe out the country's foreign debt. He chose not to, preferring to banquet in his palaces and jet off to properties in Europe, while his citizens' average annual income had fallen below $120, leaving them dependent on their wits to survive."

In the Cold War environment of the 1980s waging war against corruption was a rather hopeless affair. The FCPA was law and in time it would have a major impact. But global strategic concerns trumped matters of corporate justice in the White House in this decade, and so long as this was the case, there was scant pressure on other major industrial economies in both Western Europe and Japan to curb the propensity of their own multinational corporations to continue bribing foreign government officials to win contracts. The major global impact of the initiatives that started after Watergate to criminalize corporate bribery would only come prominently to the fore after the Cold War came to an end.

The situation was to change dramatically in the 1990s as US business put its energies into efforts to convince all other Western countries to support FCPA-type legislation and thus create a "level playing field." By 2010, however, as the Obama administration became ever more aggressive with FCPA investigations, and as the Republican Party became ever more determined to roll back all kinds of business regulation, the US Chamber of Commerce started to lobby the Congress to dilute the FCPA. It must have gone back to its mid-1970s script as it declared, "The current FCPA enforcement environment has been costly to business." It complained that FCPA investigations pursued by the US government involve companies spending "enormous sums" in legal and accounting fees, and "There is also reason to believe that the FCPA has made US businesses less competitive than their foreign counterparts who do not have significant FCPA exposure."[5]

NOTES

1. Frank Vogl, "Gulf Oil Chairman Tells 'Dismal Story' of Bribes to Foreign States," *The Times* (UK), May 16, 1975. See also, by same reporter and publication, "Huge Secret Payments by Exxon Alleged," May 20, 1975; "$750,000 Payments to Italian Politicians," May 21, 1975; "Executives Refund Oil Firm's Illegal Payments," June 27, 1975; and "Oil Firm Admits Getting Money From the CIA," July 9, 1975.

2. Frank Vogl, "How US Firm Bribed Italy's Left and Right," *The Times* (UK), July 16, 1975. See also same newspaper, "US Senate Investigator Calls for End to 'Epidemic' of Corruption by Oil Firms in Italy," July 17, 1975; "Political Bribes Paid by U.S. Firms Interest Tax Men," July 18, 1975; "Lockheed in 'Payments' Dilemma," August 4, 1975; "General Motors Admits S Korea Payments," August 5, 1975; and "Political Worries on Overseas Bribes by Companies," August 12, 1975.

3. Frank Vogl, "Mr. Simon Promises Lockheed to Raise Bribes Issue Internationally," *The Times* (UK), August 25, 1975.

4. Michela Wrong, *In the Footsteps of Mr. Kurtz—Living on the Brink of Disaster in Mobutu's Congo* (New York: HarperCollins, 2001).

5. "Restoring the Balance—Proposed Amendments to the Foreign Corrupt Practices Act," a report by the US Chamber Institute for legal reform, US Chamber of Commerce, Washington, DC, October 2010.

Chapter Eleven

Finally, Officials Embrace Anticorruption

The launching of anticorruption civil society organizations, the power of the Internet for organizing and sharing information, and, most important of all, the ending of the Cold War combined to reshape the policies of powerful official institutions and governments in the 1990s, and then on into the first decade of the twenty-first century. Reforms were consistently promoted and pushed by civil society organizations. The tempo of change and international action also benefited from the persistent anticorruption efforts of the administration of US President Bill Clinton.

This was not just because (then) Vice President Al Gore, Secretary of State Warren Christopher, Secretary of the Treasury Robert Ruben, and others deplored corruption, which they did, but also because they shared the view of US business that it was time to build a "level playing field." The United States now had the FCPA, but nobody else did, and thus, according to advocates of US business, American corporations were weakened in international competition. In addition, the Clinton administration was sensitive to mounting public concerns about taxpayer cash going from US citizens through aid agencies into the Swiss bank accounts of foreign dictators. It was time to act.

LEGACY OF COMMUNIST-ERA CORRUPTION

In July 1991, the Fund for Free Expression in Washington, DC (now part of Human Rights Watch), published a report—*Off Limits: Censorship and Corruption.* In its introduction the following events are recounted:

In November 1989, the newly-unfettered press in the German Democratic Republic hastened the end of the regime—and ultimately, the state itself—by revealing rampant self-enrichment by top government and party officials. East Germans had long understood that the regime's leaders enjoyed certain privileges, emanating from their political status, but until newspapers were freed of government control, no one had any idea of the extent to which the leaders of the supposedly austere communist vanguard had been leading lives of luxury. *Neues Deutschland*, the main party newspaper, as well as *Berliner Zeitung* and *Junge Welt*, published reports about such excesses as the 5,000-acre estate of deposed communist trade union chief Harry Tisch, who maintained a luxurious housing lodge and a 200-acre reserve for breeding wild boar. The press revealed that former party chief Eric Honecker and Gunter Mittag, who had been his top aide, maintained lavish hunting lodges at state expense near Neubrandenburg. *Berliner Zeitung* reported in late November that Mittag had been expelled from the party and would face legal action relating to his creation of a fake corporation, which acquired hard currency from East German firms that exported valuable antiquities and books.

Most damaging was the unprecedented footage on East German television of Wandlitz, the heavily wooded exclusive compound for the 23 members of the Politburo a few miles north of Berlin. Viewers saw swimming pools, saunas and greenhouses, and learned that the party elite had gardeners, two maids provided free for each house, a beauty parlor, and a store well-stocked with consumer goods generally unavailable to the proletariat. Citizens of what was formerly East Germany have hardly forgiven Honecker for these transgressions. When it was recently announced that he had left the country for medical treatment in the Soviet Union, there was widespread public protest.[1]

The ending of Communism across Central and Eastern Europe created almost a universal demand for more open, indeed democratic, government and paved the way for the explosive growth in the 1990s of anticorruption civil society groups in scores of countries, from Europe, across the Middle East, through sub-Saharan Africa, in some forty countries in Latin America and the Caribbean, and in Asia-Pacific from giant countries like India, Indonesia, and Bangladesh to the tiny islands of Vanuatu and Fiji. The 1990s would see the first international anticorruption conventions, dramatic changes in policies concerning corruption by all of the major international official organizations, such as the World Bank and the United Nations, and major shifts toward supporting good governance programs in the approaches of the major national aid agencies.

Suddenly, there was no longer any reason for Western powers to buy "friends" by using aid grants to corrupt dictators across the developing world to win their favor. The Berlin Wall was pulled down, the Soviet Union was history, Russians embraced capitalism, and the aid strategies of the United States, United Kingdom, Germany, and France—key bilateral grant-makers—came under unparalleled review.

The increasing questioning of foreign aid as the Cold War ended prompted the media and politicians to ask where so much foreign aid to poor countries had actually gone. Adding to public perceptions of huge misuse of foreign aid was an increasing number of media stories of the extravagant lifestyles of corrupt leaders from Haiti to the Philippines. In Romania, long a recipient of World Bank loans, Communist dictator Nicolae Ceausescu had built himself a one-thousand-room palace three times the size of Versailles at a cost in excess of $1 billion. From Indonesia to Zaire, staggering sums of foreign aid were widely said to have landed in the private Swiss bank accounts of national leaders.

WESTERN BLAME

It was all too easy in the early 1990s to place all of the blame for corruption in Central and Eastern Europe and across the developing world on the governments of these countries. It was easy to overlook the roles being played by bribe-paying Western corporations and by financial institutions in the West that profited from banking the illicit proceeds of Third World and ex-Soviet leaders. Moreover, the major aid agencies, from the national ones in the most advanced industrial countries to the multilateral institutions led by the World Bank, were silent on the corruption issue, as if they had no responsibility for how their funds were used—and abused—in the countries that they claimed they were helping.

Countering conventional wisdom, a rising number of experts started at about this time to become more vocal in pointing out that "the developed industrial nations of the North had much to answer for in the spreading of corruption across the developing world of the South," as globally traveled veteran businessman George Moody-Stuart stressed in TI's publication in January 1994, "Grand Corruption in Third World Development." He took the view that the habit of bribe taking and subsequently of demanding ever larger bribes by leaders of developing countries was in large measure due to the eagerness of international business executives to undermine competition through graft and kickbacks. Certainly, the manner in which top executives of giant companies discussed the routine business of paying overseas bribes in the course of the US Church Committee's hearings (see previous chapter) supports George's view.

George warned in his paper, "If the cancer of grant corruption in the South is to be eliminated, it can only be achieved by drastic surgery; and the initiative for this must come from the North."[2]

Chapter 11

THE WORLD BANK

By the 1980s the largest single source of external funding for many of the former colonies in the South was the World Bank, which had no explicit anticorruption policies, nor did it care to have any.

The World Bank is the world's largest and most dominant aid agency—headquartered in Washington, DC, it employs over ten thousand people in one hundred offices around the world; it is owned by 188 countries, whose shareholdings roughly reflect the size of their economies, with the United States as the largest single shareholder and thus the greatest influence on policy. In its fiscal year to mid-2011, the World Bank Group committed more than $57 billion in new loans for economic development purposes. The Bank is a huge tanker that turns very slowly. It is the leading intellectual and financial center of the international aid community. Its research influences thinking across the development-aid landscape and it probably has more PhDs in economics on its staff than any other institution in the world. Its policies have substantial influence on those of regional and national foreign aid agencies. Importantly, the president of the World Bank attends the summit conferences of the Group of 20, has access to government leaders across the world, and has the ability to exert considerable policy influence.

The World Bank was founded at the end World War II, and in its first half-century of existence the Bank never publicly acknowledged that billions of aid dollars were lost to corruption.

The Bank has a permanent executive board of directors appointed by governments that is cautious in all matters. The staff is organized in a highly stratified hierarchy where careers are made by accepting the status quo and not challenging policies and traditional operational approaches. In the mid-1980s, as the World Bank's director of information and public affairs, I made a trip to Kenya and on my return I sent a confidential report to my senior colleagues. I had had extensive conversations with Kenyan development experts, with Kenyan and foreign journalists, and with senior diplomats in Nairobi, and I had also visited a number of projects in rural Kenya to see how the World Bank's cash was improving people's lives.

My confidential report stressed that there were serious problems in the ways in which projects were being supervised. Some of the World Bank staff doing evaluations did so without visiting projects and just based their findings on reports from the Kenyan government. Some project evaluations were undertaken by Bank economists who had as little knowledge as I did about the complex technical issues involved in building infrastructure and where, for example, corruption could lead to use of low quality materials and shoddy work. My report also included comments by journalists that corruption in the Kenyan government was rising and that neither the diplomatic community nor the Bank appeared to be doing anything about this.

Most of the people in the top tier of the Bank who received my memorandum chose to ignore it. One vice president, however, Willi Wapenhans, who was responsible for the Middle East and North Africa, demanded that I withdraw my report. He complained about my putting pen to paper on such a controversial issue as corruption and he argued that I was unqualified to discuss issues of project supervision. He asserted that it was unacceptable for someone like me, who was not a member of the World Bank's operations staff, to circulate papers that suggested that a member government, and therefore a shareholder in the Bank, might be corrupt.

For a number of years Wapenhans had been the World Bank's vice president for East Africa and in this period he never raised the corruption issue. Earlier in his career he had senior responsibility for World Bank lending to European countries, including to the corrupt Romanian government. Executives like Wapenhans climbed the rungs of the World Bank's power structure by getting the aid funds out, making more and more loans to all and sundry, and never raising questions about corruption or democracy or human rights with the leaders of the governments with whom they negotiated World Bank projects.

Powerful bureaucrats like Wapenhans had come to see their jobs as pushing out the money to well-designed projects while being largely blind to the inadequate controls that the World Bank had in place to ensure that the cash was used honestly. He and his colleagues made minimal efforts to encourage borrowing governments to privatize industries or to look for private-sector alternatives to public utilities. They had no personal career experience with the private sector and they knew that the lending programs that they administered might decline in size, thus lowering their own prestige, if they proposed anything other than ever larger public-sector projects.

The World Bank in the 1950s and 1960s was largely staffed by expert engineers and agronomists, but under the leadership of Robert McNamara in the 1970s these experts were increasingly replaced by economists and this trend accelerated in the 1980s. At the same time, in the 1980s—as ironically a commission chaired by Wapenhans in the 1990s was to find—the World Bank was unwilling to spend sufficient cash to ensure good project supervision.

More fundamentally, top World Bank executives like Wapenhans viewed many of the senior officials in the governments they worked with as friends and they were not about to endanger their relationships by raising the corruption issue. They traveled first class, they stayed in top luxury hotels, they wined and dined with prime ministers and finance ministers and central bankers—all in the service of assisting the world's poor. Moreover, the World Bank was so supremely confident that all of its staff was honest that it saw no need to tighten its procurement monitoring systems.

From the outset in 1993, the World Bank was a top target for TI. Both Peter Eigen and I had worked at senior levels in the World Bank and we had a host of channels to the World Bank's top management. We believed that if the World Bank could adopt a strong anticorruption policy, then other aid agencies and international institutions, including the International Monetary Fund (IMF), would fall into line. We had an experienced understanding of the full scale of the World Bank's policy influence and we were determined to bring it to the anticorruption cause.

Initially, however, we were rebuffed. The World Bank's general counsel in the early 1990s, Ibrahim Shihata, told us that the subject of corruption "was too political" and could not be broached by the World Bank under its Articles of Agreement, which confined the World Bank's activities to "economic" issues. Shihata, a distinguished legal scholar, held strong views about corruption. He was a founder of the International Development Law Organization (IDLO), which has done a great deal of work training lawyers and judges in developing countries to build honest and effective legal systems. However, Shihata believed in a narrow interpretation of the World Bank's basic charter and was encouraged to take this view by Ernest Stern, the World Bank's most senior career manager. World Bank president Lewis Preston, the former CEO of the J.P. Morgan bank, was neither well versed in development issues nor interested in the corruption issue. Despite our various attempts, neither Eigen nor I could get a meeting with him.

By the spring of 1996, however, after what seemed like an eternity of campaigning by a few of us, the World Bank's leadership and its policies were set to change. Shihata had died, Wapenhans had retired, and Stern had moved to J.P Morgan. More importantly, the World Bank had a new president willing to listen to what we had to say. James Wolfensohn, multimillionaire investment banker, was not one to be intimidated by the conventional wisdom of the World Bank's staff and its executive board of directors.

Wolfensohn, an Australian Olympic fencer in his youth and a successful executive at London and New York investment banks who then built his own Wall Street investment firm, had lobbied for the leadership of the World Bank. He had campaigned to secure the sponsorship for the post from President Bill Clinton and when he was appointed in July 1995, he dove into the job with a zeal that awed the World Bank's permanent staff. He was a man on a mission. He wanted to leave his mark on history as having made a major difference in the fight against global poverty. It did not take him long to conclude that if he was to succeed, then there had to be a major reorganization of the World Bank's staff. He was impatient with a staff that consistently told him why he could not do things and how difficult it was to secure change and innovate. Temperamentally, entrepreneur Wolfensohn had little time or patience for career bureaucrats.

In January 1996, Peter Eigen had his first opportunity to meet with Wolfensohn to make TI's pitch for radical change in the World Bank's approaches to corruption. He found a well-informed and constructive listener who was keen to broaden the dialogue. He was also being pressed at the time by US Treasury Secretary Ruben to provide responses to rising media and US Congress questions about the misuse of foreign aid in general and World Bank funds in particular.

In the early spring of 1996, Wolfensohn concluded, as he told a few of us, that the World Bank had to take the lead in the anticorruption fight and the challenge now was to convince the World Bank's staff and its executive board of directors that this was the right course. He suggested that a small TI team come to the World Bank to make the case in a session scheduled from 9.00 a.m. through lunch. The audience he assembled consisted of the Bank Group's[3] top twenty-five managers.

Wolfensohn opened the meeting by saying that it was up to us to make the case that the World Bank should concern itself with corruption. He then turned the session over to us. Peter Eigen, TI's chairman, led the TI group with myself as the TI vice chairman. Our stars were Fritz Heimann, the associate general counsel of General Electric; TI managing director Jeremy Pope, the former general counsel of the Commonwealth Secretariat; and Luis Moreno Ocampo, then head of TI-Argentina.

Eigen explained the frustrations of seeing well-designed aid projects in Africa fail because of corruption. He argued that development assistance will never reach its goals so long as the World Bank and other donor agencies ignored corruption. Pope provided examples from an array of countries to show exactly how corrupt systems operated and how influential the World Bank could be to bring about change. Heimann stressed that major global corporations had key investment roles to play in the global development process, but to be effective there had to be real pressures on host governments by the World Bank in support of anticorruption reforms. He argued that the best business for the developing world results when companies are on a level playing field where none can get ahead of its competitors by paying bribes. Monitoring public-sector procurement was essential and here the World Bank could play a major role.

None of the presentations by the TI team was as effective as that given by Ocampo. With his arms constantly whirling, with his thickly accented English that at times was difficult to follow, and with the use of enormously complicated charts that sought to show how public officials extorted bribes from ordinary Argentines, he dazzled his audience. It was as much his sheer passion and the force of his character as the substance of his presentation that made the difference. He left everyone clear that whether the World Bank wanted to join the anticorruption fight or not, there was a battle raging and the good guys would win. He left the leaders of the World Bank in no doubt that if they did not join the fight, they would be seen across the world as a major part of the problem and on the side of corrupt elites.

Over lunch, Wolfensohn told us that he was sold and now he had to convince his executive board of directors. He gave the impression of being confident that he would do just that. In his World Bank annual meeting speech on October 1, 1996, in Washington, DC, he declared (perhaps recalling words spoken two decades earlier by Senator Frank Church, as well as words often used by Oscar Arias and George Moody-Stuart), "We need to deal with the cancer of corruption."

Wolfensohn went on to note, "We will support international efforts to fight corruption and to establish voluntary standards of behavior for corporations and investors in the industrialized world. . . . The Bank Group will not tolerate corruption in the programs that we support; and we are taking steps to ensure that our own activities continue to meet the highest standards of probity."[4]

GENERATING TOP-LEVEL SUPPORT

Over the course of the next twelve months, Wolfensohn campaigned to convince not only the major governments that controlled the World Bank but also other international institutions to support a robust anticorruption agenda. A vital milestone on the path was reached at the meeting of the Group of Seven Finance Ministers in Washington, DC, in spring 1997. In their final communiqué, the ministers stressed, "In view of the corrosive effects of bribery and corruption generally on the achievement of sustainable economic development, growth and stability, we welcome the increased attention to these problems in the IFIs [the official International Financial Institutions] and in the OECD." They then said, "We urge:

- The Multilateral Development Bank (MDBs) to collaborate to establish uniform procurement standards modeled on those of the World Bank and ensure strong oversight at headquarters of all facets of the procurement process;
- The IMF and the MDBs to strengthen and expand, within their own areas of responsibility, their activities to help countries fight corruption, including measures to ensure rule of law, improve the efficiency and accountability of the public sector, and promote good governance;

- The OECD countries to reach agreement on measures that will permit effective and coordinated criminalization of foreign bribery and facilitate expeditious elimination of the tax deductibility of such bribes."[5]

Wolfensohn then marched ahead, winning a total victory a few months later in September 1997 at the annual meetings of the World Bank and the IMF in Hong Kong. Corruption was the dominating development topic. The World Bank–IMF joint ministerial "Development Committee" issued a communiqué that began as follows:

> Ministers agreed that corruption and weak governance undermine macro-economic stability, private sector activity and sustainable development objectives, and may erode international support for development cooperation. They emphasized that corruption is a global problem that requires complementary actions by all countries. While stressing that member governments have the primary responsibility for combating corruption and strengthening governance, they welcomed the more active involvement of the Bank and the Fund, each within their respective mandate, in responding to member governments' requests to strengthen their institutions and performance in these areas, including the introduction of greater transparency in the public sector. They welcomed the relevant strategies and guidelines recently issued by the Bank and the Fund. The Committee stressed the importance of a consistent and even-handed approach, as well as the need to take governance issues and corruption explicitly into account in lending and other decision-making when they significantly affect project or macroeconomic and country performance. The Committee asked that the Bank and Fund report to the Committee in a year's time on the implementation of their respective strategies and guidelines.
>
> Ministers invited other Multilateral Development Banks (MDBs) to develop similar strategies and guidelines. The MDBs were encouraged, as a matter of urgency, to establish procurement procedures and oversight mechanisms of the highest standard and as uniform as possible, including anti-bribery provisions. Ministers noted the ultimate responsibility of borrowers for ensuring fair and effective procurement, and stressed the importance of MDBs increasing their assistance to help build borrower capacity and accountability.
>
> Ministers welcomed the efforts underway in other international and regional bodies to coordinate efforts to combat corruption. In particular, the Committee encouraged governments to criminalize international bribery, in an effective and coordinated way.[6]

This was the most important statement by major governments and official international agencies that had ever been made on the subject of corruption. It catapulted the issue onto the agendas of governments and aid agencies across the world. It was to lead to the IMF, the Asian Development Bank, the Inter-American Development Bank, and the European Bank for Reconstruction and Development formulating their own anticorruption policies and action plans. It served notice on the United Nations that it too had to address the corruption issue.

In the following years Wolfensohn crusaded for this cause. He gave dozens of speeches and demanded new programs and anticorruption projects from his staff. He created an internal World Bank investigative unit and he beefed up the supervision of World Bank procurement. His successors have taken up the cudgels to secure change. Change at the World Bank is slow, however, and rhetoric has consistently run ahead of action (see chapter 14).

Wolfensohn's efforts were not confined to the World Bank. He galvanized international support for anticorruption measures across the Group of Seven (the United States, Canada, France, Germany, Italy, Japan, and the United Kingdom). In so doing, he contributed significantly to another campaign that was moving toward its climax in 1997: the globalization of the US FCPA.

THE OECD ANTIBRIBERY CONVENTION

Parallel with TI's campaign to change the World Bank was a major effort to secure an international treaty to criminalize bribe paying by corporations to foreign government officials. American business, having failed in the 1980s to undo the FCPA, was now campaigning for a global effort to see that all major trading countries put a similar law in place. Maybe the motivations were different, but the objectives of TI and American business lobbies were the same when it came to this issue.

In the summer of 1993, US Secretary of State Christopher made a speech to the US Chamber of Commerce in Singapore in which he announced that the United States would campaign to see that all member countries of the OECD (the thirty most advanced industrial economies) legislated along the lines of the US FCPA to criminalize bribe paying by corporations to foreign government officials.

The International Chamber of Commerce (ICC) immediately started to mobilize as much corporate support as it could for the OECD effort. GE's Heimann was an architect of the ICC effort, just as he was of TI's enthusiasm to build strong business support for this initiative. He was now the founding chairman of TI-USA and he gathered a group of general counsels and senior executives from a range of major US corporations, including Boeing, Merck, and Enron, onto the US chapter's board of directors in an effort to strengthen the OECD campaign. GE had been fined by the US Justice Department for violating the FCPA in the 1980s and now it was the leading corporate advocate of efforts across the world to ensure that it had a level global playing field. If GE could not pay bribes, then it wanted laws everywhere that would prevent its competitors from paying bribes.

TI-USA worked hand in glove with US Undersecretary of State for Economic Affairs Daniel Tarullo (now a governor of the US Federal Reserve Board), who led the Clinton administration's efforts to secure an OECD antibribery convention, and then his successor, Al Larsen (now in private practice as a business lawyer and Heimann's successor as the chairman of TI-USA). Their skill in using every diplomatic lever they could pull to overcome powerful opposition in Europe and in Japan was formidable.

The OECD initiative was far from popular in many Western European governments. In Sweden, for example, the Bofors arms manufacturer had been caught in the 1980s in a major bribery scam involving the government of India. Swedish diplomats explained to me a decade later that it was all very well for the United States to tell its arms manufacturers not to pay foreign bribes while at the same time deploying the huge power of the White House and US embassies around the world to twist the arms of host governments to buy American products.

Sweden and other small countries, continued the diplomat, had no political and diplomatic leverage at all. He said he opposed bribery and almost all Swedes shared his view, but he could well understand that if companies from small countries wanted to compete in the arms trade with the giant American corporations, then they might resort to using kickbacks. He saw the proposed OECD Convention to bar corporate bribery as, in fact, tilting the playing field of global business in favor of the United States.

In the mid-1990s, former UK trade minister Lord Young told me in a radio discussion on corruption that British firms had to compete around the world to ensure that good jobs were maintained in the United Kingdom. To compete, he suggested, might mean doing what everyone else did and pay bribes.

Talks with UK government officials about banning bribe paying were disappointing. They did not openly say they blessed the practice, but they implied that they knew it went on and had no reason to object. The government had little confidence that its enterprises could win the big deals in fair competition, especially against the Americans and the Japanese, while they were well aware that major continental European firms routinely paid bribes.

Similar attitudes prevailed in many European governments. A senior French official told me that in the arms industry the French were forced to use bribes to compete with the major American companies, which received huge subsidies from the Pentagon and the US Export-Import Bank and enjoyed the unique advantage of—in the case of major deals—having the US president pick up the telephone to major foreign leaders and encourage them to buy American.

There was no enthusiasm in Germany for anticorruption laws. Solid German corporate executives would agree that they would never pay bribes in their private lives, but once at work the world looked different and bribery was an essential tool in global commerce. One of the remarkable mysteries was that TI's Eigen succeeded in convincing the leaders of Siemens to publicly announce that they would support an OECD antibribery pact at the very time when they were using bribes across the globe. A decade later in 2006, Siemens was found to have pushed ahead with a massive, highly organized, global bribe-paying strategy for years after the introduction of anticorruption laws.

It was a remarkable achievement of TI chapters in Europe and an admirable effort by TI's staff in Berlin, as well as by many other Europeans involved in civil society organizations, to have campaigned so effectively. They were to convince European governments to eventually support a OECD pact—US pressure alone would never have been sufficient to produce this result.

Tarullo, Larsen, and Heimann were tireless in their globe-trotting efforts to make the case for the OECD pact. Gradually, as the years went by, the momentum built toward an agreement, as was illustrated by the communiqué of the Group of Seven Finance Ministers in the spring of 1997 that explicitly urged support for an OECD Convention.

In late 1977, I went to Ottawa, together with TI managing director Jeremy Pope and TI-Canada chairman Wesley Cragg of York University, to meet with senior government officials to encourage them to take an active lead in securing an OECD agreement and become the first government to pass a national law to ratify. Top Canadian businessmen from mining company Placer Dome, GE Canada, and Bell Telephone Canada joined our presentation to senior Canadian politicians and officials. One official encouraged us hugely: then Canadian aid agency head Huguette Labelle, who a decade later, on the retirement of Peter Eigen, was elected as TI's global chair. In due course and following a great deal of work by Cragg, in particular, Canada ratified the new OECD treaty in 1998, following its general approval by OECD member countries in December 1997. At that time the OECD stated,

> The OECD Anti-Bribery Convention establishes legally binding standards to criminalize bribery of foreign public officials in international business transactions and provides for a host of related measures that make this effective. It is the first and only international anti-corruption instrument focused on the "supply side" of the bribery transaction.[7]

IMPLEMENTING THE OECD PACT

Adoption and ratification were only starting points as far as Fritz Heimann was concerned. The lifelong GE lawyer knew that the toughest job ahead was treaty enforcement. He wrote on April 21, 1998, to the head of the OECD, Secretary General Donald Johnson, and signed the letter "Fritz F. Heimann, Chair, United States Council for International Business Working Group on Bribery and Corruption." On the same day he wrote to Samuel Berger, head of the US National Security Council, now signing himself as "Fritz F. Heimann, Chairman, TI-USA." With yet another hat, this time as a leader of the ICC's effort, the indefatigable Heimann would lead the charge, which he has done ever since, to win support for effective monitoring of the enforcement of the OECD Convention. His efforts were complemented by then TI-UK chair Laurence Cockcroft and by others in TI across Europe.

As of late 2011, thirty-four OECD member countries and four nonmember countries—Argentina, Brazil, Bulgaria, and South Africa—had adopted the convention. In addition, Russia announced that it would also join the pact, following the signing by President Dmitry Medvedev at the beginning of May of legislation that criminalized foreign bribery, with a significant increase in the monetary sanctions for companies and individuals who bribe foreign public officials to gain business advantages.

As is discussed later (see chapter 14), the pact has been monitored and the findings have been disappointing. While a number of countries have seen their public prosecutors engage increasingly in sharing key information relative to investigations across national borders, the number of successful prosecutions outside of the United States of bribe-paying corporations has been modest.

For many years the UK authorities took a cynical view of the OECD agreement. Publicly they said they supported it and they claimed that their national laws were in line, but their statements were shameful hypocrisy. UK public prosecutors, under political guidance from the Tony Blair and Gordon Brown governments, determined that it was so difficult to interpret their own law that they never made a serious effort.

However, the OECD Secretariat in Paris was determined to force the UK authorities to change. It is a measure of the anticorruption momentum today that this happened and, more to the point, that the OECD was successful.

In late 2007, Prime Minister Tony Blair had shut down a Serious Fraud Squad investigation of UK arms seller BAE Systems, claiming "national security" considerations. There was outrage at this over in Paris at the headquarters of the OECD. Secretary General Angel Gurría rightly worried that if

member governments could just disregard the OECD Anti-Bribery Convention on a whim, claiming "national security," then it would not be long
before the convention was in tatters.

Gurría had played crucial roles at the helm of the Mexican government in
the late 1980s and into the 1990s in negotiating the country's massive international debts with foreign creditors and placing Mexico on a stable growth
path. He did not lack for courage. He is the first person from a developing
country to become head of the fifty-year-old OECD and he has proved to be
fearless. No sooner had Blair made his BAE announcement than Gurría went
on the attack. There was no hesitation—so typical of international civil servants—to be cautious when taking on the head of a major power on Gurría's
part. True to his character, he was blunt, forceful, and effective. He challenged the UK government both in private talks with top officials and in front
of the international media. It was just the opening salvo.

Gurría was not alone. Mark Pieth, a crusading anticorruption Swiss academic, had been chairing the OECD working group on antibribery on a part-
time basis for years and he swiftly convinced the working group of international government officials to launch an investigation of all the impediments
in the United Kingdom to meaningful anticorruption enforcement. Under
Pieth's close guidance, an extraordinary report was published in September
2008 that reads as a blatant indictment of the United Kingdom's legal hypocrisy. It called the United Kingdom's anticorruption law a sham, and demanded that the United Kingdom introduce new legislation that had teeth. It
threatened to monitor the United Kingdom's progress toward this goal on a
quarterly basis and then, just as a kicker, Pieth threatened that if the United
Kingdom did not act, other governments and aid agencies would be encouraged to take a particularly careful look at the propensity of UK firms to bribe
abroad.

Mark's leadership was forcefully followed up by a number of UK nongovernmental organizations, including TI-UK. In March 2010, the UK
Houses of Parliament enacted a brand new anticorruption law. It had teeth.

For US business, the coming into force in 1998 of the OECD Convention
was a victory in its efforts to secure a "level playing field" where all multinational companies had to abide by the same antibribery laws. More generally,
the OECD Convention, while still very much a work in progress, was a huge
step forward in developing an international anticorruption legal architecture
and bringing the major governments of the world to accept the need for
active anticorruption policies.

A LATIN PRECEDENT

The Clinton administration's concern about global corruption ran beyond the confines of business. In the spring of 1994, I received a telephone call from Richard Feinberg at the White House. He was on the National Security Council with special responsibilities for Latin America and he suggested that we get together. Much to my surprise he said he had heard about TI and the administration wanted our help.

He said he was involved in planning the first ever "Summit of the Americas," which would take place in Miami in December, and Vice President Al Gore wanted to place corruption on the agenda. He said the United States could not diplomatically raise the issue itself as this would be resented. Rather, he asked if there was a way in which TI could use its contacts in Latin America to get a government to propose that corruption be discussed.

Fortunately, TI's most prestigious advocate in the region was Nobel Peace Prize winner and Costa Rican president Oscar Arias, who jumped at the opportunity and discussed it with Ecuador's Dahik, then the chairman of TI's new Advisory Council. It was not long before the US State Department received an official request to place the issue on the summit's program.

In the immediate months before the summit, TI-USA's then managing director, Nancy Boswell, led TI efforts to mobilize civil society support for what had the potential of being the first ever declaration by heads of state of developing countries to take actions against corruption. While Nancy worked the nongovernmental organizations, the US State Department and Vice President Gore spared no efforts through diplomatic channels.

The eventual summit communiqué in Miami in December 1994 did not fall short. It was the first ever at such a heads-of-state level to explicitly call for major international anticorruption action. It was to be the prime impetus for the subsequent drafting and coming into force in 1996 of a regional anticorruption pact (the Inter-American Convention Against Corruption) under the auspices of the Organization for American States—the first regional anticorruption convention of its kind. It was also the first international anticorruption convention signed by the United States, setting an important precedent for future years.

This outcome gave impetus to TI's own efforts to build public awareness of the corruption issue in general, and of the OECD and World Bank challenges in particular. TI pressed hard for strong media support of its goals. On July 4, 1995, for example, the *Financial Times* published a long lead editorial under the banner "Attack on corruption." It stated in part:

> Opaque procedures for public procurement, inadequate funding of political parties and underpayment of officials all breed corruption. The best way to help countries reduce opportunities for such wrongdoing is to establish open

procurement procedures. The privately financed lobby group, Transparency International, has done as much as anybody to advise countries ready to take this path. It has now called for action on a broader front.

The group wants measures already introduced to combat money laundering to be used in a global fight against corruption. It also wants an international convention that would make bribery a global crime, with the perpetrators liable to pursuit and punishment by the signatory. The US already has legislation enabling it to prosecute companies for corrupt practices abroad, but its attempts to persuade other countries to follow suit have made slow progress.

EUROPE GETS ON BOARD

Running parallel with the OECD, World Bank, and Latin campaigns were efforts to ensure that that the European Union moved off the fence and firmly into the anticorruption camp. Dieter Frisch, who had resigned from the EU Commission, worked tirelessly in Brussels with many others on this agenda.

The lead was taken by the Council of Europe.[8] In 1994, justice ministers of council member countries came together at a conference in Valetta, Malta, to start discussing the corruption issue. This led to the establishment of a Council Multidisciplinary Group on Corruption (GMC), which formulated a program of action in November 1996 and developed a series of concrete measures. The most important was the establishment in May 1999, with the approval of seventeen founding-member countries, of the "Group of States against Corruption—GRECO."[9]

In January 1999, a "Criminal Law Convention on Corruption" was ready for signing by council states and it entered into force on July 1, 2002. It was closely followed by a "Civil Law Convention on Corruption," which came into force on November 1, 2003 (see appendix 4 for some key provisions of these conventions). The criminal convention is quite comprehensive and states are required to enforce its provisions, with GRECO serving to monitor performance. The convention incorporates provisions concerning enhanced international cooperation (mutual assistance, extradition, and the provision of information) in the investigation and prosecution of corruption offenses.

The Civil Law Convention on Corruption was the first attempt to define common international rules in the field of civil law and corruption. It required contracting parties to provide in their domestic law "for effective remedies for persons who have suffered damage as a result of acts of corruption, to enable them to defend their rights and interests, including the possibility of obtaining compensation for damage" (Art.1). The convention is divided into three chapters (measures to be taken at national level, international cooperation, and monitoring of implementation) and final clauses. In ratifying the convention, the states undertake to incorporate its principles and rules into their domestic law, taking into account their own particular circumstances.

GRECO's key function is to report regularly and publicly on the anticorruption efforts of countries across Europe, especially those that have applied for membership in the European Union, such as countries in the Balkans. GRECO has, in fact, put teeth into the fine council rhetoric and its reports are highly influential in the EU Commission, often to the dismay of European governments. GRECO elects its president, vice president, and members of its bureau, who are overseen by GRECO's Statutory Committee, which is composed of representatives on the Committee of Ministers of the member states that have joined GRECO and provide its budget.

The European Union's Commission and Council of Ministers have lagged behind the Council of Europe. EU member countries are signatories to the OECD Convention and to assorted other conventions, and they have placed the anticorruption issue on a host of their sectoral "to do" lists. In June 2011, the commission announced that it was establishing a mechanism for "periodic assessment of EU States' efforts in the fight against corruption." As it explained on its official EU website:

> The mechanism, part of a wider anti-corruption package, will allow for the periodic assessment of anti-corruption efforts in EU States, with a view to fostering political will, helping to step up anti-corruption efforts and reinforcing mutual trust. It will also facilitate the exchanges of best practices, identify EU trends, gather comparable data on the EU 27 and stimulate peer learning and further compliance with EU and international commitments. Moreover, the EU reporting mechanism will prepare the ground for future EU policy initiatives in the area of anti-corruption. [10]

It sounds good, but like so many official governmental pronouncements against corruption, it engenders a degree of skepticism, and rightfully so. As noted in chapter 15, EU member countries overall have mostly failed to enforce the OECD Convention and so, in effect, have done nothing to discourage multinational corporations headquartered in most EU countries (Germany is a major exception) from paying bribes to foreign governments.

THE UNITED NATIONS JOINS THE CHORUS

At the launch conference of TI in May 1993, Ahmedou Ould Abdallah, a Mauritanian who has held some of the toughest diplomatic jobs as a UN ambassador, from Burundi to Somalia, made a striking appeal. He declared,

"Corruption may have already become an integral component of the social and cultural systems of many countries. This development, unless quickly and seriously fought, will become an irreversible addiction."

Then he noted that the United Nations needs to fully address, indeed lead, the fight against corruption. He pointed out that the UN Economic and Social Council in 1972 had touched upon the corruption issue in a resolution on transnational corporations and the development process of developing countries. He stated that the council strengthened the focus in 1974 with a resolution that called for research on transnational corporations that included work on a code of conduct. Moreover, in 1975, the UN General Assembly had adopted a resolution titled "Measures Against Corrupt Practices by Transnational Corporations, Their Intermediaries and Others Involved." This called for the collection of information on corrupt practices.

Against this background, Ould Abdullah told the TI conference:

> It is essential to secure the support of a number of UN member states to prepare and sponsor a new resolution to be adopted by the general Assembly at its 29th session 1994, or at the 1995 UN's 50th anniversary. Transparency International should take action as soon as possible. With commitments and dynamic support, a comprehensive resolution could be adopted to the satisfaction of all, particularly the poor and neglected populations of the world, about two million human beings.[11]

By the late 1990s, there was barely a major multilateral official organization that had not publicly released its own anticorruption policy. The IMF proudly talked about imposing rigorous anticorruption controls on Indonesia as the Asian financial crisis developed in 1998. It declared that radical reform of the Indonesian government's public finances, its relationships with banks, and its procurement approaches were conditions of obtain IMF funding. Bilateral and multilateral aid agencies were starting to convene regional conferences on corruption.

The most prominent holdout was the United Nations, but even there the pressures were mounting. In January 1999—one year after the OECD Convention came into force—at the World Economic Forum in Davos, Switzerland, UN Secretary General Kofi Annan announced the launch of the UN Global Compact to stimulate "best practices" in global corporate citizenship. He talked about key principles concerned with the environment, human rights, and labor rights. Missing was any mention of bribery. He was asked about this and sheepishly evaded the question. One of his staff members, Georg Kell, who was to become the UN Global Compact's executive director, said that Annan wanted an anticorruption principle, but the problem was that there was no UN General Assembly declaration or agreement on the topic.

A year later, Kell made sure to invite Eigen to the UN Global Compact's first assembly in New York. Peter called on the United Nations to adopt a tenth principle in its UN Compact charter for good global citizenship. Alongside issues of human rights, labor rights, and environmental protection, Eigen called for pledges by businesses that joined the UN Global Compact that they would not pay bribes. Soon thereafter I was invited to participate in a UN Global Compact working group to look at issues that related to corruption even though the subject was not officially recognized as part of the agenda. In time, largely with Kell's efforts, it did indeed become a full part of the UN Global Compact's work and Huguette Labelle, representing TI, was appointed to the UN Compact's Governing Council.

The development of the UN Global Compact went hand in hand with another major development. The UN Secretariat was acutely embarrassed over its mishandling of the UN oil-for-food sanctions program with Iraq. A commission under Paul Volcker found huge abuse and corruption, as noted in chapter 5. The findings, taken together with the rising tide of official conventions and declarations against corruption, finally led to action by the UN General Assembly itself.

After holding out for over sixty years from discussing corruption, the General Assembly in 2003 adopted the United Nations Convention Against Corruption (UNCAC). It was formally ratified in late 2005 and by the end of 2009 more than 140 governments had signed it (see some highlights in appendix 3). It obliges governments to enforce a host of anticorruption measures. It also provides the most comprehensive set of detailed legal anticorruption requirements on governments that has ever existed. It starts by noting,

> The purposes of this Convention are: (a) To promote and strengthen measures to prevent and combat corruption more efficiently and effectively; (b) To promote, facilitate and support international cooperation and technical assistance in the prevention of and fight against corruption, including in asset recovery; and (c) To promote integrity, accountability and proper management of public affairs and public property.

Skepticism is in order about the enforcement of UNCAC with many governments quite evidently reluctant to introduce anticorruption measures in their countries. Efforts by nongovernmental organizations to see that UNCAC included monitoring provisions failed to win UN approval. In 2009, TI was a leader in coordinating more than three hundred civil society organizations from almost one hundred countries to press the United Nations to establish an effective convention-review process. The United Nations has responded and, as TI reports to its members on a regular basis, it has vowed to assess, for example, whether governments have taken sufficient action in areas such as law enforcement, whistle-blower protection, and cross-border cooperation.

The UNCAC is the formal acceptance by the governments of the world, via the UN General Assembly, that corruption is wrong and should be actively confronted. This is a milestone in the long fight to build a more honest system of governance across much of the world.

NOTES

1. Paul Glickman, Gara LaMarche, and Fund for Free Expression, *Off Limits: Censorship and Corruption* (New York: Human Rights Watch, 1991).

2. First published by Transparency International as *Grand Corruption: How Business Bribes Damage Developing Countries*, by George Moody-Stuart (Oxford: WorldView Publishing, 1977).

3. The World Bank Group consists of the International Bank for Reconstruction and Development, the International Development Association, the International Finance Corporation, the Multilateral Investment Guarantee Agency, and the International Center for the Settlement of Investment Disputes.

4. James Wolfensohn, annual World Bank meeting speech, Washington, DC, October 1, 1996, http://go.worldbank.org/SA5WLZWHO70.

5. Statement of the G7 Finance Ministers and Central Bank Governors, paragraph 17, Washington, DC, April 27, 1997.

6. "Joint Ministerial Development Committee of the IMF and World Bank on the Transfer of Real Resources to Developing Countries," Hong Kong, September 22, 1997, communiqué paragraphs 2, 3 and 4.

7. See Convention on Combating Bribery of Foreign Public Officials.

8. The Council of Europe's official website, www.coe.int, notes that the council, based in Strasbourg (France), covers virtually the entire European continent, with forty-seven member countries. Founded on May 5, 1949, by ten countries, the council seeks to develop throughout Europe common and democratic principles based on the European Convention on Human Rights and other reference texts on the protection of individuals.

9. The founding-member states of GRECO were Belgium, Bulgaria, Cyprus, Estonia, Finland, France, Germany, Greece, Iceland, Ireland, Lithuania, Luxembourg, Romania, Slovakia, Slovenia, Spain, and Sweden. Today, GRECO is supported by forty-eight European countries, plus the United States.

10. European Commission, "Commission Fights Corruption: A Stronger Commitment for Greater Results," press release, Brussels, June 1, 2011.

11. Intervention by Ambassador Ould Abdulla at the Transparency International launch conference, Berlin, May 1993.

Part 3

Moving Forward

Chapter Twelve

Justice and the Demand for Good Governance

Ordinary citizens, even in some of the most corrupt nations in the world—and some of the most dangerous for anticorruption activists—can organize and secure justice. According to a report published by TI[1]:

> Eight mothers in Zimbabwe die in labor every day, according to UN figures. The country's health system has borne the brunt of years of economic turmoil. Expectant mothers often struggle to afford the mandatory hospital delivery fee of approximately US $50, which is around a third of an average Zimbabwean's yearly income. Many have no choice but to give birth at home, without professional help.
>
> As part of their community outreach program, TI-Zimbabwe learned about how corruption was making the situation even worse. They were told that nurses in a local hospital were charging women US $5 every time that they screamed while giving birth, as a penalty for raising false alarm. Women who refused or were unable to pay their delivery fees were allegedly detained at the hospital, and charged interest on their debt until they settled it. Some say they called on family members to help them escape. Others who were eventually released reported being hassled by debt collectors who demanded both the hospital fees and additional "collection charges."
>
> On hearing this, TI-Zimbabwe wrote to the Ministry of Health and received confirmation of its receipt. After some time passed without a response, TI lawyers called the ministry but were reportedly told that their letter had been lost. So they turned instead to the Deputy Prime Minister. After meeting with TI-Zimbabwe, Thokozani Khupe called on the Minister of Health to carry out an investigation into maternal health issues as part of a broader review of the national health system.
>
> Since then TI-Zimbabwe has received no further complaints from women in the area, and has remained in close contact with local residents to ensure that this situation is not reversed. TI-Zimbabwe has also launched a broad-

based campaign to raise awareness about corruption in basic services such as
health, education and water. They are also holding workshops in local communities to encourage people to secretly record officials in the act of asking for
bribes, as proof for the police or judiciary.

Just as corrupt dictators are being toppled by massive public engagement
and new anticorruption laws are being set because of huge public protests,
systems of justice in many countries will be improved—are being improved—because of grassroots demands for good governance. The Arab
Spring and the new age of transparency underscore the power of the public's
will to secure reform. This can happen in the crucial area of justice and the
momentum of action is increasing.

Top politicians and their corrupt business partners in many countries
control the courts, the public prosecutors, and the police. As noted in chapter
9, reforms are under way in many countries, but the forces that are determined to make the justice system bow to their own narrow and crooked
needs are powerful. The demand for good governance, with demands for
justice at their core, that are coming from ordinary citizens could well be the
way, over time, for far-reaching justice reform.

This is a vital and complicated area. Without fair and honest justice, as
noted earlier in this book, the sustainability of anticorruption reforms will
always be in question. Believing that such a system of justice can be effectively promoted from the grassroots upward may be a stretch, yet today it
seems to be the most viable course. It is a core demand of many of the
protesters that have emerged in the months after the onset of the Arab Spring.
The deep political divides, for example, that emerged in late 2011 in the
Indian parliament over how best to formulate a tough new anticorruption law
centered on the demands of protesters for strongly independent powers for a
tough new anticorruption commission, while the Indian government wanted
to maintain key controls over the new commission. Similar tussles are likely
to become far more common in many countries as the anticorruption campaigns, based on mass public engagement, call for independent judicial authorities, including independent bodies that can investigate and prosecute
governmental abuses of power.

The broad public demands for justice will not only be seen in terms of
national systems and oversight of national governments. They will increasingly be seen, case by case, in terms of the lives of ordinary citizens and their
victimization by middle- and low-level public officials.

When grand corruption pervades the top echelons of power in a country,
then corrupt deals on a far smaller scale involving mid-level and low-level
officials and business people and ordinary citizens are always widespread.
For many individuals the corruption is seen as either brutal extortion or
blatant robbery. Someone may want to open a small restaurant but finds that

this is impossible without cash payments under the table to obtain all manner of licenses. A person may buy a house and then find that local authorities have declared the contract invalid and have sold the house to someone else.

Hundreds of thousands of instances of such routine corruption create bitter public resentment toward government, cynicism about politics, and often a sense of powerlessness. The inability to fight back in countries where the police and the judges are corrupt produces enormous frustrations. However, developments in just the last few years, from Bosnia-Herzegovina to Palestine to Zimbabwe, suggest that in many countries the situation is far from hopeless.

ADVOCACY AND LEGAL ADVICE CENTERS (ALACS)

Ordinary citizens in the tens of thousands in these countries and a rapidly rising number of other countries are now voicing their complaints, seeking redress, and finding the means to fight back. The development of Advocacy and Legal Advice Centers (ALACs) by TI's national chapters in more than fifty countries is a crucial dimension of citizen engagement in the war on corruption, and a remarkable success story as well.

ALACs seek to empower both victims and witnesses of corruption to address their grievances, to gather information on systemic corruption issues, and to support efforts to secure anticorruption policy changes. ALACs are the single largest global initiative promoted today by the TI movement. They assist victims of corruption to find redress by effectively using legal and media avenues in their own countries. TI's work in this area highlights the effective on-the-ground activism that many anticorruption organizations are pursuing.

There are both street offices where ALACs are able to work with citizens and Internet-based ALAC services. At the basic and general levels, ALACs, as TI-Venezuela notes on its website, can do the following:

- Guide citizens if their case relates to corruption and identify possible actions to take
- Support citizens with the preparation of actions to be taken (request for information, reporting, administrative procedures, etc.)
- Track cases and document their progress
- Present reports aimed at institutional strengthening of the organisms involved
- Provide services that are free and maintain citizen confidentiality

And, at a general level, ALACs can:

- Take a position on the case
- Report on behalf of the citizen
- Represent victims in court
- Investigate the case

Bosnia-Herzegovina, with its rolling hills and winding roads, has much of its beauty masked by a brutal history. Today, almost fifteen years after the ending of the worst war Europe has experienced since World War II, bullet holes still mark some of the oldest and most important buildings in the capital city of Sarajevo. Unemployment is said to be close to 40 percent, but the cafes of the city are full, people appear well dressed, cars abound, and life seems strangely normal. But here, in a country rich with history and culture, there flourishes an informal economy, the product of chaotic and ineffective governments (at national, regional, and local levels) and rampant corruption.

I was invited to Sarajevo to celebrate the UN "Anti-Corruption Day" on December 10, 2010, by my friends in TI-BH and to participate in a seminar that they had arranged at the national parliament building. The participants, including civil society organizers, academics, members of parliament, journalists, and business people, were open about the extent of corruption, open about the failures to enforce many laws and to act effectively against widely known conspiracies involving prominent politicians and business organizations ("the mafia," said one of my friends) and crooked judges. But none of the lawyers or politicians present wanted to claim any responsibility for trying to clean up the mess.

The benefits of action here are obvious. The underground economy provides nobody with a sense of security or hope of a better life for themselves or their children. Bosnia's access to the European Union, which could pave the way for modernization and sustained economic growth, is blocked because of corruption. In August 2011, GRECO published its "Third Round Evaluation Report" and called on the BH authorities "to take determined steps to enforce criminal legislation and become more efficient in convicting corruption offenders." GRECO also calls for more transparency and accountability in the funding of political parties and election campaigns.[2]

The scale of the country's corruption problems was indicated in a paper that TI-BH prepared for the 2010 conference. It noted, for example, that BH was ranked more corrupt than any other European country in the 2009 TI CPI (ninety-ninth position in the world ranking). The paper detailed a host of major corruption problems in the country, from abundant evidence of conflicts of interest among officeholders at all levels of the country's governments, to lack of any means to verify the real assets held by public office holders, to lack of enforcement of existing access to information laws. It concluded that overall, even though the country has adopted anticorruption laws as advocated by GRECO, the lack of implementation means that no real progress in the anticorruption fight has been made in years.

In fact, there has been some progress, but it is entirely due to the courage and the initiative of civil society. Emir Djikic and Boris Divjak, the cofounders of TI-BH, the national chapter, built an organization in the country that has become a force for change and a thorn in the side of some of the most powerful politicians. Conferences and research reports are a small part of what the chapter does. Frustrated by the scale of corruption and the failure of anyone in authority to do anything about it, they were among the very first in the TI movement, around 2004, to establish an ALAC.

It encouraged ordinary citizens to come forward and talk about how they felt cheated by governmental corruption and then the ALAC would seek to find ways to directly take up the case and secure justice. At times, just the media publicity of a complaint could be effective, while at other times, a lawyer representing the victim could create the kind of problems for the authorities that compromise solutions could be found. Sometimes, effective redress has not been possible. The Bosnian ALAC did, however, start to receive the media visibility that became increasingly troubling to the corrupt authorities. In response, these authorities started to hit back by denouncing TI, naming the members of the TI Bosnian staff, and highlighting them in the media that the government controlled to the point that their lives were placed at mounting risk.

The pressures rose and the chapter felt it had no choice other than to close its offices. But not for long. The global TI movement mobilized and protests from the European Commission and the US government, combined with international publicity (including a news report in the *Financial Times*), forced the government to relent. Today, TI-Bosnia is handling more individual ALAC corruption cases than ever.

By the end of 2011, more than one hundred thousand people had lodged complaints and cases with ALACs organized by TI national chapters in fifty-three countries. As TI noted, for example, in its 2009 Annual Report:

- Transparency Maroc opened an ALAC in January 2009 and served three hundred people during the year. The center has developed contacts with other organizations, especially in human rights, so they can refer people needing assistance. It also carried out a large-scale media and communications campaign to reach out to citizens wanting to report acts of corruption. It is now building relations with the authorities to help them detect and prevent corruption in their services.
- Transparency Rwanda's ALAC received 332 cases in its first year. The complaints covered several categories including education, health, justice, international development, children's rights, and local government. A

workshop with public partners, civil society, international organizations, and the private sector has been organized to promote awareness of the ALAC's achievements and how it can help people.

- By its first anniversary, the ALAC run by the Guatemalan TI chapter, Acción Ciudadana, had been contacted by more than eight hundred people and had pursued numerous cases of corruption. Successes included the dismissal and sanctioning of ten public officials and the submission of reports to government ministries on embezzlement and to the Judicial Council on the abuse of authority.

- After launching an ALAC, staff from TI-Fiji visited communities nation-wide, discussing corruption and providing legal assistance. Overwhelming numbers of people have since sought help with corruption-related prob-lems. The chapter gives on-the-spot legal advice, follows up with organ-izations accused of corrupt activities, drafts letters for clients, and refers them to other organizations that can assist further. The visits help empow-er people to report corruption in their communities and are arranged through networking with community leaders and by encouraging people to write in and invite TI-Fiji staff.

- TI-Azerbaijan operates five ALACs throughout the country—the first was established in 2005. In total they have received more than twenty-three thousand complaints, provided legal aid to more than 13,880 clients, and accepted 3,112 formal complaints—approximately 95 percent of which have been resolved by various public agencies to the full or partial satis-faction of clients. Contributing to the establishment of an anticorruption hotline, amendments to the criminal code (to incorporate penalties for corruption-related offences), and the writing of a draft conflict of interests law are just a few examples of the chapter's successes to create structural change.

Experienced staff of TI's secretariat have found from reviewing hundreds of cases that have been handled by ALACs that citizens are seeking a whole range of services, from sophisticated legal and paralegal services to just a place where they can unburden themselves and let off some steam against corrupt officials. The responses from ALACs also cover a very wide range, from seeking to find lawyers who can take on cases, to alerting investigative reporters, to waging significant public campaigns. The approaches that ALACs take are totally pragmatic and this builds trust, which is absolutely key to encouraging people to move from passive acceptance to active protest.

Some ALACs, note TI's experts, are building anticorruption libraries and resource centers for use by clients and community members, including how-to guides for citizens on official procedures. Some ALACs have also produced compendia of the questions most commonly asked by citizens. There is an enormous range of techniques, services, and strengths between the ALACs from one country to another.

At TI's annual meeting in October 2011, national chapter leaders from across the world discussed some of the systemic issues that arise from their ALAC work. I had not fully appreciated until I heard this discussion the degree to which the experiences gained in ALAC work, case by case, were influencing the knowledge base of the anticorruption movement and helping to set the activist agenda. As people come to complain, patterns form that may show, for example, that most cases relate to corruption in the judiciary and the police. This in turn strengthens the focus of the national chapter in its campaign work to clean up the legal system and to use its cases and data to build a powerful case for reform.

There is a marvelous story of a government official in Palestine who became increasingly angry about the degree to which government officials were using their official cars for their private purposes. Muhammad Hallaq is a middle-aged, somewhat portly employee at the Ministry of Transport who felt that the misuse of government vehicles was corruption and an abuse of office. He believed that it amounted to more than simply the theft of gasoline and the costs of car repairs that were greater because of all the nonofficial use, and which alone totaled some $18 million per month—it was also a matter of principle.

Mr. Hallaq went to TI-Palestine (AMAN) and met with Hama Zidan, the determined head of the ALAC. She took on the case and a campaign was launched that involved bumper stickers, advertising, and encouragement to citizens to report official cars used for private purposes. Night after night Mr. Hallaq would drive around shopping malls and other busy places and register the number plates of government-owned vehicles. With reports flowing to him and with his own evidence in hand he would find the drivers and confront them. Gradually, the campaign started to impact the senior levels of government, which decided to reduce access to official cars for lower-level government workers. AMAN helped to bring a case to court to challenge the decision and, in fact, secure a ruling that, barring emergency situations, almost all official vehicles could only be used for official purposes. Mr. Hallaq went to court, and when the judge ruled in his favor he said, "This is the happiest day of my life."

His joy related not simply to the misuse of government vehicles. It was a victory with far broader implications. As AMAN also saw it when it gave Mohammad Hallaq its annual Integrity Award, the case and the campaign had sensitized many Palestinians to the fact that they could participate in actions to reduce governmental abuse and start to change the very culture that for so long had seen corruption run rampant across their government's offices.

In many countries, the ALAC initiative is energizing rising numbers of people to become involved in the corruption fight in very personal ways. In a nationwide Internet ALAC in Russia, for example, citizens can voice their grievances, which is inspiring lawyers and accountants and other professionals to see the cases and to volunteer at times to come and help. Multiply the actions a thousand or ten thousand times, and the impact on governance and justice cannot be underestimated. The central goal of all the rapidly growing ALACs in so many countries is the same: to strengthen the justice system.

INVOLVING THE AID AGENCIES

The strength of civil society itself is critical to the progress that can be made to improve justice system reform in a country, as well as to build institutional capacity to curb corruption. Social networks can help to create demonstrations and protests, but sustaining reform movements demands longer-term strategies, civil society organization, and support for such organization. Overwhelmingly the support should come from the citizens themselves, but in many countries in the developing world, and in Central and Eastern Europe, international philanthropic foundations and official aid agencies can and do play important supporting roles.

Strengthening the contributions to reform by civil society ought to be a goal of the major aid agencies and they are uniquely placed, given their lending and grant-making ties to governments, to be effective in this area.

As in all other areas of international development aid, the bilateral agencies and the smaller multilateral ones look to the World Bank for leadership. Former World Bank president Robert Zoellick was acutely aware of this and of the need for his institution to come closer to civil society and be more constructive in working with civil society. Zoellick, who left the Bank in mid-2012, ensured that the World Bank is heavily engaged today in designing governance-reform programs and providing funds to governments to support them, though the results are, more often than not, disappointing.[3]

A major recommendation to the World Bank now is to take far greater advantage of civil society capacity in many countries to independently monitor governmental reform programs to ensure they are implemented, that funds designated for them are not stolen or switched to other programs, and that there is accountability. Over the last decade, the Partnership for Transparency Fund (PTF) has funded close to two hundred individual anticorruption projects developed and implemented by individual civil society organizations. This has produced an important experience base about the capabilities of civil society as an effective partner to governments and aid agencies in constructive reform programs and has highlighted the actual and potential scope for civil society to play key monitoring roles.

In 2011, Daniel Ritchie, president and CEO of PTF; Vinay Bhargava, a PTF managing director; and Kit Cutler, a consultant to PTF, authored a report based on PTF experience and aimed at the World Bank called "Stimulating the Demand for Good Governance." They chose to define this demand as "development interventions that enhance the ability and extent of citizens, civil society organizations, and other non-state actors to hold the state accountable and to make it responsive to their needs. In doing so, DFGG enhances the capacity of the state to become more transparent, participatory, and accountable in order to respond to these demands."

The PTF report stated that the World Bank's approaches to governance reform contain some serious problems that need to be addressed if civil society monitoring in countries is to be effective. The authors noted that the World Bank can only lend to governments and thus their consent is necessary before civil society can be engaged in monitoring roles. Then again, the World Bank has not developed a meaningful mechanism to provide sufficient funding to civil society to undertake independent monitoring of projects and reform programs. And many civil society groups are concerned about their independence and perceptions of conflict of interest if they take money from their own governments, even if the cash is supplied by the World Bank. Mutual distrust between civil society organizations and their governments is a common problem that aid agencies often underestimate.

These are issues of central importance in the global fight against corruption. The post–World War II architecture of international aid and development has barely recognized the roles of civil society. Over the last twenty years, however, the number of civil society organizations has grown enormously and their impact has become formidable. Nevertheless, almost all dealings between official aid agencies, especially multilateral agencies such as the United Nations and the World Bank and the IMF, are with governments. When these are corrupt governments, the prospects for serious reform being promoted by the aid agencies is at best questionable and the prospects that these authorities will engage independent civil society to monitor their reform performance are remote.

World Bank President Zoellick noted on April 14, 2011, in a speech at the Woodrow Wilson Institute in Washington, DC, "Modern multilateralism will not be a constricted club with more left outside the room than seated within. It will look more like the global sprawl of the Internet, interconnecting more and more countries, companies, individuals, and NGOs through a flexible network."

The PTF authors in their report emphasized that they were seeking qualitative and not just quantitative change in the World Bank's approaches to civil society:

> Most non-governmental organizations (NGOs) and civil society organizations (CSOs) in developing countries operate with very scarce resources, and many lack the formal systems that the Bank expects from counterparts, such as sound accounting and financial reporting processes, systematic institutional record keeping, transparent procurement and hiring processes. The lack of such systems compounds the difficulty of working with non-governmental counterparts since the Bank is required to account to its members for the way loan and grant funds are utilized.[4]

Many aid agencies have developed such complex and costly reporting systems, ostensibly to demonstrate that they go overboard to guard against internal theft of resources, that they eliminate themselves from engagement with small civil society organizations in developing countries that have no means of managing all the auditing and management requirements. Intermediaries like PTF are useful here, but many aid agencies are sometimes reluctant to use intermediaries because they claim this adds to their costs. It is a catch-22 situation in which all the claims of aid agencies that they wish to work on a practical scale with civil society organizations are undermined by rules and regulations that prevent them from doing so. Yet there is something incredible about the belief that foreign-aid funds can be efficiently and effectively used to help anticorruption reforms when the agents of change who are being funded are corrupt governments and where there is no independent performance monitoring.

In their conclusion, Ritchie, Bhargava, and Cutler called on the World Bank (and by implication the fraternity of international development aid agencies) to make far greater use of civil society organizations and their experience in the demand for good governance. The authors argued that ways have to be found to fund civil society organizations on a meaningful scale and in an independent manner; the experiences of civil society organizations need to be better understood in the World Bank; the World Bank needs to develop organizational structures that can best ensure effective work with civil society organizations, their funding, their place within World Bank strategies, and the deployment of appropriate tools to maximize impact.

It will be enormously difficult to build honest and effective systems of justice in many countries. The work of ALACs and of civil society independent monitoring of governance reforms are two complementary paths that are important in this context. The prime driver of action will be from within countries, but stronger support via multilateral aid agencies to civil society will be a very significant help.

NOTES

1. "Transparency International Annual Report 2009" (Berlin: Transparency International, 2010).

2. GRECO, Council of Europe, press release issued in Strasbourg, August 17, 2011.

3. The World Bank has published numerous evaluations of its governance work in recent years.

4. Daniel Ritchie, Vinay Bhargavia, and Kit Cutler, "Stimulating Demand for Good Governance: Eight Strategic Recommendations for Intensifying the Role of the World Bank," Partnership for Transparency Fund, July 4, 2011, www.ptfund.org/publications/special-reports.

Chapter Thirteen

The G20 Sets a Bold Agenda

Peter Eigen is a tireless campaigner, continuously traveling, giving media interviews, teaching seminars, and working the telephones to convince government officials and businessmen alike to do more to fight corruption. He spent most of his professional career in the World Bank, much of it dealing with top government officials and politicians, which built both his diplomatic skills and gave him faith in the power of persistent behind-the-scenes persuasion. No sooner was TI launched in 1973 than Peter was seeking to get meetings with senior officials in the most powerful Western governments to make the anticorruption case. Year after year, TI would be on the sidelines at summit meetings of the Group of 8 leading nations, quietly pressing its views.

Peter recognizes that the encouraging statements that leaders make will not translate into sustained action unless those leaders are consistently pressed to act on their pledges and if official actions are rigorously monitored. TI has for more than a decade, for example, monitored compliance with the OECD Anti-Bribery Convention (see chapter 15) and taken a lead, thanks to painstaking work by TI staffer Gillian Dell, in the monitoring of the implementation of the UNCAC. Progress has often been slow, but Peter has never talked about being rebuffed nor indicated disappointment. Instead, he has kept on pressing and kept on encouraging TI's national chapters to press their own governments for reforms.

In recent years, TI has evolved to run its global campaigns on two tracks: continuing Peter's networking and behind-the-scenes diplomacy, while encouraging rising mass public engagement in the anticorruption fight. Both tracks have contributed to transforming the anticorruption agenda and winning recognition for meaningful reform by major governments.

The global financial crisis in 2008/2009 increased TI's vigor to secure support for anticorruption efforts by world leaders. President Bush brought together the leaders of twenty governments to a White House conference in November 2008 to chart a crisis economic action plan and launched the Group of 20 summit[1] process to address global economic instability. TI members from across the world resolved at their 2008 annual meeting that now was the time to launch a major campaign to secure greater transparency and accountability in global finance and soon thereafter it determined that the G20 was the key target.

A TI working group was established involving TI members from Australia to France to Indonesia, supported by the TI secretariat in Berlin with expert guidance from staff member Angela McClellan. At the same time, TI's chair, Huguette Labelle, raced from the lofty establishment halls of the World Economic Forum in Davos, Switzerland, to high-level conferences at the OECD, United Nations, and World Bank to personally convince world leaders that now was the time to act. TI was not alone—many nongovernmental organizations started to lobby the G20.

Progress at first was slow, but a breakthrough came as the Canadian and South Korean governments took the helm of the G20 in 2010. Huguette was effective with her fellow Canadians and TI's Geo-Sung Kim was no less skilled in Seoul. Others in TI chapters in G20 countries, in particular, kept the pressure up with submissions to those key individuals in their governments responsible for the summit agendas. And when the lead for the G20 was handed to France at the start of 2011, TI-France, under the tireless leadership on this front of Daniel Lebègue and Jacques Terray, pushed hard on the diplomatic front and reported back to the TI working group on which issues the French were most likely to support progress (notably, anti–money laundering). The first concrete results came at the conclusion of the G20 summit in Seoul, South Korea, in November 2010, with the announcement of the "Anti-Corruption Action Plan."

The content of the G20 commitments in this declaration went well beyond the expectations of the founders of TI when they first determined to press for global anticorruption reforms in the early 1990s. None of those participants ventured to suggest back then that a time would come when the most powerful governments in the world would jointly agree and promote a detailed set of plans that placed action-oriented responsibilities on each participating government.

The anticorruption actions agreed to by the G20 have been largely overlooked by the media. The anticorruption statement was announced at exactly the same time that the G20 summit issued its macro-economic policy decisions and individual leaders held press conferences to declare major victories in determining ways to build global economic growth and reduce unemployment. The vacuous statements and the failures of the G20 on the global economic front, which spawned many headlines and comment articles in the media, overshadowed the anticorruption decisions. All the same, in time, the full significance of the comprehensive G20 anticorruption commitments will be seen as the roadmap for official international actions in this area by major governments.

The G20's Seoul plan and the subsequent G20 Cannes progress report represent both a remarkable achievement by civil society and a challenge for further action. Now these official commitments need to be translated into firm and monitorable actions. A major objective for the global anticorruption movement in the immediate years ahead will be to hold the G20's feet to the fire and to press relentlessly that the G20 governments act on their own excellent rhetoric. If the G20 process is to be meaningful, then the agreements that the members have joined together to forge need to be seen publicly to have meaning.

The Action Plan called for implementation of the UNCAC, enforcement of laws against foreign bribery, international cooperation in preventing illicit flows into G20 financial markets, and tracing and recovering stolen assets and for the protection of whistle-blowers, which have long been key requests from civil society and anticorruption fighters. In some areas, such as in the work of development-aid institutions, anti–money laundering, and repatriation of stolen assets (see chapter 15), the approaches so far made by the G20 are inadequate. Yet even in these areas the recognition by the world's leaders that much more must be done is constructive.

THE ACTION PLAN

Given the significance of the G20 commitments it is useful to consider what has been agreed on. The starting point is that part of the G20 summit's overall "Declaration," issued on November 12, 2010, under the heading "Anti-Corruption":

> Recognizing that corruption is a severe impediment to economic growth and development, we endorse the G20 Anti-Corruption Action Plan. Building on previous declarations, and cognizant of our role as leaders of major trading nations, we recognize a special responsibility to prevent and tackle corruption and commit to supporting a common approach to building an effective global anti-corruption regime.
>
> In this regard, we will lead by example in key areas as detailed in the Anti-Corruption Action Plan, including: to accede or ratify and effectively implement the UN Convention against Corruption (UNCAC) and promote a transparent and inclusive review process; adopt and enforce laws against the bribery of foreign public officials; prevent access of corrupt officials to the global financial system; consider a cooperative framework for the denial of entry to

corrupt officials, extradition, and asset recovery; protect whistleblowers; safeguard anticorruption bodies. We are also committed to undertake a dedicated
effort to encourage public-private partnerships to tackle corruption and to
engage the private sector in the fight against corruption, with a view to promoting propriety, integrity and transparency in the conduct of business affairs,
as well as in the public sector.

The G20 will hold itself accountable for its commitments. Beyond our
participation in existing mechanisms of peer review for international anticorruption standards, we mandate the Anti-Corruption Working Group to submit annual reports on the implementation of our commitments to future Summits for the duration of the Anti-Corruption Action Plan.[2]

The Action Plan was detailed in Annex III of the official Summit Declaration. It started with a call for all governments that had not yet ratified the
UNCAC to do so and ensure effective monitoring of the convention's implementation. It stressed the need for more countries to ratify the OECD Convention Against Bribery and to ensure enforcement of laws that criminalize
bribe paying to foreign government officials by corporations. Then the G20
agreed to make efforts to strengthen anti–money laundering and implement
the FATF standards calling for transparency of cross-border wires, beneficial
ownership, customer due diligence, and due diligence for "politically exposed persons."

The G20 also pledged to consider a cooperative framework to prevent
corrupt officials from being able to travel abroad with impunity and seek safe
havens. It said it would promote the use of the UNCAC, particularly those
provisions related to extradition, mutual legal assistance, and asset recovery
and offer technical assistance where needed, and encourage the signing of
bilateral and multilateral treaties. Moreover, it noted, "To support the recovery of proceeds of corruption stowed abroad, all G20 countries will adopt
measures related to, inter alia, preventing and detecting transfers of proceeds
of crime; measures for direct recovery of property; mechanisms for recovery
of property through international cooperation in asset tracing, freezing and
confiscation; measures for special cooperation in voluntary disclosure; and
return and dispose of assets."

The G20 went on with a pledge to encourage all governments to enact
whistle-blower protection rules. It said it would also encourage governments
to work with business "to combat corruption in specific sectors, by working
with industry and civil society to identify vulnerabilities in commercial transactions in a subset of specific sectors, with the goal of recommending multi-
stakeholder initiatives for improvements in propriety, integrity and transparency."

Importantly, the G20 said it would follow up on the Action Plan with a
progress report at the 2011 G20 summit in Cannes. And so in Cannes, on
November 2011, the final declaration of the leaders contained the following:

We have made significant progress in implementing the Action Plan on combating corruption, promoting market integrity and supporting a clean business environment. We underline the need for swift implementation of a strong international legislative framework, the adoption of national measures to prevent and combat corruption and foreign bribery, the strengthening of international cooperation in fighting corruption and the development of joint initiatives between the public and the private sector.

In a special statement issued in Cannes headed "Fighting Corruption," the leaders stated that their governments had begun work in areas including the recovery of assets, the fight against money laundering, whistle-blower protection, the functioning and the independence of anticorruption agencies, public-sector transparency, and international cooperation. They said that the most significant individual achievements carried out by the G20 members over the course of 2011 were the following:

- The ratification by India of UNCAC
- The decision by Russia to join the OECD Convention on Combating Bribery of Foreign Public Officials in International Business Transactions
- The entry into force in China of a law criminalizing international corruption
- The adoption by the European Commission of the Anti-Corruption package in June 2011
- The entry into force in South Korea of a law protecting whistle-blowers
- The creation of a national anticorruption agency in Saudi Arabia
- The entry into force of a new law on international corruption in the United Kingdom
- The enactment of the Dodd-Frank Act in the United States

SECURING FURTHER G20 PROGRESS

The Cannes statement highlighted linkages between world trade, tax evasion, money laundering, and corruption. To some extent this was due to the consistent concerns about corruption that have been voiced by the influential head of the World Trade Organization, Pascal Lamay. To some extent, they also reflect the rising concerns of many G20 governments with national budget deficits and the serious leakages in revenue collection that these issues create. We shall see an intensification of work on these issues by a number of G20 governments because they view progress as very much in their personal interest in coming years.

The Cannes statements included a detailed paper on foreign aid and development that explicitly emphasized that "transparency and accountability are critical elements of domestic resource mobilization." The leaders are acutely aware of the potential for corruption in procurement, as well as a host of other areas related to commerce and taxation. The G20 called, for example, on governments and multinational corporations to jointly improve their practices on the disclosure of payments by corporations to governments. Furthermore, the G20 advocated full participation by governments to strengthen international exchange of information on all aspects of tax payments.

Like the 2010 Action Plan, the Cannes Summit's Progress Report was barely noticed by the media. The summit took place in the midst of the European financial crisis, which dominated all press reporting. The anticorruption materials were also released late and only on the website of the French government, which was the host of the summit. Indeed, one could conclude that there were efforts by some officials to downplay these statements. Nevertheless, they are on the record and they provide a host of clear and monitorable commitments. The implementation of the decisions that the G20 has taken will have an enormous influence in coming years on the extent to which the corruption war can be won.

NOTES

1. The G20 is made up of the finance ministers and central bank governors of nineteen countries and the European Union: Argentina, Australia, Brazil, Canada, China, France, Germany, India, Indonesia, Italy, Japan, Mexico, Russia, Saudi Arabia, South Africa, South Korea, Turkey, the United Kingdom, and the United States.

2. www.g20.org/Documents2010/11/seoulsummit_annexes.pdf.

Chapter Fourteen

Shaping Solutions I

US ambassador Richard Holbrooke brought extraordinary passion to efforts to resolve even the most intractable political issues. In striving to end the worst war that the European continent had experienced since World War II, Holbrooke had to deal with men who used terrible power to pursue their national interests, as well as their own. The corruption that seethed through the Balkans added to the complexities of Holbrooke's challenge. Yet his goal was not just to end a war and create a roadmap for future regional security, but also to ensure that the peoples of the region saw that justice was being done. To this end it was vital; to use Klitgaard's phrase, "the people needed to fry a big fish," and no fish was larger than Serbian leader Slobodan Milosevic.

Holbrooke succeeded and the eventual trial of Milosevic told the world not only of the true horrors of ethnic cleansing and fanaticism perpetrated by this villain and his cronies but also of their personal thievery. As a result, in what I believe is a footnote to Holbrooke's remarkable skills, the Swiss authorities, for the first time in the history of a country notorious for providing secret havens to the ill-gotten gains of dictators, froze about one hundred bank accounts with more than $80 million in funds linked to the Serbian leader. In due course it would emerge that he had private accounts in numerous other countries as well.[1] The Swiss precedent would be useful in subsequent years, right through the Arab Spring when the Swiss froze accounts belonging to the former Tunisian, Egyptian, and Libyan dictators.

People can make a difference in winning the battles in the war on corruption, be they determined international diplomats, or civil society activists, or investigative reporters. It is a war that each and every day starts within countries as reforms are sought at the local, municipal, and national levels. Each country has to find its own unique path to reform that takes into account its history, its culture, and its key priority problems. Yet each national set of battles can be fortified and encouraged when it receives international support. Sometimes that can come from an extraordinary diplomat like Richard Holbrooke, but mostly it comes from years of painstaking work to build an international consensus to not only agree upon reforms but also ensure that they are implemented.

The websites of scores of nongovernmental organizations in many countries contain reams of proposals for government reforms in general and anticorruption actions in particular. They range across the many topics discussed in earlier chapters. There is no one-fits-all solution to corruption, no model of a national integrity system for one country that can just be exported and succeed in another country.

As suggested in earlier chapters, public engagement in the anticorruption fight, be it in public Arab Spring–like protests or through ALACs, are gathering momentum. Nobody underestimates the difficulties and everyone is well aware that joy at successes is all too often short-lived—a corrupt regime is hurled out of office only to see, in time, that yet another bunch of gangsters has taken power.

The anticorruption activists everywhere need all the help they can get and they are the first to admit that they cannot do it all themselves. Most of their organizations in the developing world obtain their funds from the major Western industrial countries—from bilateral and multilateral aid agencies, from major philanthropic foundations, from a few corporations, and from the generosity of individual citizens. National and international anticorruption actions can and should reinforce each other.

There are many areas where international cooperation needs to be strengthened to enhance the fight against corruption and where firm actions will help nationally based activists enormously with their battles within their countries. Much international research has been done and continues to be done on such topics as corruption and climate change, corruption and health, and education and political finance. Each of these areas is important and each could benefit from international agreements and understandings. They are, however, first and foremost national issues in their application. Each country needs to find the optimum anticorruption path in each of these and many other areas that is in tune with the national culture, with traditions, and with current economic and political realities.

Of the many areas where cross-border action is necessary, I have concentrated in this chapter and in the next one on five areas where I believe that significant progress can be achieved if there is the will to support the kind of rhetoric that has now been seen at G20 summit conferences:

1. *Development assistance*: Agencies need to undergo a total review of their anticorruption endeavors.

2. *The arms trade*: Transparency must become a meaningful and operative driver of all aspects of this massive business.
3. *Oil, gas, and mining*: The time has now come for securing extractive industries' transparency.
4. *Anti–money laundering*: We know what needs to be done; now is the time to generate the political will to act.
5. *Corporate bribe paying to foreign government officials*: The laws are on the books, but enforcement is far below what it should be—it is time this changed.

These should not be seen as separate and distinct actions, but as a combined package. Leadership in each and all of these areas needs to be bold and responsibility, first and foremost, rests with the heads of governments of the world's most powerful countries.

DEVELOPMENT AID AND CORRUPTION

There is something of an "Alice in Wonderland" quality to the idea that a foreign-aid agency can provide money to a corrupt foreign government for the express purpose of reducing corruption and then expect the objective to be attained. Corrupt governments have zero incentive to reform their ways when provided with huge amounts of foreign cash. More likely, they will just steal the cash.

The fundamental flaw in the anticorruption approaches of the major multilateral development banks that deal with the poorest countries—the World Bank, the Asian Development Bank, the Inter-American Development Bank, and the African Development Bank—is that they can only lend or make grants to governments or to wholly controlled governmental entities. When it comes to promoting good governance (as noted in chapter 11), securing full-scale independent monitoring of reform programs is imperative—after all, the recipients of the cash from these development banks are governments, many of which are corrupt.

This intensively close relationship between the development banks and their client governments is the prime reason why today, more than a dozen years after then World Bank president James Wolfensohn talked about the "cancer of corruption," that the impact on reducing corruption by the World Bank and other development banks falls far short of what is necessary.

This is a tragedy because it means that vital resources are not helping the world's poor to the degree that they should because taxpayer cash is being wasted and the reputations of the aid agencies are being soiled.

I worked in senior posts at the World Bank for nine years in the 1980s, including almost two years as its acting vice president for external relations and as a member of its top-level managing committee, which enabled me to travel across the developing world and see how the World Bank's work had improved the lives of the world's poor. It was a privilege to serve the World Bank, and I believe that the World Bank and its highly able staff have done an enormous amount of good. They have alerted the world repeatedly to the anguish of absolute poverty, they have funded pioneering agricultural and health research, and they have given grants and loans for well-designed projects that have yielded many significant benefits in many countries. It was thrilling to once travel on behalf of the World Bank to a remote village in Burkina Faso in West Africa and open a small school that the villagers told me they had been praying for and that they were convinced would create vast new opportunities for their children. Aid programs have done this thousands of times.

In the arena of governance, however, the World Bank has often been more a part of the problem than a contributor to the solution, as have the other multilateral aid agencies and many of the bilateral ones. This remains the case.

It is important in discussing aid to focus first and foremost on the World Bank. As noted previously, it leads the policies and thinking of the global aid community. An economist once described the World Bank as the Vatican of aid—its rulings are dominant, its authority enormous, and its decisions rarely if ever questioned by the professionals in the international official aid community (national aid agencies such as USAID, international agencies such as the United Nations Development Program, and multilateral agencies such as the Asian Development Bank or the African Development Bank).

In recent years, World Bank President Robert Zoellick was passionate about using the full force of the World Bank to reduce poverty and he understood that to the degree that corruption is a cause of poverty, the World Bank has an important anticorruption role to play. He was sensitive to the fact that the World Bank is owned by the nations of the world and that their representatives who sit on the executive board of directors include officials from some of the world's most corrupt regimes. He believed that the World Bank needs to expand its partnerships with civil society and that their approaches to governance and working with the Bank (as described in chapter 12) have merit. He felt the need, however, to tread carefully, perhaps too carefully.

The World Bank has undertaken substantial research on many aspects of governance that has made important contributions. Zoellick saw to it that the World Bank had an efficient internal investigative unit to detect corruption in its own operations and that it was aggressive in the blacklisting of firms that have used bribes in World Bank projects. But the World Bank has spent hundreds of millions of dollars every year in recent years on anticorruption projects and programs that are not reducing corruption.

Three months after Zoellick became the head of the World Bank, an independent panel of leading international experts issued a report on the World Bank's anticorruption work. The panel was headed by Paul A. Volcker and included Gustavo Gaviria, John Githongo, Ben W. Heineman Jr., Professor Walter Van Gerven, and Sir John Vereker. It reviewed key aspects of the World Bank's anticorruption efforts since James Wolfensohn announced a new World Bank policy a decade earlier. In their report, they stressed:

> A lack of common purpose, distrust, and uncertainty has enveloped the anti-corruption work of the Bank. The result has been to blunt the effectiveness of the measures undertaken to support the Wolfensohn initiative a decade ago, including the formation of INT (the World Bank's Department of Institutional Integrity). Ignoring the issue, or, more subtly, tacitly supporting superficial government efforts where there is little political commitment, conspires against aid effectiveness and the welfare of the country's poor. The borrowing countries are sovereign but, when deploying Bank funds and those of other donors, those providing the funds have the right and the responsibility to follow the money and to ensure that the money serves the purposes for which it is disbursed. . . . What is necessary is a fully coordinated approach across the entire World Bank Group, ending past ambivalence about the importance of combating corruption. That will require strong Bank leadership, not simply by the President and the Executive Directors but by those directly responsible for operations and for supporting staff.[2]

Then, in 2008, the World Bank's own Independent Evaluation Group (IEG) published a major study of the World Bank's lending for public-sector reform across the world for the 1999–2006 period. It stated that the World Bank has not developed a framework that adequately recognizes the long duration of the process to reduce corruption and the differences in where countries need to start. The World Bank's stance against corruption needs operational clarification in country contexts—for instance, how the extent of corruption should affect the balance between investment and budget-supporting operations.

And in yet another IEG report in 2011,[3] the focus was on new approaches introduced under Robert Zoellick in 2007 that were known as the Governance and Anti-Corruption strategy (GAC). In a lengthy, jargon-filled analysis, the authors found some technical reasons to praise aspects of the GAC's work. Yet, overall, at best it seemed that very slow progress had been achieved. The dense report, which attracted little public attention, is a blunt assessment of the failings and inadequacies of the World Bank with anticorruption projects. In its conclusions in the two-hundred-page report, the IEG noted a lack of commitment to the goals of the GAC strategy by the governments of the countries receiving World Bank funds for governance. It went on to state, for example, that "since the launch of the 2007 strategy, the Bank's operational response to GAC issues demonstrated continuity without systematic improvement as yet." It added, "Important opportunities to managing risks and developing innovative operational solutions have yet to be seized."

The World Bank and the other multilateral aid agencies need to radically change their approaches. Instead of dense reports for experts only, the World Bank should welcome and foster a broad public discussion on how development aid can indeed assist the peoples of the developing world to improve governance. It is time for the major aid agencies to respond to the class of the Arab Spring.

The aid agencies need to recognize that their staffs get too close to the governments to which they provide grants and loans and that almost always they get outsmarted by those governments. Repeatedly, officials overlook the corruption in their host governments because they see their own success and their paths to promotion in their institutions as being determined by the volume of projects they further and approve, not by saying no, halting projects, and investigating abuse.

Too often aid officials get blinded by being too close to the politicians they negotiate with. I remember in the mid-1990s having an argument with a World Bank official who was threatening sanctions against the government of Tanzania unless there were actions taken against one of the senior ministers, whom this World Bank official believed was stealing government funds. I argued that that the World Bank was pointing its finger at the wrong villain and that it was being misinformed by its close contacts at the Ministry of Finance. The World Bank official did not relent until a few months later, when the country's minister of finance suddenly died of a heart attack in the hall of a large bank in London; inside the case he had with him were thousands of dollars in cash.

In the final paragraph of her book on Kenyan corruption, *It's Our Turn to Eat—The Story of a Kenyan Whistle-Blower*, Michela Wrong writes:

> As sleaze flourished, Kenya's poverty has deepened and the slums near the stadium have spread, along with mounds of rotting rubbish on which the storks depend. Politicians, foreign aid officials and World Bank spokesmen continue to talk up Kenya's prospects, but each year I notice that there are more of these bald-headed scavengers perched above the honking *matatus* and diesel-snorting exhausts, a quiet tangible sign that inequality is growing, not diminishing.

Michela Wrong wrote movingly and with sadness about a country she loves and that has been torn apart by years of corruption fostered at the very top of its government. She is acutely aware of the double standards that abound. At one level, in press conferences and in reports and in high-level international official meetings, the World Bank consistently talks about progress, places a fine gloss on even the bad news that it cannot avoid noting, and argues that new, multimillion-dollar aid programs are going to work and creating new Kenyan prosperity. At another level, the human misery of so many Kenyans becomes ever greater, the government corruption becomes ever more visible, and the repeated failures of well-intentioned aid programs become ever more apparent. Wrong's clear message is that the Western aid organizations have been complicit in the nation's misrule.

The current model used by aid agencies is to try and get along with all kinds of regimes. They do not say there shall be no money unless an independent judiciary is in place, unless there is press freedom, unless people have the right to free assembly, or unless human rights are guaranteed. The aid agencies argue that to make these conditions would be overly intrusive in the domestic political affairs of their client countries. They seek incremental governance reforms despite a record of failure.

The aid agencies use precisely the same argument to defend their "partner" developing countries in refusing to publicly disclose, or publicly discuss, their defense spending. Aid agencies examine the budgets of governments, exclusive of the defense sector, find huge deficits, and provide funds to correct the situation. In many countries the expenditures on weapons systems are large and the corruption within those accounts is enormous, but the aid agencies ignore this. They claim it is too political. They forget that the money they give away is funded by ordinary taxpayers.

So long as these attitudes prevail at aid agencies, many of their good works will be ignored, their reputations will be tarnished, and the broad public in developed and developing countries alike will be cynical. I have heard people in Egypt and Pakistan assert that the real purposes of USAID funding in their countries is to support American consulting companies and US manufacturers that win the procurement contracts under these aid programs. However inaccurate such assertions may be, they reflect widely held perceptions and illustrate the skepticism so widespread in many developing countries about the motivations of aid agencies and their effectiveness.

There is bound to come a time when a US congressional committee investigates the World Bank's anticorruption record and finds that the World Bank's continued trust in governments that are highly corrupt has led to the waste of vast amounts of cash.

Such an investigation will only add support to the views of those like Dambisa Moyo, who argued in her book *Dead Aid*[5] that African countries would have a far greater prospect of economic growth if they refused foreign development assistance and relied on the private sector. She suggested that foreign aid has done more harm than good. Her book is dedicated to the British economist Lord Peter Bauer, a major influence on Margaret Thatcher when she was UK prime minister. Bauer led the charge in questioning the pro-government approaches of aid agencies, which he argued reduced the full potential of the private sector. There is a strong presumption among such opponents of aid that the assistance boosts the public sector and encourages corruption and inefficiency. The best antidote, they argue, is no aid and far greater roles in development for free-market competition.

Across the developing world the governmental bureaucracies have flour-ished and multiplied, constantly seeking rents from all who need a permit or a license to build a house, or qualify for a government contract, or want to start a business. Those rents stifle growth and competitiveness, even in coun-tries like China and India, which have achieved substantial economic growth. Time and again, the aid agencies have been the complicit agents of the growth of government.

At the same time, the aid agencies have failed too often to look carefully at how these governments in poor countries can pay decent wages to the rising numbers of people that are on the public sector payrolls—low pay to policemen and nurses and teachers is a prime cause of petty corruption across the developing world.

The primary fault at all aid agencies rests in the fact that almost all of their major programs involve providing loans and grants, explicitly and di-rectly, to governments. During the period in Kenya reviewed by Michela Wrong in her book, when corruption rose in the government and election fraud led to mass murders, the World Bank's representative in Nairobi was Colin Bruce. He was widely seen as close to Kenyan President Kibaki and rented his house from the Kibaki family. Soon after the 2007 elections, which after horrendous ethnic conflicts saw Kibaki hold on to office, Bruce was recalled to Washington amid considerable media controversy. He was then promoted.

It can be intimidating for a mid-level World Bank manager to sit at the large table in the board room at 1818 H Street in northwest Washington, DC, and confront the twenty-four members of the executive board representing the 188 member countries of the organization. They all want the cash to flow. They do not want to hear a manager say that loans and grants are being stopped because of corruption. They do not want to be told that the World Bank's staff refuses to provide funding to an array of World Bank member countries because their governments are corrupt.

Senior managers tell their staffs to work around the corrupt officials and ensure projects are well monitored. In many of the countries that receive substantial aid, such as those at the lower levels of the CPI's rankings, the task is impossible. But the aid agencies go ahead with all manner of balance of payments and budget-supporting programs and infrastructure project funding, and they also approve large grants for anticorruption/good governance programs. To support these programs, the aid agencies then hire large numbers of Western consultants who rarely have detailed anticorruption experience, let alone familiarity with the history, culture, and governmental conditions of the countries in which they are assigned to work. The consultants agree to contracts that explicitly deny them the right to speak publicly when they see abuse.

So often, for example, aid money will be spent on sophisticated computer systems for anticorruption commissions and for the judiciary and the police under provisions of anticorruption programs. In theory this is excellent, but useless if these government bodies are run by corrupt officials and staffed by people on subsistence-level incomes. Most anticorruption activists that I know in developing countries see the aid agencies as being too close to governments, too friendly with corrupt top politicians, and too keen to pump out the grants and the loans. So what is the right course?

Overall, the critical consideration is that it is the quality of aid, not its quantity, that should always be viewed as paramount. If economic aid cannot be seen as improving the lives of ordinary people, then it has failed. This is the sole criterion that matters. More specifically, the aid agencies led by the World Bank should at a minimum take the following steps:

1. The aid agencies should do what they do best—promote agricultural research, support infrastructure, address the basic needs of the very poor, and provide advice on economic policies. They should cease to directly promote loans and grants to governments for explicit "good governance" programs because they lack the experience, the staff, and, most importantly, the political clout to ensure effective implementation (they should support civil society as the lead in promoting good governance in countries).

2. Experience shows that progress toward better and more transparent governance almost only takes place in economies that are growing. Aid agencies—notably, the World Bank—have armies of excellent economists on their staffs and growth-oriented programs are what they should be concentrating on if they want to contribute to the anticorruption fight. In this context, the agencies should see that public officials in aid-recipient countries get decent salaries, especially in the justice system, in government procurement, and for workers providing basic social services.

3. Governments should not be given aid agency grants to introduce measures that reduce their own corruption. This is just wrong. Governments should not need cash to clean up their own houses. The World Bank and other aid agencies need to start to tell recipient

governments of all kinds of aid that the flow of funds is dependent on the host government ensuring basic good governance. This means building institutional arrangements to ensure transparency in government procurement, including defense; ensuring governmental public accountability by establishing an independent procurement oversight body that reports publicly by fully reporting all aspects of public expenditure to parliament and implementing meaningful freedom-of-information laws and regulations; ensuring that the judicial system is independent and well-funded; and guaranteeing human rights and the rights to free assembly and freedom of the press. Aid agencies should cease aid to countries that fail to take these governance measures and accept that, based on the current CPI rankings, this could mean stopping aid flows today to twenty to forty countries.

4. The World Bank and other aid agencies should change internal incentives. Executives have to be confident that their careers will not be damaged by saying no to project disbursements where they do not believe there is full transparency and accountability.

5. The governments that control the World Bank (the majority of the votes are held by the United States and the Western European industrial countries) should make a major change in the institution's Articles of Agreement and the provisions of funding for its grant-making arm, the International Development Association (IDA), which provides funds to the poorest countries, many of which also have the most corrupt governments. The World Bank is currently required to provide funds only to entities controlled by governments. If the development banks believe they can attain better results in monitoring programs and supporting anticorruption projects through the private sector or the not-for-profit sector, then they should be able do so.

6. The international aid community needs to recognize the effectiveness and momentum behind anticorruption civil society groups across the developing world and in Central and Eastern Europe and provide them with far greater financial support than is currently the case (as suggested in chapter 12). The PTF is a good example. Its grants to civil society organizations promoting anticorruption projects are rarely more than $30,000 and these are accompanied by expert planning and implementation advice by a corps of volunteers. Aid agencies just cannot operate with such small grant amounts or give small civil society organizations expert help. However, in the fight against corruption, it is exactly civil society organizations like this, which know their communities and know where rot is to be found, that can make a key difference.

7. Aid agencies should continue to investigate corruption and abuse within their own organizations and severely penalize any contracting firms that engage in bribery. The World Bank is building a sound model here that other agencies should replicate.

Bilateral aid agencies are even more political in the ways they operate than the multilateral ones. Afghanistan was receiving $4 billion a year from USAID, but in 2011 this was cut in half. The country ranks among the most corrupt in the world. Absent US assistance, many of the government ministries would collapse, which places the United States in an almost impossible conundrum. Domestic political budget pressures call for a significant reduction in the funds available to USAID. The international community looks to the United States to be the prime aid giver to Afghanistan and is unwilling to add funds should the United States cut back.

Meanwhile, the Karzai government has left little doubt that there could be political chaos, leading to significant advances for the Taliban, if the governmental bureaucracy fails, as would probably be the case without the US taxpayer billions. The US intelligence and defense communities believe the USAID support to the governmental machinery is essential to enhance the military objectives that the United States has in the country. The pressures, therefore, are formidable to keep pushing through the funds to enable Afghan government officials to get rich.

This mess exists despite the fact that the United States has been engaged in Afghanistan for more than a decade. The situation is all the worse because there is a broad unwillingness by all the officials involved in Afghanistan to hold a major meeting to discuss corruption. It is the big elephant in the room every time the donors to Afghanistan come together, yet none of the political leaders want to discuss the issue comprehensively and publicly when they gather in international meetings.

There are no easy answers to situations like this. Experience suggests that foreign aid does not reduce corruption in aid-recipient countries. Experience suggests that official aid agencies have a poor record at promoting sustained governance reforms. And experience suggests that aid agencies are not yet willing to talk as candidly about corruption to corrupt governments as they should and impose sanctions unless there are reforms. It is time that this changed.

At a minimum, a tough anticorruption stance by the multilateral aid agencies, as advocated above here, dare not be undermined by the bilateral aid agencies. There is a risk that aid-recipient countries would pressure major bilateral donors if the World Bank and other multilaterals became more conditional in the governance area. The aid agencies—bilateral and multilateral—need to maintain a solid front and stress that the money of taxpayers in donor countries will no longer be used to support the lavish lifestyle of corrupt politicians in the world's poorest nations.

DEFENSE INDUSTRY CORRUPTION

Much work has been undertaken over the last dozen years to address critical issues related to corruption and the arms trade. We now understand a great deal more about the nature of corruption in this sector, as noted in chapter 7. But it is questionable whether our knowledge is leading to measurable reductions in the volume of bribery entwined in this huge business sector, which involves international exports of more than $400 billion a year.

Unlike many other business sectors, there are intimate relationships across every aspect of activity between governments and the manufacturers of weapons systems. I once challenged a top executive of a major US company about whether he ever felt any sense of guilt about selling systems to foreign countries whose governments are thoroughly corrupt. He responded that this was not an issue for his firm, as no exports of weapons systems could be made without US government approval. If the United States determined it was in its strategic interests to see corrupt foreign governments obtain US weapons, then that was just fine with the US manufacturer.

On November 29, 2011, the *Wall Street Journal* reported that former US Marine Dakota Meyer, who holds the Medal of Honor, was in a legal dispute with BAE Systems in part because when he worked for the UK company's US subsidiary, he objected to plans to sell sophisticated weapons to Pakistan. He challenged the company, but according to the newspaper report a BAE spokesman said, "The decision to sell defense equipment is made by the State Department, not BAE."[6]

It is important to recognize the degree to which governments exert control in this area. For example:

- No major manufacturer of sophisticated weapons systems in any country can conclude an export deal without the explicit approval of its own government.
- The only legitimate purchasers of weapons systems are governments, or their designated public-sector services, such as the military.
- The research and development costs of new weapons systems are so great that companies depend greatly on government research finance.
- Individual contracts are large, involve deliveries over many years, and need to be financed in complex ways that almost always require the provision of government-sponsored export credits.

- Contracts are complicated, involving "offset" agreements under which all manner of services are embedded in the overall costs and that explicitly call for governments of the supplier and the buyer countries to actively participate.

Most contracts have unique specifications, which makes it particularly difficult to discover corruption. It is almost impossible to compare one procurement contract with another in this field, as virtually every deal is unique in its details, with the result that finding hidden costs and charges that inflate the overall bill and provide payments to agents and officials is difficult.

Making matters still worse is the fact that many governments consider all aspects of weapons systems' contracting a matter of national security and thus strictly confidential. Many governments do not even publish their defense budgets. Secrecy enables corruption. Corruption in the defense sector always adds a burden to taxpayers somewhere.

In the late 1990s, Laurence Cockcroft, a co-founder of both TI and TI-UK, started conversations with a wide circle of experts about the possibility of constructively engaging the world's largest defense industry firms to come together to discuss corruption. In early April 2001, Cockcroft organized a seminar at Cambridge University sponsored by the governments of both Sweden and the United Kingdom and also by one of the world's largest defense contractors, Lockheed-Martin Corporation of the United States. Participants came from government, academia, the media, business, and civil society from the United Kingdom, the United States, France, Sweden, Greece, Nigeria, South Africa, Russia, and India.

When it came to organizing corrupt deals, it was clear at the conference that agents in the arms sales business are central players. Arms sellers are often able to conclude broad and general agreements with agents who have large latitude. These agents often operate with "slush funds" and freedom to pay bribes free of supervision and without fear of repercussions. The acceptance and complicity of such practice by the arms exporters underscores the need for solutions that pay just as much, if not more, attention to the sellers of arms as to the purchasers.

Moreover, there is anecdotal evidence to suggest that arms sellers and their sales agents are experienced in assisting buyers to deposit their kickbacks in secret offshore bank accounts. This makes corruption all the easier and more attractive to procurement officials across the globe. Money laundering and the arms trade appear to have a long history. It is a practice that is seen to be flourishing today.

Looking back at my notes from that conference and following discussions in this area ever since, I believe there are at least ten sets of actions that can and should be undertaken to strengthen the transparency and accountability in this dangerous sector:

1. Government export credit agencies play key roles in many international-al arms sales. They might be pressured across the OECD to agree to desist from supporting weapons sales. (The argument used to counter this is that it may mean unemployment in the arms sector—a bizarre line from governments that claim to support capitalism and free markets and that would oppose massive subsidies to makers of dishwashers even though such subsidies would boost employment there and do a lot less global harm than phony employment subsidies to the arms makers.)

2. The closeness between arms manufacturers and the defense ministries in their own governments is seen by some as undermining fair competition, running counter to meaningful transparency, and securing for the industry a special advantageous lobbying opportunity. Many former military officers go to work for arms manufacturers, as do civil servants in defense ministries (Boeing paid a $600 million fine for offering a top job to the deputy head of all US Pentagon procurement a few years ago in connection with a potential $20 billion contract). The multiple conflicts of interest need to be squarely addressed in the leading industrial countries. There needs to be, at a minimum, a substantial gap, perhaps a couple of years, before a person can leave the military or a government's department of defense and join a firm that is engaged in arms sales.

3. The enforcement of the OECD Convention Against Bribery clearly has potential in constraining the use of bribes. But, to be effective, the punishments must go beyond slaps on the wrist (see the final section of this chapter). BAE Systems, for example, agreed to a $400 million fine for FCPA violations in the United States and signed an agreement with US Department of Justice that is so artfully phrased that it does not impair in any way the ability of BAE to continue to be a major contractor to the US government.

4. Major arms-procurement transactions could be subjected to "Integrity Pact" approaches, as defined by TI, which include a range of safeguards to reduce the possibility of bribery. Here competitive bidding on contracts would be independently monitored to explicitly guard against corruption. Experts could be engaged under the umbrella of civil society organizations to "referee" competing bids for contracts. The "Integrity Pact" concept, pioneered and developed by an array of TI national chapters over the years and refined and made highly effective by former World Bank operations director and TI veteran Michael Wiehen, should be a basic tool in defense sector contracting.

5. An anticorruption best practices guide for the arms trade may be a valuable tool for manufacturers and for governments. Major companies have been working in this area and its application calls for very substantial investments by firms in training employees and agents in compliance.

6. The weakness of civil society in this area in developing countries needs to be explicitly addressed. Support for "think-tanks" and research centers in developing countries that are focused on military issues could greatly strengthen the ability of civil society in these countries to strive to more directly monitor arms procurement. Very few civil society organizations in the developing world focus on this area because so much information is listed by governments as "top secret—national security." The excessive use of such a designation to keep deals secret needs to be attacked.

7. Consideration needs to be given to find ways to protect military personnel who seek to "blow the whistle" on corruption in the armed forces. In most countries there is no protection of any kind.

8. So widespread is corruption in arms in non-OECD countries that there is a natural inclination to look to the major official creditors to these countries as using their leverage to curb this sickness. Sir Samuel Brittan, former economics editor of the *Financial Times*, called at the Cambridge University meeting for tough conditionality by the World Bank and the IMF related specifically to military spending by their client countries.

9. The international institutions could also assist governments of developing countries to address the issue of low pay scales in the armed forces and in top echelons of government. To a modest degree corrections here could reduce the temptations to take kickbacks from arms sellers.

10. All governments need to sign an international pact of some kind, perhaps added to UNCAC, that specifically concerns the use of sales agents in weapons contracts. They should be subject to some form of transparent and accountable public monitoring. Trace International is a US not-for-profit organization that specializes in training agents to comply with the FCPA and the OECD Convention and would be an excellent monitor of an international agreement in this area.

Oscar Arias once told me that you could draw up a list of the world's most corrupt countries and another list of those that did most to keep their defense spending secret and the probability would be that the lists would be identical. He once publicly called on the Inter-American Development Bank to demand that all countries that received loans and grants from it should publicly disclose their arms spending. The Inter-American Development

Bank has refused to do this. I have made similar requests over the years to the World Bank without success. The World Bank, together with the IMF, claims to assist countries with stabilizing their fiscal policies, but they also claim that they have no remit to look at defense spending!

The primary reasons why the World Bank and IMF do not use their influence in this area is because their major shareholders (the Western governments) do not want them to. The home countries of the world's biggest exporters of weapons systems, led by the United States, do not want multilateral official institutions engaged in any shape or form in any aspect of the arms trade.

It would be inaccurate to paint a totally negative picture of efforts to combat defense-related corruption. The Cambridge University conference was an important first step. Under the leadership of arms expert Mark Pyman, TI-UK has been raising awareness in many parts of the world, working with governments and military establishments, on critical issues in the area of corruption and defense. Ethics training for armed forces in such countries as Ukraine and Afghanistan, as well as developing programs with NATO, are some of the activities led by Pyman and his team.

Moreover, under Mark's guidance, a landmark agreement was gradually forged over the last decade that set new standards for the ways in which European and American manufacturers of weapons systems would operate. In October 2009, the American Aerospace Industries Association (AIA) and the AeroSpace and Defence Industries Association of Europe (ASD) agreed on the "Global Principles of Business Ethics for the Aerospace and Defense Industry." This underscored the need for integrity in bidding, negotiating, and performing contracts and stressed that companies endorsing the global principles were committed to implementing the provisions. This included "Zero Tolerance to Corruption."

- Companies will comply fully with all antibribery laws applicable to the conduct of their business, such as the US Foreign Corrupt Practices Act and those laws enacted pursuant to International Conventions (including, but not limited to, the 1997 OECD Convention and the 2003 United Nations Convention against Corruption).
- Companies will not offer, promise, or provide any undue pecuniary or other advantage (e.g., payments, gifts, hospitality, as well as political contributions or charitable donations) to public officials, political parties, or political candidates, or to any private party, in order to obtain or retain business or gain any other improper advantage in the conduct of their business (hereafter "Improper Advantage"). Companies shall duly account for any payments, gifts, hospitality, political contributions, or charitable donations in their books and records and in a manner which permits reasonable traceability.

- Companies will establish and enforce policies and internal control procedures that prohibit the company and their employees, directors, and officers from offering, promising, or providing—directly or indirectly—any Improper Advantage, and will conduct training on such policies and procedures.
- Companies will make their business partners, including joint-venture partners, subcontractors, and suppliers, aware of the integrity policies of the company, and require them to refrain from offering, promising, or providing (directly or indirectly) any Improper Advantage.
- Many countries and companies prohibit facilitation payments. In recognition that such payments undermine the integrity of industry, even where such payments are not prohibited by law, companies will seek to eliminate facilitation payments.

External monitoring of the agreements would add strength to this landmark agreement. The involvement of other major manufacturers of weapons systems would also add strength here.

More generally, looking across the landscape of the arms trade, however, the world of international defense contracting is largely a black hole. Now and again there is an investigation and a prosecution, but governments and military establishments are not assigning priority to the topic. A new convention at the United Nations, while welcome, is also unlikely to change things unless a meaningful monitoring and enforcement mechanism is put in place, which is improbable. But action by the United Nations, just like the implementation of the trans-Atlantic business pact, does provide civil society with opportunities to benchmark progress, to strengthen public awareness of corruption in this sector, and to lead stronger campaigns for reform. The good news is that Global Witness and other nongovernmental organizations have an acute and urgent focus on corruption in the arms trade and the enormous impact it has on civil wars and global insecurity. They are likely to continue being relentless on this front.

OIL, GAS, AND MINERALS

At the summit conference of the leaders of the Group of 8 in Evian, France, in mid-2002, the decision was taken to establish the Extractive Industries Transparency Initiative (EITI). The goal was to shed transparency on the dealings between major global minerals companies and the governments whose countries host the world's oil, gas, and metals. Top representatives of the companies and the governments, as well as a small number of leaders of civil society, would sit together around the EITI table.

Chapter 14

In June 2003, the UK government of Prime Minister Tony Blair convened a conference to launch EITI. Blair saw himself as the father of this enterprise and in rousing good form he explained to business, government, and civil society delegates the historic importance of EITI's role and mission. He said in part:

> The extraction of oil, gas and minerals from the ground underpins our modern life style. We depend on predictable supplies. Around the world there are millions of jobs in this sector. Some 3.5 billion people live in countries dependent upon their natural resource wealth for improving standards of living. They are directly affected by the way the revenues are used. . . . Some people underestimate the importance of transparency. Together with improving standards of governance and democratic accountability it is a central plank of a wider accountability agenda. This, in turn, is essential to improve development and the prospects of achieving the Millennium Development Goals for global poverty reduction.
>
> Conversely, a lack of transparency undermines public confidence in the legitimacy of the state. When there is corruption, it is always the poor who suffer most. We need to use transparency in revenue and financial management to allow people to hold government to account and build public trust. Increased transparency will also help to create the right climate for attracting foreign investment, and encourage an enterprise culture. Governments need to create this favorable environment, but companies have an interest in promoting transparency too. Transparency should help companies to reduce reputational risk, to address the concerns of shareholders and to help manage risks of long-term investments. And transparency is a positive contribution to development as it increases the likelihood that revenues will be used for poverty reduction.[7]

It would be another three years before EITI would get up and running. That this happened was in large part due to the determination of Peter Eigen, who had retired as chair of TI and became the first EITI board chair in early 2007. A secretariat was established in Oslo, Norway. EITI's work has proved to be arduous and fraught with repeated failures of action despite much good rhetoric. Many countries and big companies have joined EITI and it assumed under Eigen's leadership the basic membership strength, as well as an organizational structure, to become a useful player. Its lack of any enforcement mechanisms, however, makes it unlikely that it can reach its potential. Neither companies nor governments face any sanctions for noncompliance with the sunshine mandates that EITI seeks to promote. Major international efforts are needed to build on EITI's fruitful early years and ensure the organization gains greater authority, especially vis-à-vis oil and gas companies.

The goals of EITI are strongly supported by leading civil society organizations, which are not resting on their EITI laurels, however, when it comes to pressing their case. Considerable pioneering research and campaigning work to force oil, gas, and mining companies to declare their royalty payments to foreign governments has been undertaken by the Publish What You Pay coalition, the Revenue Watch Institute, and Global Witness. In 2008, TI published a landmark study, *Report on Revenue Transparency of Oil and Gas Companies*. It followed an earlier report by Global Witness of the behaviors of oil companies vis-à-vis host countries.

As TI researcher Dr. Juanita Olaya started to develop the TI project, she was almost overwhelmed by the sheer magnitude of the operations of the companies that she was looking at. Oil export revenues alone were estimated at US$866 billion in 2006. This was equivalent to approximately 1.8 percent of gross world product for that year and more than half of the combined gross domestic product of the fifty-three lowest-income nations in the world.

The TI research looked in-depth at forty-two oil companies in twenty-one countries of operation to determine on the basis of their published materials how substantially they reported information on their revenues. The companies were directly surveyed for comments and for responses to findings. The study found that "a majority of leading oil and gas companies are far from transparent when it comes to the payments they make to resource-rich countries, leaving the door open to corruption and hampering efforts to fight poverty."[8]

The TI research sought to evaluate the leading companies in terms of their current policies, management systems, and performance in areas relevant to revenue transparency in their upstream operations. Revenue transparency in this context included the following: (1) corporate action where disclosure can contribute to improved accountability in the management of extractive revenues, (2) payments to host governments, and (3) and corporate anticorruption programs. A complex system of scores was assigned to place the findings for each company evaluated within a high, middle, and low range relative to their revenue transparency.

Companies that made it into the "High Performers" category included BG Group, BHP Billiton, Nexen, Petro-Canada, Shell, StatoilHydro, Talisman Energy, and Petrobras. Significantly, their example undermined arguments by some of the firms that to reveal details on revenue transparency would place them at a competitive disadvantage. After all, if giants like Shell and BHP could strive for substantial transparency, then why could not many more? The list of "Low Performers" included China National Offshore Oil Corporation (CNOOC), China National Petroleum Corporation (CNPC), Exxon-Mobil, INPEX, Kuwait Petroleum Corporation, Lukoil, Oil and Natural Gas Corporation Ltd., and Petronas.

Led by the Revenue Watch Institute and the Publish What You Pay coalition, both strongly supported by George Soros's Open Society philanthropy, major US legislation was secured in 2010. Thanks to their work, including the direct interventions with some key US senators by Soros, the US 2010 financial reform legislation includes provisions calling on oil, gas, and mining companies to provide independently audited annual statements to the US SEC on all of their payments to foreign governments. This could involve hundreds of firms. The first filings are likely to be made in 2013.

The European Commission in Brussels is likely to follow the US lead and press for greater revenue transparency by the EU extractive industries companies. If these initiatives work, then within a few years a major stream of new data will enter the public domain.

We may learn as a result just how much cash flows from the companies to the host governments in resource rich countries, but then what?

Neither the Chinese nor the Russians are likely to press the corrupt governments to change their ways. Nor are the British or French authorities likely to do much here unless there is strong American leadership. For this to happen, the US government has to delink from the powerful oil and gas lobbies, which means, among other things, that it needs to accelerate its efforts at promoting alternative sources for domestic demand to imported oil.

Importantly, once there is greater clarity on just how much cash the companies pay the host governments, the next area of attention has to be on just what the governments then do with the cash. Actions are needed to make it far harder for corrupt governments to launder their cash internationally, and much easier for the citizens of the countries that have been robbed to repatriate the stolen cash from overseas. In these areas, US leadership will be crucial.

NOTES

1. According to a news report in the *Observer* (UK) by Yvonne Ridley in London and Shraga Elam in Zurich on June 27, 1999, "President Slobodan Milosevic has salted away billions of dollars in secret bank accounts, beyond the reach of NATO. Requests to freeze Milosevic's assets in Swiss bank accounts were made nearly six months ago, and it now appears that his financial advisers have switched to the notoriously secret principality of Liechtenstein. According to American and British intelligence reports earlier this year, Milosevic had assets in Switzerland, Greece, Cyprus and Russia. 'We had indications from within Belgrade on 19 April that there were frantic moves to switch his assets to safer tax havens including Liechtenstein, but obviously NATO had different priorities,' a British intelligence source told The Observer."

2. Report of the "Independent Panel Review—The World Bank Group, Department of Institutional Integrity," September 13, 2007. This panel consisted of the following individuals: Paul A. Volcker, chair, former chairman of the US Federal Reserve Board; Gustavo Gaviria, a leading coffee industry executive in Colombia; John Githongo, former permanent secretary of governance and ethics in Kenya and founder of TI-Kenya; Ben W. Heineman Jr., former senior vice president and general counsel of the General Electric Company; Walter Van Gerven, former advocate-general of the European Court of Justice; and Sir John Vereker, former permanent secretary of the UK Department for International Development. This quote is from paragraph 11 of the introduction, page 9.

3. "World Bank Country-Level Engagement on Governance and Anticorruption—An Evaluation of the 2007 Strategy and Implementation Plan," Independent Evaluation Group, World Bank, 2011.

4. Michela Wrong, *It's Our Turn to Eat—The Story of a Kenyan Whistleblower* (London: Fourth Estate, 2009).

5. Dambisa Moyo, *Dead Aid: Why Aid Is Not Working and How There Is a Better Way for Africa* (New York: Farrar, Straus, & Giroux, 2009).

6. Julian Barnes, "Decorated Marine Sues Contractor," *Wall Street Journal*, November 29, 2011.

7. Tony Blair, address at the launch conference of the Extractive Industries Transparency Initiative (EITI), Lancaster House, London, United Kingdom, June 17, 2003.

8. Transparency International, *Promoting Revenue Transparency: 2008 Report on Revenue Transparency of Oil and Gas Companies*, April 26, 2008. See also follow-up report by Transparency International, published March 2011 (www.transparency.org).

Chapter Fifteen

Shaping Solutions II

"Money laundering is the conversion of criminal incomes into assets that cannot be traced back to the underlying crime,"[1] state academics Peter Reuter and Edwin M. Truman.

Money has been smuggled across national borders for centuries, to hide the wealth of powerful people, to avoid the payment of taxes, to create cash safe havens for all manner of gangsters. Crucial to the success of corrupt leaders is their ability to launder their ill-gotten gains. Their ability to outsmart sophisticated international investigators is considerable. Money laundering is the art (some may call it a science, given its current sophistication) of converting illegally secured cash into legitimate assets. It involves criminals—from assorted heads of states to drug-traffickers, tax evaders, and terrorists—in transferring their ill-gotten gains through networks of agents and international financial institutions into investments (bank savings accounts, real estate, stock market equities and bonds, etc.) in the names of organizations and individuals with no known criminal ties.

Launched by Raymond Baker in Washington, DC, in 2006, Global Financial integrity (GFI) has become one of the most authoritative and independent sources of research on illicit financial flows of cash, as well as the foremost advocate for reform. Baker combines a passion for exceptionally detailed research with a passion for seeing that justice for the world's poor is secured through governmental actions to curb money laundering.

"Illicit Financial Flows from Developing Countries over the Decade Ending 2009," published by GFI in December 2011 and authored by Dev Kar, GFI's lead economist, and GFI economist Sarah Frietas (see appendix 4) concluded that the developing world lost $903 billion in 2009 in illicit flows. This is by no means due to corruption alone. The authors use the term "illicit financial flows" to refer to money that is illegal in its origin, transfer, or use and reflects the proceeds of corruption, crime, and tax evasion. This includes corporate avoidance of customs duties, value-added tax (VAT), and income taxes, which account for an estimated 60 percent of the total. The study utilized multiple economic models, which were combined and "tested" to determine the most reliable estimates. The findings were based on macro-economic trade and external debt data maintained by the International Monetary Fund and the World Bank. The authors stated that from 2000 to 2009, developing countries lost $8.44 trillion in all forms of illicit outflows. Conservatively estimated, illicit flows increased in current dollar terms by 14.9 percent per annum from the beginning until the end of the decade.

Baker has defined three forms of illicit and corrupt money that cross borders: proceeds of bribery and theft by government officials; proceeds of criminal activities such as drug trading, racketeering, counterfeiting, contraband, and terrorist funds; and proceeds of tax-evading and laundered commercial transactions. In a statement to the Ways and Means Committee of the US House of Representatives on March 30, 2009, Baker said:

> The US is at a critical juncture. Recent events have underscored the severity of the problem of offshore financial centers, banking secrecy, and loopholes in current US laws as well as how these enable illicit financial practices such as tax evasion and fraud. Abusive offshore schemes are depriving the US of approximately $100 billion a year at a time when the economy is in a recession and the resources are strained.

Over many years there have been initiatives of many kinds to curb money laundering. Much of the focus in the 1980s and 1990s was on the drug trade and the ability of the drug mafias to launder their cash. After September 11, 2001, the focus expanded significantly to the terrorist networks and their means of using all manner of illicit channels to obtain and hide cash and to make payments to arms traders. Compared to drug cartels and terrorists, the money-laundering activities of corrupt government officials and politicians have mostly been of secondary importance to major governments seeking to reduce overall opportunities for money laundering.

The criminals intent on money laundering are skilled and have sophisticated advisors. Corrupt public officials and the enterprises who bribe them are not averse to paying significant sums to transfer the illicit funds across the globe, through all manner of dummy companies and offshore financial centers, to eventually park the money in respectable and liquid investments, mostly in Western Europe and in North America.

In July 2011, Financial Action Task Force (FATF), the international official agency with the lead mandate to pursue anti–money laundering efforts, published a report titled "Laundering the Proceeds of Corruption." FATF underscored the fact that while some "politically exposed persons" (PEPs)[2] directly place their illicit cash in domestic bank accounts, most prefer to go through international channels. To illustrate this, FATF's report noted the case of Augusto Pinochet, the former president of Chile:

> Pinochet was assisted by his US-based bank (and its U.K. branch) in setting up corporate vehicles in order to both hide his assets and shield them from the reach of asset freezing and confiscation or civil recovery orders. Specifically, Pinochet was able to set up offshore shell corporations and a trust in 1996 and 1998, even after a Spanish magistrate had filed a detailed indictment against Pinochet for crimes against humanity and issued world-wide freezing orders.[3] These corporations, established in jurisdictions that at the time had weak AML controls, were listed as the nominal owners of the US bank accounts and other investment vehicles that benefited Pinochet and his family. The bank's KYC documentation listed only the corporations, not Pinochet, as the owners of the accounts, despite the fact that the bank knew that Pinochet was the beneficial owner (since the bank itself had set up the corporations). The bank has since been convicted of AML-related criminal charges. [4]

In recent years, FATF developed a black list of rogue countries that served as convenient and secret shelters for dirty money and started to push for sanctions against them. There has been some progress. Some national authorities have proved to be willing to reform at a faster pace than others. However, from Cyprus to the Cayman Islands, from the island of Jersey to Liechtenstein, the opportunities for corrupt officials to find mechanisms to deposit their cash and launder it through diverse channels into the mainstream of global finance remain formidable.

FATF, established in 1989 and headquartered at the offices of the OECD in Paris, made many policy recommendations in its first decade and issued many reports, but it became increasingly evident that its effectiveness depended crucially on the support it received for its proposals from the governments of the countries that control the world's most important financial centers—the United States, the United Kingdom, and Switzerland, in particular. These governments gave FATF token support at best.

The US Treasury tended to pursue its own course and take little interest in FATF. In the mid-1990s, as it became increasingly alarmed about the rising level of drugs entering the United States from Latin America, the Treasury decided to "follow the money" and was soon questioning many US banks about some of their large deposits from Latin America. Some major cases brought by the Treasury, and highly publicized by US congressional hearings, alerted top US bankers to the reputational risks that their institutions were facing by being associated with cash from the drug cartels and from corrupt Latin American politicians.

In 1999, the US Senate Permanent Sub-Committee on Investigations, chaired by Senator Carl Levin, called Citigroup top executive John Reed to testify. Mr. Levin said that what disturbed him was a "rogues' gallery" of Citibank private bank clients. He said they included Raul Salinas de Gortari, a convicted felon and the brother of the former Mexican president Carlos Salinas; Asif Ali Zardari, who has served prison time for corruption and is now president of Pakistan; President Omar Bongo of Gabon; and Sani Abacha, the deceased former president of Nigeria.

Soon thereafter I received a telephone call from Shaukat Aziz, then the executive vice president of Citigroup's private wealth management operations. I had briefly met Aziz a few years earlier when I had the opportunity to introduce TI to a group of American business leaders. Now, Aziz wanted a meeting. He explained that every bank needed to comply with US regulations that called on banks to "know their customers," which meant that banks needed to ensure they had full knowledge of the real owners of all deposits in their banks and how major depositors had come by their cash. Citi was under great pressure, as were other US banks, to rigorously apply the rules. The problem was that competitor foreign banks were not under similar pressures, he said. He added that he would like TI to work as a catalyst in bringing the world's leading banks together to formulate voluntary agreements for the full international application of "know your customer" rules and he would provide major support to this initiative.

Somewhat to my surprise, I learned soon thereafter that the leading Swiss banks were also highly concerned about being publicly seen as the places where crooked politicians and drug czars deposited their cash and that, as a result, they were interested in entering the kind of conversation that Aziz wanted to launch. In due course UBS in Switzerland took the lead and invited TI and representatives of ten major global banks to a meeting at its training center outside of Zurich in Wolfsberg in 1999. A further set of meetings, including another at Wolfsberg with a dozen major banks, led to the formulation of the "Wolfsberg Principles" in late 2000. This was a voluntary code of conduct and the first of its kind. It came about just after its chief architect, Aziz, left Citi to become Pakistan's finance minister (he was his country's prime minister from 2004 to 2007).

There was skepticism from the start about whether the banks were sincere, but this became moot after the terrorist attacks on New York's World Trade Center. The subsequent "Patriot Act," which included tough provisions in its Title 3 on anti–money laundering, placed banks on notice that severe penalties would arise if they were seen taking deposits from terrorist groups. Banks, it was very strongly argued, needed to "know their customers." Pushing hard for these reforms was Senator Levin, acutely mindful of the horror stories that his Senate committee had investigated in earlier years.

The Wolfsberg Group continued to meet and issue new anti-money-laundering statements from time to time. Its importance declined for four reasons, however: first, representation in the meetings moved from senior banking executives with major policy powers to the corporate lawyers, whose basic approaches were conservative and defensive; second, having come together in large part because of the convening skills of TI, the bankers decided they no longer needed TI and this muted the pressure within the group to face the real issues and be bold; third, the founding banks were satisfied to restrict the size of their group and never seek to expand to include a far larger number of international financial services firms; and, finally, the need for voluntary actions was reduced by the legal requirements in the US Patriot Act.

Concerns about terrorist money laundering pushed the broader issues onto the summit agendas of the G8 and later the G20 and provided FATF, at last, with greater support and authority. And then, as a result of the 2008 financial crisis, a completely new factor entered the equation: the US Internal Revenue Service, more keen than ever to boost revenues for a US budget facing massive deficits, decided that a potential source of cash was to go after Americans who were laundering cash through offshore banks and financial entities to evade US taxation.

Whereas in the past Manhattan District Attorney Robert Morgenthau had looked at times as if he was the lone investigator of major tax evasion and the activities of the offshore money centers (see chapter 6), now Interpol was engaged alongside a host of public prosecutors in various countries who were starting to obtain information.

German authorities had known for years that many wealthy Germans evade taxes by opening secret bank accounts in Luxembourg, Liechtenstein, and Switzerland, but the Berlin government did nothing. Equally disinterested have been governments in Rome as large numbers of Italians routinely smuggled cash across the border from Italy into Switzerland. The French and British governments have long known that all manner of crooked foreign leaders have large cash deposits in banks in London and Paris, but nothing has been done. The official excuse often is that there is no proof that the money was not honestly earned, which appears laughable when it is noted that the late president Sani Abacha of Nigeria was depositing more than $1 billion a year in European banks in the mid-1990s!

And then many thousands of Americans had long sought to avoid taxes by opening secret Swiss accounts. In 2009, the US authorities went after the biggest bank in Switzerland. It investigated, charged, and settled for a fine on the UBS of over $700 million and an agreement to reveal the names to the US tax authorities of up to fifty-two thousand American accounts. This emboldened the German authorities to start pressing the major Swiss banks for names.

The global money-laundering issues are finally emerging on the broader public radar screen, thanks in part to the financial crisis and the focus of the media. For example, the *New York Times* opined in an editorial on August 22, 2009:

> More international cooperation is needed to determine standards of compliance with newly devised tax information exchange agreements and police them. And pressure should be brought on recalcitrant countries like Panama. If Switzerland can be persuaded to get out of the tax haven business anyone can.

Gradually the major governments have come to appreciate that illicit financial flows are on such a scale that they threaten the stability of the global financial system and that, as a result, there are profound systemic reasons in addition to matters of tax evasion, terrorist funding, and containing the drug cartels for a far larger assault on all those institutions and regimes that support the global money-laundering business. In an evolutionary process, from one year to the next, the leading governments have ratcheted up their commitments and their actions in this area. At the G20 Cannes Summit on November 3 and 4, 2011, the leaders jointly issued a special paper titled "Tax Havens and Non-Cooperative Jurisdictions." This noted:

> In action to counter money laundering and the financing of terrorism, the FATF has identified 12 jurisdictions whose strategic deficiencies constitute a threat to the international financial system and which the States are advised to take into account: Iran and North Korea present the most serious deficiencies and the FATF has explicitly called for countermeasures to be taken against these non-cooperative jurisdictions ("enhanced due diligence" procedures by the banks). Cuba, Bolivia, Ethiopia, Kenya, Myanmar, Nigeria, Sao Tomé & Principe, Sri Lanka, Syria, and Turkey have made what the FATF considers to be insufficient progress.

For all of the heightened focus of the G20 on money laundering and for all of the heightened effectiveness of FATF, it remains a fact that the scale of current money laundering is enormous and the expert criminals in this area always seem to be a few steps ahead of the authorities. The question has to be asked about just how sincere key G20 countries, as well as important money centers like Austria, Switzerland, Hong Kong, and Dubai, are about ending the money-laundering games. Without question, many financial-services firms operating in many countries make significant profits from the trade and manage to exercise sufficient political influence to dampen the anti-money-laundering ardor of some major government authorities.

As the Arab Spring developed in early 2011, the Swiss banking authorities announced that they were freezing 470 million Swiss francs ($511 million) in the bank accounts of Tunisian and Egyptian politicians and a further

360 million Swiss francs ($391 million) of Libyan assets. The actions, for which the Swiss expected applause, highlight the failure of Swiss laws and regulations to effectively enforce "know your customer" rules on its banks. How could a bank believe that the top politicians of any country could legitimately earn tens of millions of dollars?

Why did the Swiss authorities only act after the leaders of these countries were kicked out of office or, in the case of Libya, denounced by the United States and NATO?

Which other corrupt leaders around the world have Swiss bank accounts today?

The vast number of public statements by many authorities is not matched by concrete action. The issue is not just one of clamping down on many aspects of money laundering with particularly tough sanctions on countries and territories that engage in helping crooks, including tax evaders, as well as on banks that do not enforce tough "know your customer" rules. Far more is needed because, as has been shown in so many other situations highlighted in earlier chapters, there are real victims of these money-laundering crimes. TI vice chair Akere Muna has been playing a major role in promoting international efforts to secure the repatriation of stolen assets and he is blunt and forthright in underlining how important this issue is to people across sub-Saharan Africa—a fact that does not seem to be adequately appreciated by the banking regulators in such money center capitals as London, New York, and Zurich.

The fact is that the cash has been stolen from the citizens of countries by their leaders. Those citizens deserve major international support in terms of ensuring that the illicit deposits found in foreign banks in the names of the corrupt leaders, their families, and their cronies are repatriated.

The Nigerian government of Olusagan Obasanjo authorized then Police Commissioner Ribadu to make strenuous efforts to secure repatriation to Nigeria of the vast fortune that was stolen in the 1990s by Sani Abacha and his family. Ribadu's efforts were of crucial importance in uncovering the complicity of some major European authorities in assisting the crooks. The FATF report noted the following:

> Abacha is safely estimated to have embezzled between USD 2-4 billion during his four and a half year rule. The governments of at least three of the countries involved in receiving suspect Abacha funds—the US, UK, and Switzerland— have concluded that their financial institutions conducted inadequate due diligence in their handling of those accounts. A 2000 report of the Swiss Federal Banking Commission, for example, reviewed the actions of Swiss banks—to ascertain whether [the banks] had fully adhered to due diligence requirements . . . as set out in banking law and other applicable legislation in accepting and handling funds from the entourage of the former president of Nigeria, Sani Abacha. Its review identified five banks with shortcomings and six banks

in which there were instances of serious omissions and serious individual failure or misconduct. This included ignoring indications of the possible suspicious origin of the funds, not passing relevant information to high levels in the bank and misjudging the customer relationship.

The Commission did note that none of the accounts except one were in Abacha's name, and that none of the account holders identified themselves as prominent political figures, but that the banks nevertheless should have been more cautious, particularly in dealing with regions which have a history of corruption. The UK likewise conducted an investigation in 2001 of Abacha money that passed through UK financial institutions. Of the twenty-three UK banks investigated because of possible links with Abacha accounts, fifteen were found to have significant money-laundering control weaknesses. Within those banks, the FSA (Financial Services Authority) found forty-two personal and corporate account relationships that were linked to the Abacha family and close associates. It estimated that those accounts were responsible for a total turnover between 1996 and 2000 of USD 1.3 billion in Abacha money. The US Senate likewise found a US-based bank (with branches in the UK) to have failed to engage in an appropriate level of due diligence with regard to money funneled through accounts of two sons of Sani Abacha. The Senate noted that no client profiles existed for the accounts for a time period in which $47 million passed through the accounts, and when profiles were created, they repeatedly failed the bank's own internal quality review.[5]

Even when the foreign deposits are identified, it can take years before they are repatriated. All manner of legal issues are raised by either the families of the crooked leaders or by the banking institutions themselves. The questions that arise are absolutely absurd, for they suggest that there might be a controversial issue about the legitimacy of the deposits, as if some head of state could legitimately enjoy earnings running into hundreds of millions of dollars (or even billions, as was the case with Abacha). The prevarication and delays all suggest that the major governmental authorities in major money center locations are not nearly as enthusiastic to deal with money laundering as their fine G20 and FATF public statements might suggest.

Appalled by the hypocrisy, TI-France, under the courageous leadership of Daniel Lebègue and Jacques Terray, decided several years ago to convince France's public prosecutors to undertake an investigation into the assets held in France in the names of three West African political leaders: Denis Sassou-Nguesso of Congo-Brazzaville, Omar Bongo Ondimba of Gabon (who died in June 2009 and was replaced by his son), and Teodoro Obiang of Equatorial Guinea. In each case, these are leaders of countries that are major oil suppliers to France. The leaders are vastly wealthy, while their citizens are among the poorest people in Africa. The French government fought TI-France's court actions.

At the funeral in Gabon of Omar Bongo, President Sarkozy was publicly taken to task for allowing French courts to look into the affairs in France of the Bongo family. No matter that the investigations found that the Bongos owned thirty-nine French properties, seventy bank accounts, and nine luxury cars; President Sassou-Nguesso's family had eighteen properties and 112 bank accounts; and President Obiang's family, according to both French evidence and US Senate investigations, had assets in the United States and France that rivaled those of the Bongos and the Sassou-Nguessos.

As Tom Burgis, correspondent for the *Financial Times*, wrote, "Gabon was ruled for 41 years by Omar Bongo—Africa's longest-serving ruler at his death last year. While most of the country languished in penury, Gabon's thirsty elite made the country the world's highest per capita consumer of champagne."[6]

These African rulers enjoyed the patronage and protection of the French government, however. Aiding and abetting their plunder has been routine for French governments for years. There are no indications that the French authorities believe that they can afford to change their policies without placing the contracts of their oil companies in jeopardy. But France's Supreme Court decided in November 2010, in a headline-grabbing major decision, to side with TI-France against the French government. It ruled that the application for a full investigation by the criminal court is admissible.

The Supreme Court's decision saw the appointment of an investigating judge and the opening of a judicial inquiry. TI-France had been instrumental earlier in exposing multiple bank accounts owned by the three corrupt African leaders, as well as very extensive real estate holdings. But even if the courts now discover vast holdings of financial assets in the names of the leaders and their cronies, it is questionable whether there will be any official effort by the French government to see that the assets are repatriated in some form to their rightful owners: the citizens of these three African countries.

At best, efforts to curb money laundering and to secure the repatriation of stolen assets are works in progress. Decisions like the one taken by the French Supreme Court suggest that a unified establishment front protecting the cash of corrupt foreign leaders is less secure than it was just a few years ago. The decision by the Swiss authorities to freeze the assets of fallen dictators is a positive sign, although the Swiss need to do far more. The effective investigations by US authorities that have compelled the Swiss government to change key bank secrecy laws are another indicator of progress. New legislation is under consideration in the US Congress to enhance transparency of bank accounts and close some of the loopholes that still enable rogues to deposit cash in the US financial system. Moreover, more meaningful exchanges of information between governments on tax evasion are now being seen than ever before.

There is still a vast mountain to climb, but the momentum right now is upward and the pressures on FATF member countries to translate rhetoric into action are increasing. Raymond Baker and Carl Levin and their staffs, TI-France, Global Witness, and a rising number of others keep pushing for meaningful action. Without further progress the world's most corrupt leaders will continue to feel confident that they can transfer enormous sums of cash belonging to the peoples of their countries into private jets, mega-yachts, and lavish luxury homes from California to the South of France.

BUSINESS AND BRIBE PAYING

Be it at meetings of G20 or in other international fora where top government officials meet, the anticorruption rhetoric is robust, but time and time again the action that has been pledged is nowhere to be seen. No test of the sincerity of major governments in this context is clearer than that relating to their relationships with multinational corporations.

Most businessmen are honest. However, some businessmen believe that their firms must bribe to win foreign orders and that their international success is important for their home countries in terms of jobs and foreign currency earnings. Everyone knows that such bribery is illegal. The acid test of whether governments mean their anticorruption rhetoric comes in terms of their willingness to investigate and to prosecute companies for paying bribes to foreign government officials. On this basis, most governments are failing the test very badly.

As noted, the United States legislated the Foreign Corrupt Practices Act in 1977. The OECD Convention on Combating Bribery of Foreign Public Officials in International Business Transactions was adopted in 1997 and by the end of 2011 a total of thirty-eight countries had approved national legislation that is consistent with this treaty. These laws make it a criminal offense for a company to bribe foreign government officials.

Many people engaged in civil society anticorruption activism across the world have an abiding distrust of business, especially large multinational corporations. They see these corporate leviathans striding the globe, a law unto themselves. They are seen as using all manner of subsidiaries and affiliates, offshore bank accounts, consultants, and legal advisors in dozens of countries to create complex entities that can act as they please everywhere in order to maximize profits. They are seen as bribing foreign governments and having such influence over their home governments that they have no fear of being prosecuted.

The facts on investigations and prosecutions frequently make it difficult to argue with many of these skeptics in civil society. TI[7] and Trace International publish annual independent assessments of the enforcement of the FCPA and the OECD Convention (see appendix 5). The major findings in TI's mid-2011 review were as follows:

- *Active Enforcement*: seven countries—Denmark, Germany, Italy, Norway, Switzerland, the United Kingdom, and United States
- *Moderate Enforcement*: nine countries—Argentina, Belgium, Finland, France, Japan, Korea (South), Netherlands, Spain, and Sweden
- *Little or No Enforcement*: twenty-one countries—Australia, Austria, Brazil, Bulgaria, Canada, Chile, Czech Republic, Estonia, Greece, Hungary, Ireland, Israel, Luxembourg, Mexico, New Zealand, Poland, Portugal, Slovak Republic, Slovenia, South Africa, and Turkey

TI's report, under the direction of Fritz Heimann, a co-founder of TI, and Gillian Dell, a member of the TI secretariat's staff who for many years has been tracking the implementation of key anticorruption conventions, concluded its 2011 report with a warning:

> There is now active enforcement in seven countries, which represent 30 per cent of world exports, and moderate enforcement in nine countries, which represent 20 per cent of world exports. However, there is little or no enforcement in 21 countries, which represent 15 per cent of world exports. There has been no change in these numbers in the past year. This trend raises concern about whether the Convention is losing forward momentum. Continued lack of enforcement in 21 countries a decade after the Convention entered into force, notwithstanding repeated OECD reviews, clearly indicates lack of political commitment by their governments. And in some of those with moderate enforcement, the level of commitment is also uncertain. This is a danger signal because the OECD Convention depends on the collective commitment of all parties to ending foreign bribery.

Tracelooks at all forms of enforcement against corporate bribery, covering not only the OECD Convention but also foreign prosecutions of international bribery. In its "Trace Global Enforcement Report 2011" the organization summarized conditions by noting the following:

New Developments

- Foreign bribery enforcement by countries other than the United States actually *fell* in 2010, while the United States surged ahead with a more than a doubling of its formal enforcement figures between 2009 and 2010.

- Nigeria, Italy, and South Korea lead enforcement activity worldwide for domestic or "inbound bribery," defined as the bribery of their own government officials by foreign companies. Nigeria's rate of domestic enforcement rose from one to twelve in the past year, largely due to the Nigerian government's aggressive pursuit of multinational companies that had recently settled Foreign Corrupt Practices Act investigations in the United States. First-time domestic bribery investigations were initiated in several countries, including Croatia, Cuba, Georgia, Israel, Latvia, and Poland.
- The financial-services sector has been subject to a rapid increase in enforcement, with the number of actions involving the industry more than doubling over the past year from eleven to twenty-six cases/investigations. This is largely due to the US SEC's new probes into financial firms over possible bribery in connection with sovereign wealth fund investments.

Ongoing Trends as Found by Trace International

- Just twenty-four countries have pursued enforcement of their foreign bribery laws and just forty have pursued enforcement of their domestic bribery laws against foreign citizens or companies in the last thirty-four years. There is considerable overlap in the countries that have pursued both.
- The United States has pursued 3.5 formal foreign bribery enforcement actions for every one enforcement action pursued by all other countries since the year 2000.
- The United States aggressively pursues foreign companies and individuals for foreign bribery violations. One out of every five Foreign Corrupt Practices Act matters involves a company headquartered outside of the United States or an individual employed or retained by such a company.
- The United Kingdom continues in a strong second place for the enforcement of foreign or "outbound" bribery.
- The largest number of enforcement actions involves alleged bribe payments to officials in China, Iraq, and Nigeria.
- The extractive industries sector has been the subject of international anti-bribery enforcement actions more than any other sector.
- Government officials of OECD countries received alleged bribes at a rate significant in comparison to the rate in non-OECD countries.

There is some good news. A law prohibiting foreign bribery was passed by the Russian parliament and signed by President Medvedev and Russia has indicated it will work with the OECD. Both China and India have approved laws against foreign bribery by Chinese and Indian companies. The US Justice Department and the US SEC continue to pursue major investigations on a substantial scale and in many instances these have required cooperation from foreign governments, which has been increasingly forthcoming. And most importantly in terms of recent developments, the United Kingdom revised its antibribery law so that it is now in full compliance with the OECD Convention and this is seen by the UK Serious Fraud Squad as significantly increasing the prospects for successful prosecutions.

Four sets of actions are now needed, at a minimum, to significantly curb the propensity of multinational corporations to bribe foreign government officials:

1. A far more vigorous campaign needs to be waged against the major Western governments that ratified the OECD Convention but are not enforcing it.
2. The media and civil society need to be far more aggressive in monitoring the ethical performance of corporations relative to their declared public policies.
3. The OECD Convention and the FCPA need to be toughened by eliminating a loophole that allows the payment of small bribes.
4. Prosecutors and judges need to rethink the punishments for those who do pay bribes to foreign government officials and they need to ensure that the real victims of these crimes are compensated.

TI and the OECD itself have been somewhat too diplomatic in their annual reviews of the nonenforcement by so many countries of the OECD Convention. They have found technical, legal, and bureaucratic reasons as excuses. The fact is that, for example, if the Canadian government wanted to enforce the law, it could. Canada has an outstanding reputation for business integrity, despite the vagaries at times of some small, publicly quoted mining companies. It is inexplicable that Canada should not be a leader in enforcement. It is difficult to find any articles in the prominent Canadian media that highlight this evident governmental failure.

In many countries the time has come for the media and civil society to examine far more closely the diverse linkages between governments and major multinational corporations. Are these corporations providing substantial funds to political campaigns in, for example, Italy and Japan that lead governments not to investigate OECD Convention violations by domestic firms?

Are some major companies bluntly telling their governments that corporate prosecutions of major domestic enterprises will directly result in domestic job losses? One of the reasons former prime minister Tony Blair in the United Kingdom gave for quashing investigations into foreign bribery by BAE Systems was the risk of losing UK jobs!

Governments are not enforcing the OECD Convention that they have ratified because they see short-term national disadvantages in doing this. The feckless approaches of the governments (named above as moderate and low enforcers) should be highlighted by the national media and civil society organizations in these countries. At the moment, the noncompliance is mostly below the radar screen by governments, and companies like it this way.

At a minimum, civil society and the media should strive to shame governments into enforcing the laws. For a long time, for example, the German authorities did little to remind corporations that a new law had been passed in the late 1990s and companies could no longer go around the globe paying bribes and then expensing them against their German taxes. The Siemens case, however, which showed how one of Germany's largest global enterprises was charging into scores of markets with envelopes full of cash for politicians and officials, was an acute embarrassment. Ever since, the scale of official investigations in Germany into international corporate bribery has increased sharply.

In Switzerland, the government had to be shamed into finally accepting that crooked actions in the banking sector were doing enormous damage to the country's reputation and to that of its leading banks, which had suffered greatly in the global financial collapse of 2008. In that year, as noted earlier, US action on tax evasion by American citizens led to charges against the country's biggest bank, UBS, by the US authorities. The bank was keen to settle the case and did so with a fine in excess of $750 million and an agreement to hand over some 4,500 names of Americans who had accounts with UBS. Then, however, the Swiss government stepped in and said that the bank could not violate Swiss law and provide the United States with the names. Hard bargaining ensued, and more and more adverse publicity in Switzerland itself about a government that protected American tax cheaters mounted. In the end, the public scorn hurled on the Swiss authorities resulted in key changes in Swiss secrecy laws.

Many people in civil society are on a different wavelength to those in business who talk about corporate social responsibility, doing the right thing, and demonstrating that ethical business is not an oxymoron. A negative perspective is strengthened by the seemingly endless reports in the media of many countries of corporate malfeasance.

How could a global giant like Olympus of Japan hide losses of billions of dollars year after year for a decade?

How could the board of directors of an old Wall Street brokerage company called MF Global allow a new chief executive officer to ignore all of the firm's risk-management guidelines, replace the chief risk officer, and drive the enterprise into bankruptcy within two years of joining it?

How could so many US financial institutions convince very poor people to buy homes and assume mortgage liabilities that they had no hope of servicing and then sell such mortgages, packaged into securities, to investors who were kept in the dark about how worthless the papers really were?

And how could the board of directors of the New York Stock Exchange (NYSE), knowing that the NYSE sets clear governance standards for all listed companies and is seen to be the ethical guide for all major corporations, agree in 2003 to a compensation contract for its then CEO, Richard Grasso, that amounted to more than $200 million—far in excess of NYSE's net profit?

The US Ethics Resource Center (ERC) has done superb work with many corporations in assisting them to examine their business ethics and to establish sophisticated systems that can win the support of employees, customers, shareholders, and other stakeholders. They have been in the forefront of warning corporations that all the ethics rules and credos in the world are useless if the CEOs do not serve as high-profile models of integrity and thus set the right tone at the top.

The work that ERC has in many aspects been replicated in an increasing number of countries and leads many business leaders to argue that all the tales of malfeasance in the press only reflect the behaviors of a tiny percentage of all corporations. The Enron scandal in 2001, however, made the titans of the world's largest enterprises recognize that they needed to do far more to ensure that in-house ethics codes are comprehensive and complied with and that peer pressures should mount to secure a more responsible overall image for business. The Grasso scandal, which only came fully to light because of investigations by then New York attorney general Eliot Spitzer, added to broad public perceptions that the leaders of American business had lost their moral compass.

It was against this background that a number of CEOs of major multinational corporations met several years ago in Davos, Switzerland, at the annual gathering of the World Economic Forum (WEF) to formulate and then embrace corporate antibribery codes developed by TI and the International Chamber of Commerce. Fritz Heimann had drafted TI business principles soon after TI's launch in the early 1990s and Laurence Cockcroft and Jeremy Pope pursued work in this area later in the decade, and Jermyn Brooks, formerly on TI's staff and now a member of its board of directors, took the work further and presented it at meetings of the WEF in Davos. These included protection of whistle-blowers and the commitment of firms to run training programs for their employees to explain the OECD Convention and the importance of corporate compliance with it. The WEF embraced these efforts, which gave them substantial business support. The latest iteration of the work in this area is a report titled "Business Principles for Countering Bribery" by TI and Social Accountability International, which leads with these mandates: "The enterprise shall prohibit bribery in any form whether direct or indirect; the enterprise shall commit to implementation of a program to counter bribery."[8]

The models for the approaches that companies accepting these principles could follow were set in the late 1990s by companies like Rio Tinto and Shell. The latter, for example, emerged from major scandals to review all of its ethics-training programs and corporate values. I once attended a meeting in Houston, Texas, of the company's top executives from across the world and participated in a session on how country directors could ensure that all of their employees abided by the corporate standards. Serious debates took place that emphasized the difficulties in countries as varied as China and Nigeria (where Shell had major operations) in applying the Shell standard that "Shell companies insist on honesty, integrity and fairness in all aspects of their business and expect the same in their relationships with all those with whom they do business."[9]

Experience shows that companies, just like governments, all too often allow their rhetoric to run well ahead of their actual practice. The willingness by corporations to walk the talk depends crucially on the degree to which their actions are monitored.

Civil society and the media need to do a far better job at monitoring the compliance by corporations with their ethics codes. They need to be aggressive in naming names of senior executives and companies that act unethically. They need to do more to confront senior executives about alleged abuses of ethics codes and not be brushed aside by corporate lawyers. And when companies are actually prosecuted for wrongdoing, then civil society and the media should highlight the leaders of these firms and underscore to the public that the behavior cannot be attributed to just some big corporation but is rather directly due to the management failures of the top executives.

More specifically, civil society and the media need to draw more public attention to a key loophole in the OECD Convention and the FCPA that, in effect, enables companies to claim that they are acting legally and ethically, while all the time paying bribes to foreign government officials.

Prevailing international FCPA-type laws mostly contain a clause concerned with "facilitating payments." This allows firms to make supposedly small payments to foreign government officials to facilitate themselves and their products, for example, through customs, passport controls, roadside police blocks, and so forth. These "grease payments," sometimes called "speed payments," are seen by many in business and by the Western parliaments that enacted the antibribery laws as essential in many countries to enable business to move ahead. The argument is that in many poor countries the lower-level officials in customs and immigration and other agencies that interact with foreign firms are paid so badly that small cash payments by foreign firms are expected and routine.

Across civil society in the developing world these "facilitation payments" are not seen this way. Rather, they are seen for what they really are—bribes.

A few years ago I undertook an informal survey by asking friends in TI national chapters in a dozen countries to share their views on how "facilitating payments" are perceived in their countries. Nobody suggested that they are a legitimate means of augmenting the low pay of public officials. Responses included the following:

- From the former central bank governor of Botswana, Quill Hermans: "Bribery and corruption in all their forms are as repugnant to ordinary Botswana as they are in Western Europe and North America . . . most Botswana tend to regard corruption as something which 'foreigners' initiate, if reports and editorials in the newspapers are any indication of local sentiment."
- From Shaukat Omari, head of TI-Pakistan: "The multinationals are probably a cause for most of the corruption or the 'culture of corruption' that now exists in Pakistan. It seems harsh and this is not to deny that the Pakistani companies do not indulge in bribery, I am sure that they do, but the culture of 'Baksheesh' has been definitely supported on its way by the multinational corporations."
- From the former managing director of Transparencia in Brazil, Claudio Weber Abramo: "There's no country in the world that accepts bribery ('facilitating payments') in its laws. Here the matter is reinforcing the state in order to guarantee the rule of law."

Imagine the reaction in the United States if a foreign firm sought to pay an immigration official to speed up the granting of a work permit, or sought to pay another government official a small amount in cash to secure an environmental permit?

In the United States, it is likely to take far longer than it is in, say, Kenya or Indonesia for a foreign firm to get either a work permit or an environmental permit; yet multinational corporations that would not dream of offering bribes in the United States do so routinely in many developing countries.

For some years, Fritz Heimann, reflecting widespread views in US industry, argued with me that the "facilitation payments" clause in the FCPA was essential. Jermyn Brooks also took the view that to eliminate it from the OECD pact would risk losing a good deal of business support. Alexandra Wrage of Trace International, by contrast, was one of the first influential people in US business to call bluntly for the ending of the practice and the closing of the loophole. Today, the OECD's leadership agrees that "facilitation payments" are bad. So far it has not secured sufficient political support to amend the convention, nor has there been any effort to change the US FCPA in this respect. Indeed, the US Chamber of Commerce is now running a campaign to try and weaken the FCPA.

The most important action that can be taken to curb foreign bribery by multinational corporations is, quite simply, to implement Professor Robert Klitgaard's dictat and "fry some big fish."

It is rare that an individual is sent to prison for violating the FCPA in the United States, let alone in any other country, or that a very large fine is imposed on an individual. In almost all cases, the US Justice Department and the SEC or their equivalents in a few other countries, such as the United Kingdom and Germany, are willing to agree on a corporate fine without the company involved having to formally admit guilt. The fine is ultimately paid for by the shareholders, who did not encourage the criminal acts in the first place. The settlements rarely name the names of corporate individuals. Hardly any CEOs of companies that have paid fines as a result of FCPA-type investigations have ever lost their jobs on this account.

There have also been negligible actions against accounting firms. Auditors have been willing time and time again to bury the bribes paid by corporations in the corporate balance sheets, or at least overlook such payments, and assist the corporations in hiding their criminal acts.

If judges in the United States and in Europe were to reflect on the misery that results for very poor people from the paying of bribes to foreign government officials, then they may have a clearer understanding of why today's settlements are inappropriate. The courts operate as if these are victimless crimes. It is up to judges to determine whether the settlements that are reached between the companies and the justice officials are to be accepted. They should be rejected unless there is both greater attention to the personal responsibilities of senior executives for bribe paying and unless the victims of the bribery are given prominent positions in the court proceedings.

Companies see the fines as just slaps on the wrist. Not until CEOs are sent to prison for the foreign bribe paying pursued on their watch by their enterprises will the FCPA and the OECD Convention have a major impact. Not until auditors recognize that they too are at risk by going along with the bribe payments made by their corporate clients will there be greater restraints on this corporate practice.

In this respect an important precedent was established in the United Kingdom. On February 5, 2010, the UK Serious Fraud Squad (SFO) went to court to announce a settlement agreement with BAE Systems that involved a fine of £30 million arising from one aspect of a case involving the sale of radar equipment to Tanzania. In a coordinated move, the US Department of Justice announced on the same day that it had reached an agreement with BAE involving a fine of $400 million with regard to alleged bribery payments by the firm on contracts for Saudi Arabia, Tanzania, the Czech Republic, and Hungary. In neither the UK nor the US actions was BAE forced to admit guilt. Typically, the matter would have ended then and there, but the UK decision created a media furor and the presiding judge, Mr. Justice Bean at the Crown Court in Southwark in London, was unhappy. Why was the United Kingdom treating the firm so lightly when a vastly greater fine was being imposed in the United States?

The SFO argued that under the former UK law it had a weak hand when dealing with the case and that it had determined that the prudent course was to leave it to the Americans to focus on a series of BAE violations of the FCPA in several countries, while it concentrated on the Tanzanian case. Here, because the settlement with the SFO did not compel BAE to admit guilt, Mr. Justice Bean found that he lacked the power to impose a much harsher fine than that agreed to by the SFO with BAE, even though the court documents showed that offshore companies were used to hide payments made to an agent who obtained more than £12 million in a £40 million deal.

Not all was lost, however. The SFO had decided and the judge agreed that the real victims of the situation were the citizens of Tanzania. They had suffered because a foreign firm had connived with the Tanzanian authorities to involve questionable payments and inflate the cost to Tanzanians of the equipment purchased. It was decided that BAE Systems had to ensure that £29.5 million (the £30 million fine less court penalties) went to the Tanzanian people. This is the first time that the real victims in a developing country have ever been compensated as a result of actions brought in a major developed country against an alleged bribe-paying multinational company.

In almost all settlements in the United States and in the court proceedings to secure approval of the settlements, the victims are never mentioned. It is unthinkable that a murderer would be placed on trial without the name of the person having been murdered mentioned in the charge. Yet major multinational corporations, such as Siemens and BAE Systems and Halliburton, agree to pay fines to settle FCPA violations and not a single cent goes to the people of the countries where the illicit payments were made. The victims are ignored.

The UK action, however, did not lead immediately to any cash going from BAE Systems to the Tanzanian people, which prompted an investigation by UK parliamentarians. They wanted to know why the money had still not been paid by mid-2011. In late November 2011, the UK House of Commons issued a report[10] that castigated both the company and the UK government for the nonpayment. The investigation found that BAE had no idea how to ensure that its payment supported benefits for ordinary Tanzanians rather than landing in the pockets of crooked governmental officials. The problem was significant because of the very close and mostly opaque ties between the key civilian and military leaders in Tanzania. BAE engaged an independent group to ponder the matter and the months rolled by. Meanwhile, the SFO posed the problem to the United Kingdom's aid ministry, the Department for

International Development, which came up with a proposal to add the sum to existing UK aid for education in Tanzania and to develop a special monitoring system to ensure the money really did go into the country's schools.

Not only has this proposal been finalized, but the approach will also serve as a precedent for the future. It can be expected that as the SFO beefs up its investigations and prosecutions, which it says it is doing, eventual fines will go through the development assistance channel to benefit the real victims of corporate foreign bribe paying.

This needs to be a precedent for all prosecutions in all countries of OECD Convention violations. It needs to also be accompanied by explicit prosecutions of those individuals in companies that were involved in the bribe payments. And, I believe, in the case of major bribery involving tens of millions of dollars and pounds and euros, the CEOs should personally be held to account. Such actions may strike terror in to the hearts of CEOs. Just as the top executives of firms that cooked their balance sheets, like Tyco and Enron, went to prison for long terms, so the top executives of bribe-paying firms should understand that they personally will suffer greatly.

NOTES

1. Peter Reuter and Edwin M. Truman, *Chasing Dirty Money—The Fight Against Money Laundering* (Washington, DC: Institute of International Economics, 2004), 9.

2. Official agencies develop acronyms for seemingly everything, so FATF talks about PEPs (politically exposed persons)—that is, public officials.

3. Riggs National Bank in Washington, DC, had long been the banker to US presidents and the diplomatic corps in the US capital. But a series of problems, including the prominent Pinochet scandal, damaged Riggs significantly. In 2004 it agreed to a $25 million fine as a result of an investigation into the secret Pinochet deposits by the US Office of the Comptroller of the Currency; a year later it settled another investigation with the US Department of Justice for $16 million. In March 2005 it was acquired by the PNC financial services group and the Riggs name disappeared.

4. Financial Action Task Force, "Laundering the Proceeds of Corruption," paragraph 53, July 2011. This excellent report provides an overview of official international actions against money laundering.

5. FATF July 2011 report on "Laundering the Proceeds of Corruption."

6. Tom Burgis, "Gabon to Get $4.5 bn Asian Investment," *Financial Times*, August 15, 2010.

7. Transparency International, "Progress Report 2011: Enforcement of the OECD Anti-Bribery Convention" (Berlin: Transparency International, 2011). The report places countries in three categories in terms of the degree to which they enforce the OECD Convention's mandates:

• *Active Enforcement*: Countries with a share of world exports of more than 2 percent (the eleven largest exporters) must have at least ten major cases on a cumulative basis, of which at least three must have been initiated in the last three years and at least three concluded with substantial sanctions. Countries with a share of world exports of less than 2 percent must have brought at least three major cases, including at least one concluded with substantial sanctions and at least one pending case, which has been initiated in the last three years.

- *Moderate Enforcement*: Countries that do not qualify for active enforcement but have at least one major case as well as one active investigation.
- *Little or No Enforcement*: Countries that do not qualify for the previous two categories. This includes countries that have only brought minor cases, countries that only have investigations, and countries that have no cases or investigations.

8. Transparency International, "Business Principles for Countering Bribery." The most recent edition is from February 2009 (www.transparency.org).

9. "Dealing with Bribery and Corruption—A Management Primer," Shell, 2003.

10. House of Commons, "Financial Crime and Development—International Development Committee," report, November 2011.

Chapter Sixteen

Making a Difference

Peruvian author and 2010 Nobel laureate Mario Vargas Llosa could have chosen many themes for an after-dinner talk in Mexico City before sixty of the most powerful bank executives in Latin America. He decided to talk about corruption.

It was a private dinner in spring 2010 and the bankers sat in rapt attention as their guest speaker, in effect, castigated them for failing to play leading roles in the fight against corruption. Calmly and firmly, he appealed to his audience to recognize that they had responsibilities that went beyond making profits. He called on them to contribute to cleaning up the corrupt governments that rule in so many parts of Latin America and to challenge public attitudes that see efforts to bring about change as hopeless. He implied rather heavily that the bankers, who may have long been part of the problem, could now become part of the solution.

Vargas Llosa's lamented that complacency about corruption is one of the gravest political problems facing the region. People believe, he said, that nothing can be done about corruption and such a thought is dangerous for the region's democracies.

Vargas Llosa's comments were depressing, especially since he comes from a country that has hurled a former president in prison for corruption. He is also experienced enough to know how significant the improvement has been over the last few decades in securing governmental accountability in many Latin American countries. His message was powerful and perhaps had some impact on the bankers.

The fact that he was able to make his speech at all to this conservative group of powerful business leaders is a symbol, I believe, of just how far we have come in changing the broad environment within which corruption issues can be discussed and where, indeed, constructive proposals can be con-

255

sidered. Just a few years ago, top Latin American bankers would not have given a guest speaker a lengthy ovation after he called on them to join in the fight against corruption.

Vargas Llosa raises a major issue, because the success of the anticorruption movement depends on transforming those who are complacent about corruption into activists.

In this context it is critical that widely prevailing views that corruption is a cultural phenomenon are powerfully rejected. Many people do believe that corruption is so deeply entrenched in the fabric of so many societies and in the minds of so many people that its power will overwhelm all the efforts to secure sustainable and fundamental change.

I find this a cynical view that implies that most people are inclined, when given the chance, to be dishonest, and that most people in public life, like most business people, are dishonest. The fact is that corruption, like other crimes, abounds when conditions permit it to thrive. In some countries, such as Sweden, Denmark, Finland, Iceland, New Zealand, and Canada, to name just a few, the combination of formidable enforced laws against the abuse of public office, good living standards, and a strong public emphasis in communities and schools on the ethic of serving others all contribute to low levels of corruption. Given the right conditions, from the appropriate educational systems to strong economic growth opportunities, there could be many more countries that enjoy the same sort of ethics as these that are widely seen as mostly clean of corruption.

The temptations of abusing office for personal gain are substantial for all who attain the highest political positions in their countries. But not all top officeholders seize the opportunity to commit crimes. Those who do steal from the public purse do so because they believe they can get away with it— they are driven both by greed and by the arrogance to believe that they will never be prosecuted for their crimes. There is nothing cultural about such abuse of entrusted power.

A SENSE OF BALANCE

Books and newspaper articles about corruption highlight the crooks and the villains and pay insufficient attention to the good guys. This book has placed the heroes of civil society activism in the foreground, but beyond their particular stage, it is important to look more broadly and get a sense of perspective and balance.

There are powerful officials in many countries with opportunities to steal who do not do so, just as there are powerful business people with opportunities to bribe who resist the temptation.

I was a board director of an international gold-mining company for some years and in this capacity I frequently visited Tanzania in the 1990s. I participated in many meetings with then minister of energy and mining Jakaya Kikwete (now Tanzania's president) and there was never a suggestion of a bribe being requested or paid. There were times when it looked as if our corporate requests for exploration and mining licenses were being indefinitely delayed, suggesting that bribes might be needed to ensure progress, and yet repeatedly Kikwete intervened to ensure that all contracts were honestly arrived at.[1]

Discussions of corruption often lead to generalizations that are not just wrong but also tarnish many good people who stand up for what they believe to be right, irrespective of the personal risks. Too often, for example, African politicians are described as a group as corrupt. The inaccuracy of this perception is shown in the personal meetings and relationships with people like Uganda's former comptroller general Ruzindana, Nigerian finance minister Ngozi Okonjo-Iweala, former Nigerian World Bank vice president for Africa Oby Ezekwesili (a remarkable leader who played important roles in supporting and promoting TI in its early years and then went on to hold key posts in the government of Nigeria before joining the World Bank), former top Kenyan government anticorruption official John Githongo, and former Botswana president Festus Mogae—each of whom has made powerful stands against governmental abuse that doubly put to shame such corrupt African leaders as President Mugabe of Zimbabwe, President al-Bashir of Sudan, and others who have been highlighted in earlier chapters in this book.

Similarly, in business, I believe that the bribe-paying firms are a small minority. There are many top executives who have a passion for operating their firms with integrity. I served once on the board of directors of the US ERC and at one meeting I mentioned corruption in Bangladesh, whereupon the board chairman Raymond Gilmartin (then chairman and CEO of the giant pharmaceutical company Merck) sharply interrupted to say, "We will not do business in Bangladesh. The ethical standards there of the government just do not allow us to operate in accord with our corporate standards!"

In many countries, other considerations need to be taken into account when looking at the causes of corruption—here too, however, culture has nothing to do with the motivations. There are many mid-level officials in many developing countries who seek to obtain bribes for the services that they have the power to grant. Their actions are wrong, but their reasons for seeking special favors are more complex than the greed and arrogance of their most senior official superiors.

I remember a mid-level mining ministry official in Tanzania who noted that in our company's mining agreement with the government we had agreed to set aside funds for the training of Tanzanian geologists. He suggested that he would look kindly toward our firm if some of those education funds might be used to send his oldest son to school and then to university in Australia, Canada, or the United Kingdom. He was asking us to bend the rules. He was seeking to abuse his office. He explained that his income was modest and there was no way in which he could secure a decent education for his son. He believed that if his son had a chance of an education overseas, then he would be able to make real advances in life. He was sincere. The amounts he sought were not great. But his request was wrong and we said no.

But his motivation was not power and personal greed, nor was he driven to make his pitch by cultural factors. He wanted to help his son to have brighter opportunities in life. The solution was not to allow him to extort bribes, but rather to find ways whereby officials in his position and many others can earn sufficient sums that they can save and use those savings to support good educations for their children. Singapore has for many years understood far better than almost any other country that decent salaries for government officials are a vital safeguard against corruption.

And then there are millions of people in many developing countries who are on the government's payrolls in very lowly positions and whose incomes often are below what they need to feed, clothe, and house their families. They may be ordinary policemen, customs officials, officials at passport controls, assistants in government offices that grant driving licenses or permits to open a shop or build a small addition to a house. They may be schoolteachers who can influence a decision as to whether or not a child finds a place at school. Or they may be nurses at the emergency ward of a hospital who can decide which patients might get to see a doctor. They do not seek bribes because it is in their culture, but because they feel driven to supplement their paltry incomes into order to survive. They will not change their ways through cultural training, but rather by the provision to them of what they deserve—decent wages. Their prospects of obtaining such wages will be hugely enhanced if the theft by mid-level and senior government officials in their countries is ended.

A TIPPING POINT

An Indian friend who attended one of the mass rallies led by Anna Hazare said to me that a remarkable change is coming to his country. He believes that the parliament's actions to approve antibribery legislation, after approving a major freedom of information law a few years ago, will represent what he called the "tipping point." He believes India is reaching the point of no return on a long road toward curbing corruption. The degree of actual reform right now may not be great, but the direction is right and this is what is absolutely crucial.

I believe that there are rising numbers of people in many countries today who hold a similar view about their own national situations. The broad public complacency that Vargas Llosa discussed may be giving way to the "Wake Up" sirens of mass public engagement.

The Arab Spring, as suggested at the outset of this book, will be seen in due course as a seminal event. It has unleashed mass public engagement against the abuse of power with a force and on a scale that cannot be quashed or subdued. So much has happened in the last two decades on the anticorruption front, and yet today one senses that what lies ahead will be still more exciting and productive.

Those who still see few prospects for meaningful anticorruption reforms probably underestimate the absolute determination and the skill of individual women and men who are at the forefront now in challenging public authorities. As I have sought to underscore throughout the pages of this book, people do make a difference. They do so, not only because of their pragmatic leadership as organizers and campaigners, but also at a deeper level as sources of inspiration.

J. C. Weliamuna is a seemingly low-key, mild-mannered man with nerves of steel. He talks with no emotion about the threats that have been made on his life and on those of his colleagues in TI-Sri Lanka, of the safe houses that have had to be rented for him and his staff, and the bomb threats made on the office and on his home. He almost casually admits that TI-Sri Lanka spends far more time than it would like having to plan for basic security. From July 2000 to the end of 2010, J. C. was the executive director of this TI national chapter.

He knows that the dangers of taking on the Sri Lankan authorities are very high, but he suggests that there is no alternative. His country's potential is constantly undermined by widespread corruption. He does not discuss his fears; he presses ahead knowing that the cause of anti-corruption is absolutely crucial to alleviating massive human misery in his country.

I once used the example of Sri Lanka in a conversation with George Soros in asking his advice at a time when an increasing number of TI leaders across the world were facing mounting personal dangers. He responded by noting that the fact that they were being threatened indicated the extent to which they are having an impact. Soros is right. J. C. and many TI colleagues are making an enormous difference in their countries, waking up the public at large to the abuse at the top of government, promoting reforms, canvassing for media attention, and setting the base for eventual governance change. The greater their impact, the greater the personal risks that they and their colleagues are taking, because their success is viewed by those in authority as a threat.

At an annual meeting of TI a few years ago, when representatives of over eighty national chapters came together, a colleague suggested that all those who faced serious personal threats ought to meet over a dinner to discuss their experiences and what they could do. People from forty national chapters turned up at the dinner, from Pakistan and Venezuela, from Zimbabwe and Nigeria, from Russia and, of course, Sri Lanka.

Chills went down my spine when TI friends told of receiving telephone calls late at night and hearing someone introduce himself as a "friend" and then quietly suggest that there may be serious risks if the local TI chapter continued to look into the affairs of the government. From that event, Casey Kelso from TI's Berlin secretariat and Sion Assidon from TI-Morocco took the lead in building a TI "safe" system to trigger immediate international alerts the moment anyone associated with TI got into trouble. I believe one of the first times the system was tested was on news of the kidnapping of J. C. Weliamuna—a horrible story that ended well with his release and safety.

The civil society activists are the heroes of the war on corruption, yet their work is made possible by the actions of many others who do not face the same personal risks, but who certainly need to be recognized. A number of them have been mentioned in earlier chapters and briefly highlighting just a few illustrates what a diverse array of people are now contributing in very different ways to the common goal of building societies where justice serves all citizens well, and where transparent and accountable public institutions thrive.

LEADERS

Philanthropist George Soros has used his Open Society Foundation to support the Publish What You Pay coalition of over six hundred civil society organizations that has led the fight for greater transparency in the oil, gas, and mining sectors. Soros has never thought about short-term campaigns. In June 2002, he wrote an article in the *Financial Times* that promoted the objectives of Publish What You Pay, and in 2010 he was using the same arguments in telephone calls to key US politicians to push the Publish What You Pay agenda.[2] When it looked as if efforts to include oil and gas industry transparency clauses in the 2010 US financial reform legislation were running into trouble, Soros called to speak with Senator Richard Lugar, the highly influential Republican leader, to plead the case.

From the earliest days of the fall of Communism in Eastern and Central Europe, Soros has used his energy and hundreds of millions of dollars of his own money to support democracy and human rights, transparent and accountable government, and the fight against corruption. Soros understands far better than most of the governance "experts" in the international aid agencies what really works in helping poorer countries to transition to open government. He meets with the activists, he listens and advises, and he puts his own cash behind his rhetoric. He takes risks here, knowing well that in this very dangerous arena there will be failed organizations and failed projects, but that there is no such thing as a straight path from dictatorship to democracy.

I met Alexandra Wrage in 1999 when I was invited by the US defense industry contractor Northrop Grumman to talk to corporate executives about the FCPA and the work of TI. Alexandra was on the company's legal staff and spent a great deal of time evaluating the firm's foreign sales agents and training them to comply with the FCPA. A year later, she came to Prague for a major TI international anticorruption conference and conversations there convinced her to establish the not-for-profit business membership organization Trace International. No single organization has been more effective in working with multinational corporations across the world to train agents and sales intermediaries, to monitor them, and to build a strong anticorruption initiative in this vital area.

Wrage's travels across the globe each year bring her into contact with business leaders who share her belief that the best competitive environment is one free of corporate bribery. Together these firms and Trace are walking the talk in the private sector in ways that are more effective than most of the range of not-for-profit organizational efforts that seek to convince companies to sign anticorruption pledges. She understands business in the international competitive arena very well and she was the first leader in the business community to make a strong and clear call to end "facilitating payments," recognizing the potential and actual confusion in the minds of corporate employees and agents and other business intermediaries in having to draw a line between what are illegal bribes and so-called legal grease payments.

Raymond Baker, as noted in the previous chapter, has enormous influence on the debate today on illicit financial flows. He became a researcher after a long business career. Finding a desk at the Brookings Institution in Washington, DC, he started to analyze a vast array of international trade and financial transactions. He concluded that enormous sums of cash were secretly crossing national borders, mostly from the poor countries to the rich—sums that were ten times as great as the amounts of foreign aid that flowed into developing countries. As Baker's research deepened and his findings attracted increasing expert interest, he founded a think-tank, Global Financial Integrity, which is now making a significant research contribution and influencing the international foreign aid community.

Mark Pieth has probably been the single most influential public official in the anticorruption fight over the last fifteen years, and he is only part time on the public payrolls. He is a professor of law from Basel, Switzerland, and heads a research and consulting firm involved in anticorruption. He served alongside Paul Volcker on the special UN investigation into UN bribery associated with the food-for-oil schemes that involved Iraq in the 1990s. He has also advised the Wolfsberg Group of bankers in their work on anti–money laundering.

Mark's prime claim to fame relates to his chairmanship of the OECD's Working Group on Bribery, which oversees compliance by governments with the OECD Convention. He makes exceptional efforts to strive to press governments to enforce the convention. He demonstrated his steel determination when, on grounds of national security, the UK government some years ago decided to quash investigations into BAE Systems' alleged bribery related to the sale of weapons systems to Saudi Arabia. Mark undertook a thorough review of the United Kingdom's antibribery law at the time and issued a scathing report that said, in effect, that the British government was totally insincere in claiming to be supportive of the OECD Convention. He said the United Kingdom needed an entirely new law and made detailed suggestions about its content. In 2010, a law was approved by the UK Parliament that reflected Mark's demands.

Chilean Dani Kaufmann is now the president of the Revenue Watch Institute in New York, while American Robin Hodess has her desk at TI in Berlin. Neither of them are academics by inclination or practice. Both are scholars, however, and they have played crucial leading roles in developing pragmatic, applied anticorruption research for more than a decade.

Dani created the corruption research work of the World Bank from scratch. Together with highly able colleagues, he built the World Bank Institute into a leading center of governance data from across the developing world. The voluminous reports that he managed and developed have highlighted to dozens of governments the key areas of vital governance reform, the major trends and multi-country findings that help to shape policy. He played a particularly important role in influencing—indeed, educating—World Bank president James Wolfensohn, who for almost a decade was the leading public official on the world stage advocating greater international action to curb corruption.

The building of TI's formidable research output, including its numerous reports and its indexes, owes a great deal to Robin's determination and hard work. She joined TI from the Carnegie Council on Ethics in New York and was fortunate to gradually take over the research lead in TI from Jeremy Pope and Fredrik Galtung, who in particular had created such high-quality research tools as the CPI and the TI Source Book. Robin has expanded the volume of research products, found resources to create a host of new research tools of practical use to national chapters and other civil society organizations, initiated rapidly expanding exchanges of work between academics across the world, and strengthened the quality of TI research reports.

Paul Steiger, the head of *ProPublica* in New York, is probably the foremost anticorruption journalist in the United States. Paul is in the vanguard of finding ways to use web-based approaches and a nonprofit structure to work with established newspapers and television organizations to maximize the scale and scope of investigative journalism at a time when recession and technological change are forcing major reductions in editorial budgets at the mainstream traditional media. In joint ventures, for example, with US TV's *Frontline* and the *New York Times*, *ProPublica* has leveraged its talents to have an increasing impact in the anticorruption field in America.

The war on corruption is often played out in the courtrooms. Here, extraordinary lawyers of courage are making an enormous difference: people like Patrick Fitzgerald in Chicago, who confronted the full scale of former Vice President Cheney's wrath; Eva Joly, who went after some of the biggest names in French industry and politics at great personal risk; Luis Moreno Ocampo, who has gone from prosecuting Argentinean generals to taking the lead in The Hague at the ICC against the villains of modern-day genocide; and Kamal Hossain from Bangladesh, who for more than half a century has fought every anticorruption case that has crossed his path, be it in his home country or in the international justice arena.

The leaders mentioned in the pages of this book are just a small number of the rising total of women and men across the globe in so many different walks of life that are now joining forces. They are driving the anticorruption train, engineering ways for it to run faster, carry a bigger load, and brush aside many of the obstacles on the tracks.

BUILDING UNDERSTANDING AND SUPPORT

For most of those engaged in the war on corruption, the central core objective is to alleviate some of the massive human misery that engulfs more than 30 percent of all the people on our planet. Corruption is not the sole cause of such misery. But it is a major cause. We should care. While massive charities, such as the Red Cross, consistently remind the broad public in more affluent countries of the hardships of the world's poor, they rarely mention corruption. It is as if they too take it for granted.

The fight against corruption demands that the huge charities supporting the world's poorest peoples be more vocal in public about both the damage done by corruption,and the need for public support to ensure that the fight against corruption is won. More of these charities should join the anticorruption coalitions and use their public influence to strengthen public understanding of the crucial linkages between corruption and human misery.

The victims of corruption in highly developed industrial countries are not as hard hit as the victims in the very poorest countries, but they also suffer. Public officials in municipal governments across much of the world it seems, rich and poor, often have overly close relationships with local property developers and construction firms and companies that provide such public services as transportation and garbage collection. A few politicians get rich, their business buddies get rich, and the taxpayers suffer the consequences.

As noted earlier, we are all victims. At times corruption seems almost as rampant in my home city of Washington, DC, as in the distant places that I visit in developing countries. As the final pages of this book were being written, a member of the Washington City Council resigned from the council and agreed to plead guilty to charges of corruption. The city that is home to the US Supreme Court and the White House is no stranger to corruption in local politics. Commenting ahead of a local election in Washington, DC, *Washington Post* editorial writer Colby King lamented in August 2010 that the candidates were not debating allegations of corruption and cronyism in City Hall, and he noted, after all, "Nothing is more corrosive to good government than officials who abuse the public trust."[3]

The world must recognize the victims of corruption. It must see how corruption is just as grave a curse as hunger and natural disasters. It must understand that corruption is not about economic models and criminal investigations, first and foremost, but about the anguish of hundreds of millions of people trapped in terrible poverty, with their dignity and their self-respect stripped from them by self-serving public officials.

We need to ask, for example, why the German public prosecutors did not demand prison time for the most senior former executives and board directors of Siemens whose corporate bribes added to the sum of human misery. Did those prosecutors not fully understand that the leaders of this global giant corporation needed to be held fully and personally accountable as their company bribed to win metro transit business in Venezuela and in China and to get contracts for high-voltage transmission lines in China; power plants in Israel; mobile telephone networks in Bangladesh; telecommunications projects in Nigeria; national identity cards in Argentina; medical devices in Vietnam, China, and Russia; traffic-control systems in Russia; refineries in Mexico; mobile-communications networks in Vietnam; and power stations and equipment in Iraq (under the United Nations oil-for-food program)?

And, across the OECD, in those thirty-eight countries that have ratified a convention to criminalize corporate bribe payments to foreign officials, prosecutors and judges should hold bribe-paying CEOs to account; they should tell the courts about the real victims of the kickback schemes and publicly decry the undermining of democracy and trust in government that these corporate actions of greed inflict.

Justice will come slowly, but it will come.

For every corrupt injustice that abounds, there are now individuals willing to stand up from Moscow to New York to say, "This is wrong," and to mobilize public support to fight the injustice. Their numbers are growing.

When the supporters of Prime Minister Putin tried to rig the 2011 elections, a blogger, Aleksei Navalny, decried the theft and took to the Internet, where his blog was read by thousands of Russians who took to the streets and called for national protests. He was arrested and imprisoned for two weeks and when he was set free he was hailed as a national hero across Russia's social media, and the number of readers of his blog grew. He is part of a new generation that understands that even the most corrupt political leaders can be undermined by the power of mass public engagement—everyone is now learning from the Arab Spring.

President Teodoro Obiang of Equatorial Guinea hired US public relations consultants to improve his image; not long thereafter he was invited by *Time*, *Fortune*, and CNN to participate in a conference in New York to celebrate Africa's progress. Obiang's public relations team also suggested that there be a $3 million Obiang Prize administered by UNESCO. In times past he may have gotten away with this. Leading the charge against Obiang's public relations stunts was Mary Robinson, former president of Ireland, former top UN official for human rights, and tireless civil society activist for human rights. Her criticisms were not isolated. UNESCO was to hear loud and clear the protests of a coalition of ninety-six nongovernmental organizations.

Time and again it is civil society coalitions and individual activists, from bloggers to former national presidents, from Navalny to Robinson, who are saying no to the powerful. Across so much of the world today there are anticorruption and pro-democracy activists who are moving from the sidelines to the center of the public stage, calling on great reserves of personal courage, to be the voice of the public conscience and who, in this new age of transparency, get their messages out to vast audiences through social media. They are fearless in decrying the humbug of those in power.

DEFENDING CIVIL SOCIETY

The more successful civil society activists are, the more they will be attacked. Just as the rapid spread of Internet-based information is seen as threatening to those in power and leading to efforts at censorship by corrupt governments, so are those same governments striving to weaken civil society. Much more needs to be done to protect—indeed, to strengthen—civil society organizations today. Few top public officeholders have been as determined to fight this vital fight while explicitly supporting the anticorruption agenda as US secretary of state Hillary Clinton. Speaking in Krakow, Poland, to an international civil society group on July 3, 2010, she stressed that

> Poland actually is a case study in how a vibrant civil society can produce progress. The heroes of the solidarity movement, people like Geremek and Lech Walesa and Adam Michnik, and millions of others laid the foundation for the Poland we see today. They knew that the Polish people desired and deserved more from their country. And they transformed that knowledge into one of history's greatest movements for positive change.
>
> . . . Over the last six years, fifty governments have issued new restrictions against NGOs, and the list of countries where civil society faces resistance is growing longer. In Zimbabwe, the Democratic Republic of Congo, physical violence directed against individual activists has been used to intimidate and silence entire sectors of civil society. Last year, Ethiopia imposed a series of strict new rules on NGOs. Very few groups have been able to re-register under this new framework, particularly organizations working on sensitive issues like human rights. The Middle East and North Africa are home to a diverse collection of civil society groups. But too many governments in the region still resort to intimidation, questionable legal practices, restrictions on NGO registration, efforts to silence bloggers.

But Clinton then said,

> Today, meeting together as a community of democracies, it is our responsibility to address this crisis. Some of the countries engaging in these behaviors still claim to be democracies because they have elections. But, as I have said before, democracy requires far more than an election. It has to be a 365-day-a-year commitment by government and citizens alike, to live up to the fundamental values of democracy, and accept the responsibilities of self-government. Democracies don't fear their own people. They recognize that citizens must be free to come together to advocate and agitate, to remind those entrusted with governance that they derive their authority from the governed. Restrictions on these rights only demonstrate the fear of illegitimate rulers, the cowardice of those who deny their citizens the protections they deserve. An attack on civic activism and civil society is an attack on democracy.

The secretary of state announced the creation of a special fund to help to protect embattled NGOs, adding, "For the United States, supporting civil society groups is a critical part of our work to advance democracy. But it's not the only part. Our national security strategy reaffirms that democratic values are a cornerstone of our foreign policy. Over time, as President Obama has said, America's values have been our best national security asset."

Two days later on July 5, 2010, at a meeting with civil society leaders in Yerevan, Armenia, Clinton underscored the US government's commitment by emphasizing that "democracy requires not just elections, but open dialogue, a free exchange of ideas, government transparency and accountability, and above all, an empowered citizenry, who constantly work together to make their country fairer, juster, healthier, and freer."

WINNING

Fighting corruption in some countries may prove to be just too difficult. These are the failed states. Most countries, however, do not live in utter chaos and it is here where the fight against corruption will be seen as making real progress. A great deal has already been done in many countries and there is no turning back. Yes, there will be reverses and we should never underestimate the cunning of corrupt officials, but the momentum to move ahead and build on the gains that have been won with such difficulty will be sustained.

There is an Everest of corruption still to climb. Two decades ago we could look at the mountain from afar and dream. Today, we have reached base camp. We are living the dream. We rejoice at each small victory and we mourn most bitterly when friends are murdered and imprisoned.

When we take stock and see the activism that abounds in scores of countries, note the heightened media attention on corruption, recognize that progress that is being made on the rule of law, see the gathering pressures to enforce the new anticorruption conventions, and read the ambitious declarations from the summits of the world's most powerful leaders, then we have reason for hope.

A paradigm shift is under way from broad resignation and acceptance of corruption to recognizing that the fight against corruption can and will produce substantive victories in the immediate years ahead. The climb to the summit will continue, and its tempo will accelerate.

On December 10, 2011, three African women received the Nobel Peace Prize: Ellen Johnson-Sirleaf and Leymah Gbowee, from Liberia, and Tawakkol Karman, from Yemen. Thorbjørn Jagland, chair of the Norwegian Nobel Committee, concluded his speech in Oslo with a quotation from the American author and civil rights advocate James Baldwin, who wrote, "The people that once walked in darkness are no longer prepared to do so."

Mr. Jagland added, "Make a note of that!—all those who wish to be on the right side of history."

NOTES

1. It has been suggested to the author at times that this view of the leadership of the Tanzanian government is too generous. The statements made in this book reflect the author's own experience and are made within the context of his own dealings with leading members of the Tanzanian government in the mid-1990s as a director of a Canadian company that was called Sutton Resources (subsequently acquired by American Barrick).

2. George Soros, "Transparent Corruption—Oil and Natural Resource Companies Should Make Clear How Much Money Is Being Taken by Officials, Says George Soros," *Financial Times*, June 13, 2002.

3. Colbert I. King, "D.C. Mayor Contest Must Get Substantive on Schools, Corruption," *Washington Post*, August 21, 2010.

Appendix 1

Transparency International's Corruption Perceptions Index 2011

Please note that for a country/territory to be included in the ranking, it must be included in a minimum of three of the CPI's data sources. Thus, inclusion in the index is not an indication of the existence of corruption but rather depends solely on the availability of sufficient information.

The 2011 CPI draws on seventeen data sources from thirteen institutions. The information used for the 2011 CPI is survey data from these sources gathered between December 2009 and September 2011. The CPI includes only sources that provide a score for a set of countries/territories and measure perceptions of corruption in the public sector. TI ensures that the sources used are of the highest quality. To qualify, the data collection method must be well documented and the methodology published to enable an assessment of its reliability.

Sources included in the CPI 2011:

1. African Development Bank Governance Ratings 2010
2. Asian Development Bank Country Performance Assessment 2010
3. Bertelsmann Foundation Sustainable Governance Indicators
4. Bertelsmann Foundation Transformation Index
5. Economist Intelligence Unit Country Risk Assessment
6. Freedom House Nations In Transit
7. Global Insight Country Risk Ratings
8. IMD World Competitiveness Yearbook 2010
9. IMD World Competitiveness Yearbook 2011
10. Political and Economic Risk Consultancy Asian Intelligence 2010
11. Political and Economic Risk Consultancy Asian Intelligence 2011
12. Political Risk Services International Country Risk Guide

Rank	Country	Score		Rank	Country	Score
1	New Zealand	9.5		46	Bahrain	5.1
2	Denmark	9.4		46	Macau	5.1
2	Finland	9.4		46	Mauritius	5.1
4	Sweden	9.3		49	Rwanda	5.0
5	Singapore	9.2		50	Costa Rica	4.8
6	Norway	9.0		50	Lithuania	4.8
7	Netherlands	8.9		50	Oman	4.8
8	Australia	8.8		50	Seychelles	4.8
8	Switzerland	8.8		54	Hungary	4.6
10	Canada	8.7		54	Kuwait	4.6
11	Luxembourg	8.5		56	Jordan	4.5
12	Hong Kong	8.4		57	Czech Republic	4.4
13	Iceland	8.3		57	Namibia	4.4
14	Germany	8.0		57	Saudi Arabia	4.4
14	Japan	8.0		60	Malaysia	4.3
16	Austria	7.8		61	Cuba	4.2
16	Barbados	7.8		61	Latvia	4.2
16	United Kingdom	7.8		61	Turkey	4.2
19	Belgium	7.5		64	Georgia	4.1
19	Ireland	7.5		64	South Africa	4.1
21	Bahamas	7.3		66	Croatia	4.0
22	Chile	7.2		66	Montenegro	4.0
22	Qatar	7.2		66	Slovakia	4.0
24	United States	7.1		69	Ghana	3.9
25	France	7.0		69	Italy	3.9
25	Saint Lucia	7.0		69	FYR Macedonia	3.9
25	Uruguay	7.0		69	Samoa	3.9
28	United Arab Emirates	6.8		73	Brazil	3.8
29	Estonia	6.4		73	Tunisia	3.8
30	Cyprus	6.3		75	China	3.6
31	Spain	6.2		75	Romania	3.6
32	Botswana	6.1		77	Gambia	3.5
32	Portugal	6.1		77	Lesotho	3.5
32	Taiwan	6.1		77	Vanuatu	3.5
35	Slovenia	5.9		80	Colombia	3.4
36	Israel	5.8		80	El Salvador	3.4
36	Saint Vincent and the Grenadines	5.8		80	Greece	3.4
38	Bhutan	5.7		80	Morocco	3.4
39	Malta	5.6		80	Thailand	3.4
39	Puerto Rico	5.6		86	Bulgaria	3.3
41	Cape Verde	5.5		86	Jamaica	3.3
41	Poland	5.5		86	Panama	3.3
43	Korea (South)	5.4		86	Serbia	3.3
44	Brunei	5.2		86	Sri Lanka	3.3
44	Dominica	5.2		91	Bosnia and Herzegovina	3.2

Rank	Country	Score		Rank	Country	Score
91	Liberia	3.2		134	Niger	2.5
91	Trinidad and Tobago	3.2		134	Pakistan	2.5
91	Zambia	3.2		134	Sierra Leone	2.5
95	Albania	3.1		143	Azerbaijan	2.4
95	India	3.1		143	Belarus	2.4
95	Kiribati	3.1		143	Comoros	2.4
95	Swaziland	3.1		143	Mauritania	2.4
95	Tonga	3.1		143	Nigeria	2.4
100	Argentina	3.0		143	Russia	2.4
100	Benin	3.0		143	Timor-Leste	2.4
100	Burkina Faso	3.0		143	Togo	2.4
100	Djibouti	3.0		143	Uganda	2.4
100	Gabon	3.0		152	Tajikistan	2.3
100	Mexico	3.0		152	Ukraine	2.3
100	Sao Tome & Principe	3.0		154	Central African Republic	2.2
100	Suriname	3.0		154	Congo Republic	2.2
100	Tanzania	3.0		154	Côte d'Ivoire	2.2
112	Algeria	2.9		154	Guinea-Bissau	2.2
112	Egypt	2.9		154	Kenya	2.2
112	Kosovo	2.9		154	Laos	2.2
112	Moldova	2.9		154	Nepal	2.2
112	Senegal	2.9		154	Papua New Guinea	2.2
112	Vietnam	2.9		154	Paraguay	2.2
118	Bolivia	2.8		154	Zimbabwe	2.2
118	Mali	2.8		164	Cambodia	2.1
120	Bangladesh	2.7		164	Guinea	2.1
120	Ecuador	2.7		164	Kyrgyzstan	2.1
120	Ethiopia	2.7		164	Yemen	2.1
120	Guatemala	2.7		168	Angola	2.0
120	Iran	2.7		168	Chad	2.0
120	Kazakhstan	2.7		168	Democratic Republic of the Congo	2.0
120	Mongolia	2.7		168	Libya	2.0
120	Mozambique	2.7		172	Burundi	1.9
120	Solomon Islands	2.7		172	Equatorial Guinea	1.9
129	Armenia	2.6		172	Venezuela	1.9
129	Dominican Republic	2.6		175	Haiti	1.8
129	Honduras	2.6		175	Iraq	1.8
129	Philippines	2.6		177	Sudan	1.6
129	Syria	2.6		177	Turkmenistan	1.6
134	Cameroon	2.5		177	Uzbekistan	1.6
134	Eritrea	2.5		180	Afghanistan	1.5
134	Guyana	2.5		180	Myanmar	1.5
134	Lebanon	2.5		182	Korea (North)	1.0
134	Maldives	2.5		182	Somalia	1.0
134	Nicaragua	2.5				

13. Transparency International Bribe Payers' Survey
14. World Bank—Country Performance and Institutional Assessment
15. World Economic Forum Executive Opinion Survey (EOS) 2010
16. World Economic Forum Executive Opinion Survey (EOS) 2011
17. World Justice Project Rule of Law Index

The CPI is mostly an assessment of perceptions of administrative and political corruption. It is not a verdict on the levels of corruption of entire nations or societies or of their policies and activities. Citizens of those countries/territories that score at the lower end of the CPI have shown the same concern about and condemnation of corruption as the public in countries that perform strongly. Furthermore, the country/territory with the lowest score is the one where public-sector corruption is perceived to be most prevalent *among those included in the list.* There are more than two hundred sovereign nations in the world, and the 2011 CPI ranks 183 of them. The CPI provides no information about countries/territories that are not included.

Appendix 2

Transparency International's Bribe Payers' Index 2011

Rank	Country	Score
1	Netherlands	8.8
1	Switzerland	8.8
3	Belgium	8.7
4	Germany	8.6
4	Japan	8.6
6	Australia	8.5
6	Canada	8.5
8	Singapore	8.3
8	UK	8.3
10	USA	8.1
11	France	8.0
11	Spain	8.0
13	South Korea	7.9
14	Brazil	7.7
15	Hong Kong	7.6
15	Italy	7.6
15	Malaysia	7.6
15	South Africa	7.6
19	Taiwan	7.5
19	India	7.5
19	Turkey	7.5
22	Saudi Arabia	7.4
23	Argentina	7.3
23	UAE	7.3
25	Indonesia	7.1
26	Mexico	7.0
27	China	6.5
28	Russia	6.1
	Average	*7.8*

TI Bribe Payers' Index (BPI) 2011 (Note: Scores based on business executives' responses when asked how often firms with which they do business from a given sector engage in bribery [0 = always, 10 = never]. Bribe Payers' Index 2011. © 2011 Transparency International. All rights reserved. [See http://www. transparency.org])

The 2011 Bribe Payers' Survey was conducted in thirty countries worldwide, as listed in this table. They were selected as recipients of large inflows of foreign direct investment and imports, and to achieve a good regional balance in countries surveyed. In each country a minimum of one hundred senior business executives were interviewed, except in China, where eighty-two business executives were surveyed. In total, 3,016 business executives were interviewed. In each country, executives from a range of business sectors were surveyed with an oversampling of large and foreign-owned firms.

The BPI was carried out on TI's behalf by Ipsos Mori between May 5 and July 8, 2011. Ipsos Mori drew on a network of partner institutes to carry out the survey locally, through telephone or face-to-face interviews in each country, where appropriate, and online in the United States.

Rank	Sector	Score
1	Agriculture	7.1
1	Light Manufacturing	7.1
3	Civilian Aerospace	7.0
3	Information Technology	7.0
5	Banking and Finance	6.9
5	Forestry	6.9
7	Consumer Services	6.8
8	Telecommunications	6.7
8	Transportation and Storage	6.7
10	Arms, Defense and Military	6.6
10	Fisheries	6.6
12	Heavy Manufacturing	6.5
13	Pharmaceutical and Healthcare	6.4
13	Power Generation and Transmission	6.4
15	Mining	6.3
16	Oil and Gas	6.2
17	Real Estate, Property, Business and Legal Services	6.1
17	Utilities	6.1
19	Public Works Contracts and Construction	5.3
	Average	*6.6*

Perceptions of Foreign Bribery by Sector (Note: Scores based on business executives' responses when asked how often firms with which they do business from a given sector engage in bribery [0 = always, 10 = never]. Bribe Payers' Index 2011. © 2011 Transparency International. All rights reserved.)

Nineteen sectors were scored and ranked using the same methodology as the 2008 BPI. The 2011 Bribe Payers' Survey, on which the index is based, asked business executives how common bribery was in the sectors with which they have business relations; how often three different types of bribery were perceived to occur in each sector: (1) bribery of low-ranking public officials; (2) improper contributions to high-ranking politicians to achieve influence; and (3) bribery between private companies. Answers were given on a five-point scale. This was then converted to a ten-point scale in which 0 indicates that companies in that sector are perceived to always pay bribes and 10 that they never pay bribes.

Appendix 3

Summary Highlights from the United Nations Convention Against Corruption

The General Assembly in 2003 adopted the United Nations Convention Against Corruption (UNCAC). It was formally ratified in late 2005 and by the end of 2009 more than 140 governments had signed it. It obliges governments to enforce a host of anticorruption measures. It provides the most comprehensive set of detailed legal anticorruption requirements on governments that has ever existed.

Article 1 of the Convention reads as follows:

> The purposes of this Convention are:
>
> a. To promote and strengthen measures to prevent and combat corruption more efficiently and effectively;
> b. To promote, facilitate and support international cooperation and technical assistance in the prevention of and fight against corruption, including in asset recovery;
> c. To promote integrity, accountability and proper management of public affairs and public property.

And Article 65 deals with implementation of the convention:

> 1. Each State Party shall take the necessary measures, including legislative and administrative measures, in accordance with fundamental principles of its domestic law, to ensure the implementation of its obligations under this Convention.
> 2. Each State Party may adopt more strict or severe measures than those provided for by this Convention for preventing and combating corruption.

The detailed convention covers an extensive range of issues and, unquestionably, if every government that has signed UNCAC were to adhere to the final article, then this would be a much better world. Some of the key provisions, in brief, are as follows:

- Article 5 stresses the importance of critical issues of transparency and accountability in national legal systems.
- Article 9 explicitly focuses on public procurement and calls upon public authorities to "take the necessary steps to establish appropriate systems of procurement, based on transparency, competition and objective criteria in decision-making, that are effective, inter alia, in preventing corruption."
- Article 10 highlights the issue of secrecy in public administration and calls for actions to secure greater freedom of information.
- Article 11 calls upon governments to safeguard the integrity and independence of the judiciary by preventing opportunities for bribery.
- Article 12 expressly raises issues of corporate governance by calling for strengthened regulatory and legal actions to curb private-sector corruption.
- Article 14 hones in on anti-money-laundering matters to boost prevention, strengthen reporting, and tighten regulation of financial institutions.
- Articles 15 and 16 decry the bribery of national and foreign government officials and call for actions to stop such practice.
- Article 33 underscores the need to protect people who report acts of corruption.
- Article 43 stresses the need for international cooperation to curb corruption and calls for strengthened actions.

Appendix 4

Issues Related to the Council of Europe's Criminal and Civil Law Conventions on Corruption

The Council of Europe in January 1999 approved a "Criminal Law Convention on Corruption," which entered into force on July 1, 2002. It was closely followed by a "Civil Law Convention on Corruption," which came into force on November 1, 2003.

The criminal convention is quite comprehensive and states are required to enforce its provisions, with the Group of States Against Corruption (GRECO) serving to monitor performance. The convention incorporates provisions concerning enhanced international cooperation (mutual assistance, extradition, and the provision of information) in the investigation and prosecution of corruption offenses.

The Criminal Law Convention of the Council of Europe covers the following forms of corrupt behavior normally considered as specific types of corruption:

- Active and passive bribery of domestic and foreign public officials
- Active and passive bribery of national and foreign parliamentarians and of members of international parliamentary assemblies
- Active and passive bribery in the private sector
- Active and passive bribery of international civil servants
- Active and passive bribery of domestic, foreign, and international judges and officials of international courts
- Active and passive trading in influence
- Money laundering of proceeds from corruption offenses

- Accounting offenses (invoices, accounting documents, etc.) connected with corruption offenses

The Civil Law Convention on Corruption was the first attempt to define common international rules in the field of civil law and corruption. It required contracting parties to provide in their domestic law "for effective remedies for persons who have suffered damage as a result of acts of corruption, to enable them to defend their rights and interests, including the possibility of obtaining compensation for damage" (Art. 1). The convention is divided into three chapters (measures to be taken at the national level, international cooperation, and monitoring of implementation), and final clauses. In ratifying the convention, the states undertake to incorporate its principles and rules into their domestic law, taking into account their own particular circumstances.

The Council of Europe's Civil Law Convention deals with the following:

- Compensation for damage
- Liability (including state liability for acts of corruption committed by public officials)
- Contributory negligence: reduction or disallowance of compensation, depending on the circumstances
- Validity of contracts
- Protection of employees who report corruption
- Clarity and accuracy of accounts and audits
- Acquisition of evidence
- Court orders to preserve the assets necessary for the execution of the final judgment and for the maintenance of the status quo pending resolution of the points at issue
- International cooperation

Appendix 5

Global Financial Integrity—Illicit Financial Flows

Africa = 22.3 percent	
Middle East and North Africa (MENA) = 19.6 percent	
Developing Europe = 17.4 percent	
Asia = 6.2 percent	
Western Hemisphere = 4.4 percent	
Top ten countries with the highest measured cumulative illicit financial outflows between 2000 and 2009	
1	China: $2.74 trillion
2	Russia: $504 billion
3	Mexico: $501 billon
4	Saudi Arabia: $380 billion
5	Malaysia: $350 billion
6	United Arab Emirates: $296 billion
7	Kuwait: $271 billion
8	Nigeria: $182 billion
9	Venezuela: $179 billion
10	Qatar: $130 billion

Global Financial Integrity: Real Growth of Illicit Flows by Regions, 2000–2009 (*Source*: Global Financial Integrity, "Illicit Financial Flows from Developing Countries over the Decade Ending 2009" [December 2011]. © GFI.)

Appendix 6

Enforcement of the Foreign Corrupt Practices Act and the OECD Anti-Bribery Convention—Trace International and Transparency International Surveys

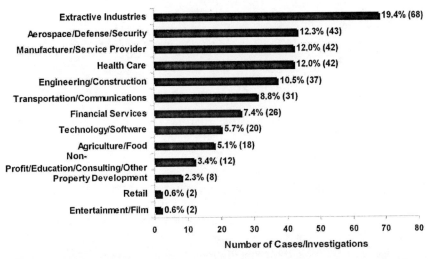

International Enforcement Activity by Industry, 1977–July 2011: Enforcement by Business Sector (This table provides an updated summary of bribery enforcement activity in the US and internationally. Trace International, "Global Enforcement Report 2011." © Trace.)

283

Appendix 6

Country	Enforcement [1]				Share of World Exports, % 2010 [II]	Share of Foreign Investment, % for 2009 (outward)
	Total Cases		Investigations Under Way			
	2010	2009	in 2010	in 2009		
Active Enforcement						
Denmark	14 [III]	14 [III]	1	1	0.8	0.9
Germany	135	117	22	24	8.2	8.4
Italy	18	18	2 [IV]	3 [IV]	2.9	4.6
Norway	6	6	1	1	0.9	0.6
Switzerland	> 35	30	0 [IV]	0	1.6	2.6
United Kingdom	17 [V]	10	26	24	3.5	13.3
United States	227	169	106	100	9.8	15.7
Moderate Enforcement						
Argentina	2	2	0 [IV]	0	0.4	0.1
Belgium	4 [IV]	4 [IV]	0 [IV]	0	2	2.5
Finland	6	5	3	5	0.5	0.4
Japan	7	7	0 [IV]	0	4.5	3.7
Korea (South)	17	17 [IV]	0	1	2.9	0.8
Netherlands	9	7	3	0	3.3	1.6
Spain	11	11	0 [IV]	1	2	6
Sweden	2 [IV]	2 [IV]	4	5	1.2	1.9
Little or No Enforcement						
Australia	1	1	3	4	1.4	1.2
Austria	0	0	5 [IV]	4 [IV]	1.1	1.6
Brazil	1	1	8	4	1.3	0.4
Bulgaria	4	3	0	1	0.1	0.1
Canada	2	2	23	1	2.5	2.7
Chile	2	0	2	0	0.4	0.2
Czech Republic	0	0	0	0	0.8	0.2
Estonia	0	0	0	0	0.1	0.1
Greece	0 [IV]	0 [IV]	0 [IV]	0 [IV]	0.3	0.3
Hungary	27	27	2	0	0.6	0.2
Ireland	0	0	0 [IV]	0 [IV]	1.1	1
Israel	0	0	0	0	0.4	0.4
Luxembourg	2	—	Some [IV]	—	0.5	0.5
Mexico	0	0	0	0	1.7	0.4
New Zealand	1	0	1	2	0.2	0.1
Poland	0	0	0	0	1	0.2
Portugal	4	4 [VII]	6	0	0.4	0.3
Slovak Republic	0	0	1	1	0.4	0.4
Slovenia	0	0	2	2	0.2	0.1
South Africa	0	0	5	1	0.5	0.2
Turkey	0	0	5	4	0.9	0.1

1. Case numbers are cumulative, starting from convention entry into force; investigations numbers are those ongoing in the year listed.
2. Numbers from the OECD Working Group on Bribery 2010 Annual Report.
3. Cases all related to UN oil-for-food program. Some of these cases may have been brought for sanctions violations.
4. Number of unknown or based on media reports.
5. Includes 2011 cases.
6. Belgium has brought ten additional cases on behalf of EU institutions.
7. Number of corrected form last year's report.

Foreign Bribery Enforcement in OECD Convention Countries (This table provides an overview of the annual analysis of compliance and enforcement of the OECD pact that is published by Transparency International. © Transparency International 2011)

Index